Pediatric Nursing Test Succe

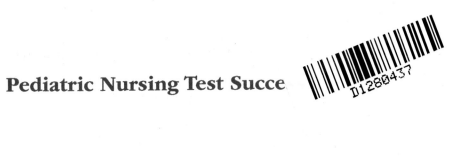

Susan Parnell Scholtz, PhD, RN, is an associate professor of nursing at Moravian College, Bethlehem, Pennsylvania. She has been a Nursing Care of the Child educator since 1978. Susan received a bachelor of science degree in nursing from the Pennsylvania State University and received a master's degree in nursing care of the child from the University of Pittsburgh with a focus as a clinical nurse specialist. She completed her PhD at Widener University in 2003 and studied the effects of expressive writing on students' apperception of threat related to clinical education. Susan is certified as an ELNEC-Pediatric Palliative Care Nurse Educator and as a school nurse through the State of Pennsylvania Department of Education. In 2011, she was reappointed as a NCLEX-RN® item writer. In addition to teaching nursing to both undergraduate and graduate students, Susan also has been involved in the development and implementation of a first-year seminar that focuses on student writing as well as facilitation of a successful transition to college. In 2002, Susan was awarded the Pennsylvania State Nurses Association's Nursing Education Excellence Award and was a Nightingale Awards of Pennsylvania Finalist for Excellence in Nursing Education. In 2011, she received the St. Luke's Hospital Nursing Excellence: Nurse Educator Leadership Award. She has published a chapter in Moyer and Price's *Nursing Education: Foundations for Practice Excellence*; *"A Risk Worth Taking"* in Hudacek's *Making a Difference: Stories From the Point of Care, 2nd ed.*; and wrote several chapters in *Instructor's Resource CD-ROM, Effective Leadership & Management in Nursing, 6th edition*. She has written NCLEX-RN questions in D'Amico's *Health Assessment in Nursing* and *Pharmacology for Nurses*.

Vicki A. Martin, MSN, RN, is a pediatric nursing instructor at Francis Marion University, Florence, South Carolina. She has been a nurse for 23 years and has experience in nursing education, pediatrics, medical–surgical, infusion, and community health. She received her associate's degree from Florence-Darlington Technical College (1991) and a bachelor of science in nursing degree from the University of South Carolina (2000). She completed a master's of science in nursing degree with specialty in nursing education from Walden University (2008). Vicki has taught LPN, RN, BSN, and RN-BSN students over the past 8 years. She supervises graduate nursing students in pediatrics in community settings. She also received certification as an online instructor from Central Michigan University (2011). She serves the community as a Head Start clinical nurse liaison/consultant, CPR instructor for the American Heart Association, Reach to Recovery volunteer for the American Cancer Society for breast cancer patients, and is currently certified to serve as a guardian ad litem for abused children in Florence County, South Carolina. Vicki has written an article on pediatrics that was published in *Nursing2013*, "Using Distraction Techniques with Children." She published a chapter in 2013 on the faculty role in the college/university setting in: Reflection in Hunt's *The New Nurse Educator*. She has experience in research/statistics from 2007 to 2011 with Laerdal Medical and Medical Education Technologies, Inc. involving technology advancements with high-fidelity human patient simulators to enhance student learning within college nursing programs. Vicki has received funding for research on three grants at Francis Marion University. She is currently a doctor of nursing practice (DNP) student at Chatham University.

Frances H. Cornelius, PhD, MSN, RN-BC, CNE, CHSE-A, is clinical professor, chair of the MSN Advanced Practice Role Department, and coordinator of informatics projects at Drexel University, College of Nursing and Health Professions. Fran has taught nursing since 1991 at several schools of nursing. She taught community health at Madonna University (Livonia, Michigan), Oakland (Michigan) University, University of Pittsburgh, and Holy Family College (Philadelphia, Pennsylvania). Fran taught Adult Health and Gerontology at Widener University School of Nursing until 1997 when she began teaching at Drexel. In 2003, she was a Fellow at the Biomedical Library of Medicine. She is a certified nurse informaticist and has been the recipient of several grants. She has collaborated on the development of mobile applications as coordinator of informatics projects, including the Patient Assessment and Care Plan Development (PACPD) tool, which is a PDA tool with a Web-based companion, and the Gerontology Reasoning Informatics Programs (the GRIP project). She is the co-editor/chapter author of Cornelius/Gallagher-Gordon's *PDA Connections*, an innovative textbook designed to teach health care professionals how to use mobile devices for "point-of-care" access of information. She has written 6 book chapters and has published 19 journal articles on her work. She has been an invited speaker for 33 presentations and has delivered more than 60 peer-reviewed presentations mostly in the United States, but also in England, Spain, Portugal, Czech Republic, Canada, and Korea. She is a member of Sigma Theta Tau International, the American Informatics Association, the American Nursing Informatics Association, the International Institute of Informatics and Systemics, NANDA, the American Nurses Association, and the Pennsylvania State Nurses Association.

Ruth A. Wittmann-Price, PhD, RN, CNS, CNE, CHSE, ANEF, is chairperson and tenured professor in the Department of Nursing, Francis Marion University (FMU), South Carolina. She is a fellow in the National League for Nursing Academy of Nursing Education. Ruth has been an obstetrical/women's health nurse for 35 years. She received her AAS and BSN degrees from Felician College in Lodi, New Jersey (1978, 1981), and her MS as a perinatal clinical nurse specialist from Columbia University, New York, New York (1983). Ruth completed her PhD at Widener University, Chester, Pennsylvania (2006), and was awarded the Dean's Award for Excellence. She developed a mid-range nursing theory "Emancipated Decision-Making in Women's Health Care." Besides continuing her research on decisional science, she studies nursing educational practice. She was the director of nursing research for Hahnemann University Hospital (2007–2010) and oversaw all evidence-based practice projects for nursing. Hahnemann University Hospital was awarded initial Magnet status (American Nurses Credentialing Center) in December 14, 2009. Ruth has taught all levels of nursing students over the past 15 years and completed an international service-learning trip (2007) to rural Mexico. Prior to her chairperson position at FMU, Ruth was the coordinator for the nurse educator track in the DrNP program at Drexel University, Philadelphia, Pennsylvania (2007–2010), and participates on dissertation committees for Drexel University and Widener University. Ruth is author or coauthor of 11 books including *Nursing Education: Foundations for Practice Excellence* (2007), which won the *American Journal of Nursing* Book of the Year Award in 2007, and *Nursing Concept Care Maps for Safe Patient Care* (2013). For Springer Publishing Company, she has written *Fast Facts for Developing a Nursing Academic Portfolio: What You Really Need to Know in a Nutshell* (2012) and coedited *Certified Nurse Educator (CNE) Review Manual, Second Edition* (2012). She is also the series editor of the Nursing Test Success series, which includes maternal–child nursing, fundamentals of nursing, medical–surgical nursing, and community health nursing books.

Pediatric Nursing Test Success:
An Unfolding Case Study Review

Susan Parnell Scholtz, PhD, RN
Vicki A. Martin, MSN, RN
Frances H. Cornelius, PhD, MSN, RN-BC, CNE, CHSE-A

Series Editor
Ruth A. Wittmann-Price, PhD, RN, CNS, CNE,
CHSE, ANEF

SPRINGER PUBLISHING COMPANY
NEW YORK

Springer Publishing Company, LLC
11 West 42nd Street
New York, NY 10036
www.springerpub.com

Acquisitions Editor: Margaret Zuccarini
Composition: S4Carlisle Publishing Services

ISBN: 978-0-8261-7136-8
e-book ISBN: 978-0-8261-7137-5
eResources ISBN: 978-0-8261-7151-1

A list of eResources is available from www.springerpub.com/scholtz-ancillary

14 15 16 17 / 5 4 3 2 1

The author and the publisher of this Work have made every effort to use sources believed to be reliable to provide information that is accurate and compatible with the standards generally accepted at the time of publication. The author and publisher shall not be liable for any special, consequential, or exemplary damages resulting, in whole or in part, from the readers' use of, or reliance on, the information contained in this book. The publisher has no responsibility for the persistence or accuracy of URLs for external or third-party Internet websites referred to in this publication and does not guarantee that any content on such websites is, or will remain, accurate or appropriate.

Library of Congress Cataloging-in-Publication Data

Scholtz, Susan Parnell, author.
 Pediatric nursing test success : an unfolding case study review / Susan Parnell Scholtz, Vicki A. Martin, Frances H. Cornelius.
  p. ; cm. — (Unfolding case study review)
 Includes bibliographical references and index.
 ISBN 978-0-8261-7136-8—ISBN 0-8261-7136-2—ISBN 978-0-8261-7137-5 (e-book)—
ISBN 978-0-8261-7151-1 (eresources)
 I. Martin, Vicki A., author. II. Cornelius, Frances H., author. III. Title. IV. Series: Unfolding case study review (Series)
 [DNLM: 1. Child—Case Reports. 2. Child—Problems and Exercises. 3. Nursing Care—Case Reports. 4. Nursing Care—Problems and Exercises. 5. Child Development—Case Reports. 6. Child Development—Problems and Exercises. 7. Health Promotion—Case Reports. 8. Health Promotion—Problems and Exercises. 9. Nursing Diagnosis—Case Reports. 10. Nursing Diagnosis—Problems and Exercises. 11. Pediatric Nursing—methods—Case Reports. 12. Pediatric Nursing—methods—Problems and Exercises. WY 18.2]
 RJ245
 618.92'00231—dc23
                                   2014013313

Special discounts on bulk quantities of our books are available to corporations, professional associations, pharmaceutical companies, health care organizations, and other qualifying groups. If you are interested in a custom book, including chapters from more than one of our titles, we can provide that service as well.

For details, please contact:
Special Sales Department, Springer Publishing Company, LLC
11 West 42nd Street, 15th Floor, New York, NY 10036-8002
Phone: 877-687-7476 or 212-431-4370; Fax: 212-941-7842
E-mail: sales@springerpub.com

Printed in the United States of America by Bradford & Bigelow.

This book is dedicated to my daughter, Susan Elisabeth Scholtz, RN, BSN, who epitomizes a learner who was unwavering in her quest for excellence in her own nursing education. As I watched her journey toward her goal and witnessed her competency, compassion, and gentleness toward her patients evolve, my own passion for nursing and teaching has been re-energized.

—Susan Parnell Scholtz

To my family and friends who have supported me through this publishing endeavor. I know you have given up countless hours to assist me in this dream. To my colleague, boss, and friend, Ruth Wittmann-Price, your support and guidance have brought this dream to fruition. Words cannot thank you enough. Bless you and I love you!

—Vicki A. Martin

Contents

Preface

This textbook is designed to enhance nursing students' understanding of the multifaceted concepts inherent within the nursing care of children. Utilizing a developmental approach, various issues are addressed within the growth and development, health promotion, and management of acute, chronic, and terminal illnesses categories. Knowledge acquisition, comprehension of the material, and application of theory to clinical practice are facilitated through the use of electronic technology and connection to useful web links.

Case studies lay the foundation for the student to understand a disorder within the context of a situation. Instead of learning about diseases in a "silo" approach where a student answers question after question about a myriad of diseases, the unfolding case study approach gives the learner an active and multidimensional perspective on health care problems. Once an answer selection is made, the student can check his or her response by reviewing the correct answer at the end-of-chapter answers section that includes the rationale for each correct answer. Unlike other NCLEX review books, this book builds content and evaluation right into the case scenarios, facilitating active learning as students work through the compelling and increasingly more complex unfolding case studies.

More than 390 NCLEX-style questions have been constructed by experienced nurse educators to broaden the student's mastery of key concepts in the nursing care of children. These questions are embedded within the cases to evaluate learning as the case unfolds. Questions include true or false, multiple choice, matching, select all that apply, ordering, calculation, and fill in the blank. Diligent completion of these exercises will aid the student in mastery of the content and will prepare students for tests such as course examinations, standardized assessment tests, and the NCLEX-RN®. The personalization of patient care content stimulates clinical reasoning and decision making, unlike answering question after question in isolation.

In addition to the plentiful NCLEX-style questions, the student is referred to electronic resources that will be useful not only in this circumstance but also in clinical practice.

Appropriate web links and resources are incorporated into the unfolding cases as a means to further replicate realistic clinical situations in which the point-of-care/point-of-need access to information is utilized for clinical decision support. In the e-book, clicking on the link will take the student directly to that website to study additional content, which could be as interactive as watching a procedural video on YouTube. **A list of these web links and eResources is available from www .springerpub.com/scholtz-ancillary.** Mobile resources such as PubMed and Agency for Healthcare Research and Quality guidelines, as well as others, are utilized for this purpose. A review of these electronic resources will heighten the student's or new graduate's awareness of valuable tools that can be accessed online.

We hope you can envision yourself as the professional nurse in each of these pediatric patient-centered unfolding case studies and gain a greater understanding of the challenges embedded in each situation. As you evolve both professionally and personally in the profession of nursing, always seek resources that will enrich your commitment to lifelong learning and develop your competency as a professional nurse.

Susan Parnell Scholtz
Vicki A. Martin
Frances H. Cornelius

Nursing Test Success

With Ruth A. Wittmann-Price as Series Editor

Maternal-Child Nursing Test Success:
An Unfolding Case Study Review
Ruth A. Wittmann-Price, PhD, RN, CNS, CNE, CHSE, ANEF,
and Frances H. Cornelius, PhD, MSN, RN-BC, CNE, CHSE-A

Fundamentals of Nursing Test Success:
An Unfolding Case Study Review
Ruth A. Wittmann-Price, PhD, RN, CNS, CNE, CHSE, ANEF,
and Frances H. Cornelius, PhD, MSN, RN-BC, CNE, CHSE-A

Community Health Nursing Test Success:
An Unfolding Case Study Review
Frances H. Cornelius, PhD, MSN, RN-BC, CNE, CHSE-A,
and Ruth A. Wittmann-Price, PhD, RN, CNS, CNE, CHSE, ANEF

Medical–Surgical Nursing Test Success:
An Unfolding Case Study Review
Karen K. Gittings, DNP, RN, CNE, Alumnus CCRN, Rhonda M. Brogdon,
DNP, MSN, MBA, RN, and Frances H. Cornelius, PhD, MSN, RN-BC, CNE,
CHSE-A

Leadership and Management in Nursing Test Success:
An Unfolding Case Study Review
Ruth A. Wittmann-Price, PhD, RN, CNS, CNE, CHSE, ANEF,
and Frances H. Cornelius, PhD, MSN, RN-BC, CNE, CHSE-A

Pediatric Nursing Test Success:
An Unfolding Case Study Review
Susan Parnell Scholtz, PhD, RN, Vicki A. Martin, MSN, RN,
and Frances H. Cornelius, PhD, MSN, RN-BC, CNE, CHSE-A

Pediatric Nursing Test Success

1

Human Growth and Development

Susan Parnell Scholtz

Unfolding Case Study #1-1 ▨ Maddie

Maddie is a 6-month-old infant whose birth weight was 7 pounds 5 ounces, head circumference was 16 inches, and her length was 21 inches. She presents to the clinic with her parents for a well child visit.

Exercise 1-1: *Calculation*
You weigh Maddie at her visit and document her weight as 15 pounds, head circumference as 16 inches, and length as 25 inches. You plot her measurements on the chart and determine her percentiles for height and weight. What percentile is she in terms of weight and length?

 eResource 1-1: Consult your mobile device and open the World Health Organization's STAT GrowthCharts™ (download from: goo.gl/BEyqAf [Android] or goo.gl/qdaGY2 [iOS]): [Pathway: STAT GrowthChart™ → Enter gender, age, length and weight into the appropriate fields]

Exercise 1-2: *Fill-in*
How would you interpret these findings in relation to her percentile and other female infants of the same age?

 eResource 1-2: In order to plot Maddie's weight go to:
■ The Centers for Disease Control and Prevention's (CDC)'s website (www.cdc.gov.growthcharts) and download the Birth to 36 Months: Length for Age and Weight for Age profiles. Plot the appropriate weight and height to determine the percentile each parameter falls within.

Answers to this chapter begin on page 10.

■ Utilize Online Child Growth Chart Calculators at
  ■ Baby Center: [Pathway: goo.gl/6YtwJM → Enter child's sex, age, length, weight, and head circumference → View the percentile each parameter falls within]
  ■ MedCalc Interactive Growth Chart: [Pathway: www.medcalc.com → Select "Pediatrics" → Select "Growth Charts" → Enter age, sex, height, weight, and head circumference → Select Combined HC-for-Age and Weight-for-Length Birth to 36 Months → Select "Create Growth Chart" to view results]

You also listen to Maddie's heart and lungs and assess Maddie's gross motor development during her visit.

Exercise 1-3: *Multiple-choice question*

Which findings would indicate that Maddie has met gross motor age-appropriate milestones?
  A. Maddie is able to pull herself to a stand.
  B. Maddie can sit alone without support.
  C. Maddie can roll from her back to her abdomen.
  D. Maddie can grasp a rattle with her fingers.

Maddie's father asks you for suggestions about appropriate play for her.

Exercise 1-4: *Select all that apply*

Based on an understanding of growth and development, and safety, select all toys that would meet Maddie's needs.
  ❑ Brightly colored latex balloons
  ❑ Push–pull toys
  ❑ Teething toys
  ❑ Books with bright pictures
  ❑ Brightly colored soft toys
  ❑ Stacking blocks

 eResource 1-3: To reinforce your teaching regarding normal growth and development, you provide the following resources from Baby World:
■ Reading materials regarding normal 6 month development: goo.gl/T2pTr7
■ Videos:
  ■ *Baby on the Move: Sitting:* goo.gl/PlKvkz
  ■ *Baby on the Move: Crawling:* goo.gl/uFhJ9o

Maddie's parents are very attentive to your teaching and you provide them with literature about age-appropriate activity. You also review with them home safety for a 6-month-old. Their next visit is established in another 3 months when Maddie will be 9 months old. At that time you will prepare them for safety issues that involve a child that is more mobile.

Answers to this chapter begin on page 10.

Unfolding Case Study #1-2 — Omar

You go out to the waiting room to call in your next patient, Omar, and notice two toddlers are sitting side by side in the playroom, each is playing with a truck. There is very little interaction between the two children.

Exercise 1-5: *Multiple-choice question*
The scenario described in Unfolding Case Study #1-2 is an example of:

    A. Stranger anxiety

    B. Regressive behaviors

    C. Cooperative play

    D. Parallel play

Fifteen-month-old Omar is taken to the examination room with his father. You know his mom is a nurse and works days so you have established a rapport with Omar's father from the previous visits.

    Omar's father is unemployed and stays home with the children.

Exercise 1-6: *Select all that apply*
Which findings would indicate that Omar has met gross motor age-appropriate milestones?

    ❑ Walks well

    ❑ Stoops and recovers a ball

    ❑ Walks up steps

    ❑ Builds a tower of two cubes

    ❑ Jumps

Omar's dad asks you, "When should I introduce a cup for him to drink his whole milk?"

Exercise 1-7: *Multiple-choice question*
Based on an understanding of growth and development of a 15-month-old, you state:

    A. "Omar should only be drinking low-fat milk."

    B. "Omar can begin to drink from a cup now."

    C. "Omar should still be drinking formula from a bottle."

    D. "Omar will not have the necessary fine motor skills until he is 2."

You do parent teaching regarding development from 15 to 18 months with Omar's father and provide him with written information. Omar's father is of Indian descent but was educated in English in his native country and can read and write English well.

Exercise 1-8: *Select all that apply*
Which of the following teaching points should you make in your instruction?

    ❑ Potty training should be completed during this time.

    ❑ Offer the child push–pull toys.

    ❑ Allow the child to dress himself.

    ❑ Use child-resistant covers and cupboard closures.

    ❑ Gradually introduce table foods.

Answers to this chapter begin on page 10.

In order for you to provide the best instruction for parents who come to the clinic with their children, you realize that you must fully understand the psychosocial milestones in human growth and development. You are also asked to precept a student nurse today. The student's name is Harold and he is a second-degree student that is back to nursing school after a career as a chiropractor.

Exercise 1-9: *Matching*

Match the psychosocial milestone in Column A with the correct stage of development in Column B.

Column A	Column B
_____The child takes pleasure in completing tasks	A. Infancy: Trust versus mistrust
_____The child begins to form attachment to the parents.	B. Toddler: Autonomy versus shame and doubt
_____The child asserts free will to initiate a task.	C. Preschool: Initiative versus guilt
_____The child engages in imaginative play and interactions.	D. School age: Industry versus inferiority
_____The child's focus turns to the importance of acceptance.	E. Adolescent: Identity versus role diffusion

 eResource 1-4: To reinforce Harold's understanding of developmental milestones, you direct him to the CDC's website to:
- Review materials: goo.gl/ccsYiX
- Watch a video, *Baby Steps: Learn the Signs. Act Early*: goo.gl/yxMffc

Harold observed that a child in the waiting room started crying when his mother left the room to go to the restroom. He has some additional questions about separation anxiety.

 eResource 1-5: You encourage Harold to use his mobile device to access Medscape to learn more about separation anxiety:
- Online: [Pathway: www.medscape.org → Under the tab "Reference," select "References & Tools" → Enter "Separation anxiety" into the search field → Under the "Overview" tab, review "Background"]
- On your mobile device, you can access the same information: [Pathway: Medscape → Enter "Separation anxiety" into the search field → Under the "Overview" tab, review "Background"]

You and Harold continue to discuss developmental levels of children before you call for the next patient. Harold is very thankful because he knows this will help him on his next pediatric test.

Answers to this chapter begin on page 10.

Exercise 1-10: *Matching*

Match the cognitive milestone in Column A with the correct stage of development according to Piaget in Column B.

Column A	Column B
_____ Child looks for a ball that is hidden under a pillow.	A. Sensorimotor
	B. Preoperational
_____ Child is able to conserve mass.	C. Concrete operations
_____ Child is able to understand a hypothesis.	D. Formal operations
_____ Child is egocentric and believes everyone sees three mountains in the same way as he or she does.	

You tell Harold that your next patients are 4- and 5-year-olds and they are good ages to review developmental activity. You call the next patient to the examination room.

Unfolding Case Study #1-3 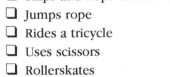 Ethan and Annie

The next patients you see are 4-year-old Ethan and his 5-year-old cousin, Annie. They are brought in by their grandmother since their parents work. Ethan and Annie are developing well and are cared for in a multigenerational home in which the grandmother takes responsibility for childcare when her children, the parents of Ethan and Annie, are at work. The grandmother takes good care of the children but speaks Spanish and very limited English.

Exercise 1-11: *Select all that apply*

You and Harold perform a Denver Developmental Screening on 4-year-old Ethan. Which of the following tasks should Ethan be able to demonstrate?

- ❏ Skips and hops on one foot
- ❏ Jumps rope
- ❏ Rides a tricycle
- ❏ Uses scissors
- ❏ Rollerskates

e **eResource 1-6:** To reinforce his understanding of normal development for Ethan, Harold refers to the CDC website and reviews the content regarding expected milestones for a 4-year-old: goo.gl/Agdvy2

Annie shows you a cut on her finger that she got in preschool and tells you the story about how it happened. She is a very social little child who speaks clearly in English and both she and Ethan can speak in Spanish also. While Annie is waiting for you to finish Ethan's examination, Annie unloads her "pocketbook" and she cuts figures from a piece of construction paper and hands the figure to Harold and instructs him to glue a design on it.

Answers to this chapter begin on page 10.

Exercise 1-12: *Multiple-choice question*

The type of play that Annie is portraying is known as:

     A. Parallel play

     B. Dramatic play

     C. Solitary play

     D. Associative play

e   **eResource 1-7:** To provide the grandmother a handout that explains normal growth and development for children Annie's and Ethan's ages, Harold prints out the CDC's educational handout, *Act Early*, Spanish edition, which provides an easy-to-understand overview of developmental milestones: goo.gl/9tz3Dn

Ethan and Annie's grandmother has a handwritten note from Annie's mother that asks about immunization needed for Annie to start kindergarten in the fall.

Exercise 1-13: *Select all that apply*

Which of the following immunizations are recommended by the CDC for the 5-year-old school-age child?

     ❑ Yearly seasonal influenza vaccine

     ❑ Pertussis vaccine (Tdap)

     ❑ Human papillomavirus

     ❑ Inactivated polio vaccine

     ❑ Hepatitis B

e   **eResource 1-8:** Harold uses his mobile device to access the CDC's *Childhood Immunization Schedule*: goo.gl/86NxtF

You write the answers on the paper that the grandmother presents so she can take them home to the family. You also give her an appointment to see Annie 1 month before the start of kindergarten to get all her immunizations up to date. Ethan needs a 5-year-old appointment in a year. You and Harold continue to discuss immunizations. You tell Harold that there are many resources available that he can download onto his mobile device that can be accessed from the CDC's website.

e   **eResource 1-9:** You give Harold the web address, goo.gl/RnkWwh
     ■ Harold downloads *Healthy Children* from the American Academy of Pediatrics (AAP) and reviews immunization schedules for 5-year-olds.
     ■ Harold also downloads *Shots by STFM* from the Group on Immunization Education of the Society of Teachers of Family Medicine.

e   **eResource 1-10:** As Harold browses the CDC's website, he discovers the mobile versions of the Vaccine Information Sheets (VIS) for health care providers to provide to patients. He writes down the link to share with you: m.cdc.gov/VIS

Answers to this chapter begin on page 10.

Unfolding Case Study #1-4 ░ Jessica

The next patient that you see is Jessica who is a developing 10-year-old. Jessica is with her mother and is not happy about being at the clinic. Jessica believes the clinic is for "babies." Her mother has been taking her to the clinic since birth and you have watched Jessica grow and meet all of her milestones. This is very important since you know that Jessica was 9 weeks preterm at birth. Today you want to assess her gross cognitive development.

Exercise 1-14: *Multiple-choice question*
Which of the following assessments would indicate that the child is in the concrete operations stage of cognitive development?
   A. The child is using formal logic to problem solve.
   B. The child is able to set priorities based on problem solving.
   C. The child is able to conserve mass.
   D. The child moves from egocentric thought and develops awareness of others.

Jessica's mother states that she would like to talk about Jessica's sexual development since she is prepubescent and showing signs of breast development. You ask Jessica's mom if she is comfortable speaking about this with Harold in the room and if she would prefer him to wait outside. Jessica looks annoyed that her mother has even brought this subject up. While you are outside the examination room with Harold you ask him to review female and male maturation stages and give him two case studies to review. One case is about a 16-year-old girl with heavy bleeding and the second is about male development.

Exercise 1-15: *Ordering*
Order the steps of sexual maturation in females from 1 to 4, beginning with the first stage and ending with the last stage.
_____ Menarche
_____ Development of breast buds
_____ Pubic hair growth
_____ Axillary hair growth

Exercise 1-16: *Ordering*
Order the steps of sexual maturation in males (from 1 to 4) beginning with the first stage and ending with the last stage.
_____ Deepening of the voice
_____ Facial hair growth
_____ Pubic hair growth
_____ Enlargement of the testes

Answers to this chapter begin on page 10.

eResource 1-11: To reinforce your teaching, you provide Jessica's mother with a handout, *Positive Parenting Tips for Healthy Child Development: Middle Childhood (9–11 Years of Age)*: goo.gl/Npl9gH

Exercise 1-17: *Multiple-choice question*

Also in the clinic is a 16-year-old female who has a history of heavy bleeding with her menstrual cycles. As a result, she is experiencing iron deficiency. Which of the following foods should be encouraged to increase her iron levels?

    A. Dark leafy green vegetables and citrus fruits

    B. Peanut butter, jelly, and bananas

    C. Seafood and yellow vegetables

    D. Beans and dairy products

 eResource 1-12: To support patient teaching regarding dietary management of iron deficiency, you:

    ■ Print out the CDC's patient information regarding *Iron and Iron Deficiency*: goo.gl/2JkMy6

    ■ Provide an audio recording from WebMD, about *Iron-Rich Foods*: goo.gl/trJmSb

Exercise 1-18: *Multiple-choice question*

Another patient, Andy, a 16-year-old boy, views himself as competitive, athletic, and masculine. This image of oneself is known as:

    A. Gender schemes

    B. Androgyny

    C. Gender identity

    D. Gender stereotype

Talking to Jessica's mother with Jessica in the room was beneficial and Jessica did ask questions about what she can expect next in her development. Jessica does not need another appointment for a year unless there are concerns between that time frame. After the appointment with Jessica, Harold discusses his exercise and case study answers with you. Harold is very happy that you are reviewing material he will need for his upcoming pediatrics test. You and Harold call the next patient from the waiting room.

Answers to this chapter begin on page 10.

Unfolding Case Study #1-5 ▨ Frankie

Six-year-old Frankie is being seen for a follow-up visit. He had his arm cast removed a week ago and you are checking the movement in his wrist. He had sustained a wrist break by falling off a piece of playground equipment at school.

Exercise 1-19: *True or false*
_____ Prior to puberty, the child's bones are soft and flexible, which predisposes them to fractures.

Exercise 1-20: *Select all that apply*
Which findings would indicate that Frankie has met fine motor age-appropriate milestones?
- ❑ Ties shoelace
- ❑ Cuts with scissors
- ❑ Prints first name
- ❑ Plays a musical instrument
- ❑ Weaves potholders on small looms

eResource 1-13: To reinforce your teaching for Frankie's mother, you provide a printout from the CDC website: *Positive Parenting Tips for Healthy Child Development: Middle Childhood (6–8 Years of Age):* goo.gl/LgCgGu

Exercise 1-21: *Select all that apply*
Which of the following strategies facilitate social development in the school-age child?
- ❑ Reinforce competitive behaviors in organized sports.
- ❑ Encourage children to select activities based upon their own interests.
- ❑ Emphasize teamwork and fair play in organized sports.
- ❑ Limit involvement to one organized sport.

Answers to this chapter begin on page 10.

Answers

Exercise 1-1: *Calculation*

You weigh Maddie at her visit and document her weight as 15 pounds, head circumference as 16 inches, and length as 25 inches. You plot her measurements on the chart and determine her percentiles for height and weight. What percentile is she in terms of weight and length?

Weight 26th percentile and height 25th percentile

Exercise 1-2: *Fill-in*

How would you interpret these findings in relation to her percentile and other female infants of the same age?

Interpretation of Findings: Seventy-five percent of infants Maddie's age are taller and 74% of infants Maddie's age weigh more than Maddie

Exercise 1-3: *Multiple-choice question*

Which findings would indicate that Maddie has met gross motor age-appropriate milestones?

A. Maddie is able to pull herself to a stand—NO, this milestone does not occur until approximately 10 months.

B. Maddie can sit alone without support—NO, this milestone occurs at approximately 8 months.

C. Maddie can roll from her back to her abdomen—YES

D. Maggie can grasp a rattle with her fingers—NO, this is an example of a fine motor milestone that occurs at 6 months.

Exercise 1-4: *Select all that apply*

Based on an understanding of growth and development, and safety, select all toys that would meet Maddie's needs.

❑ Brightly colored latex balloons   NO, this is a safety hazard. The child could bite into the latex and aspirate.

❑ Push–pull toys   NO, the child does not walk until 12 months.

☒ **Teething toys**   **YES, first teeth are erupting.**

☒ **Books with bright pictures**   **YES, stimulates the senses.**

☒ **Brightly colored soft toys**   **YES, children like to manipulate and mouth.**

❑ Stacking blocks   NO, children do not have the fine motor skills until 9 to 12 months.

Exercise 1-5: *Multiple-choice question*

This scenario described in Unfolding Case Study #1-2 is an example of:

A. Stranger anxiety—NO, stranger anxiety presents at 6 to 8 months and resolves.

B. Regressive behaviors—NO, this is normal play for a 2-year-old.

C. Cooperative play—NO, this type of play is seen in preschoolers.

D. Parallel play—YES

Exercise 1-6: *Select all that apply*

Which findings would indicate that Omar has met gross motor age-appropriate milestones?

☒ **Walks well**   **YES, child can walk independently.**

☒ **Stoops and recovers a ball**   **YES, will use a wide-based stance.**

❑ Walks up steps   NO, does not achieve this until 18 months.

❑ Builds a tower of two cubes   NO, this is a fine motor skill.

❑ Jumps   NO, this skill typically occurs after the second birthday.

Exercise 1-7: *Multiple-choice question*

Based on an understanding of growth and development of a 15-month-old, you state:

A. "Omar should only be drinking low-fat milk."—NO, toddlers must drink whole milk for brain development.

B. "Omar can begin to drink from a cup now."—YES, weaning should begin.

C. "Omar should still be drinking formula from a bottle."—NO, toddlers must drink whole milk for brain development.

D. "Omar will not have the necessary fine motor skills until he is 2."—NO, he is developmentally able to meet this fine motor skill milestone.

Exercise 1-8: *Select all that apply*

Which of the following teaching points should you make in your instruction?

❑ Potty training should be completed during this time—NO, child is not physiologically ready for potty training until a minimum of 18 months.

☒ **Offer the child push–pull toys—YES, this will foster gross motor development.**

❑ Allow the child to dress himself—NO, the child does not have the necessary fine motor skills.

☒ **Use child-resistant covers and cupboard closures—YES, prevent poisoning in this curious age group.**

☒ **Gradually introduce table foods—YES, introduce all major food groups.**

Exercise 1-9: *Matching*

Match the psychosocial milestone in Column A with the correct stage of development in Column B.

Column A	Column B
__D__ The child takes pleasure in completing tasks.	A. Infancy: Trust versus mistrust
__A__ The child begins to form attachment to the parents.	B. Toddler: Autonomy versus shame and doubt
__B__ The child asserts free will to initiate a task.	C. Preschool: Initiative versus guilt
__C__ The child engages in imaginative play and interactions.	D. School age: Industry versus inferiority
__E__ The child's focus turns to the importance of acceptance.	E. Adolescent: Identity versus role diffusion

Exercise 1-10: *Matching*

Match the cognitive milestone in Column A with the correct stage of development according to Piaget in Column B.

Column A	Column B
__A__ Child looks for a ball that is hidden under a pillow.	A. Sensorimotor
__C__ Child is able to conserve mass.	B. Preoperational
__D__ Child is able to understand hypothesis.	C. Concrete operations
__B__ Child is egocentric and believes everyone sees three mountains in the sameway as he or she does.	D. Formal operations

Exercise 1-11: *Select all that apply*

You and Harold perform a Denver Developmental Screening on 4-year-old Ethan. Which of the following tasks should Ethan be able to demonstrate?

☒ **Skips and hops on one foot—YES, this milestone is met during the preschool years.**

❑ Jumps rope—NO, this milestone is met during the school-age years.

☒ **Rides a tricycle—YES, this milestone is met during the preschool years.**

☒ **Uses scissors—YES, this milestone is met during the preschool years.**

❏ Rollerskates—NO, this milestone is met during the school-age years.

Exercise 1-12: *Multiple-choice question*

The type of play that Annie is portraying is known as:

A. Parallel play—NO, this play is seen in toddlers whereby they play near each other but have little interaction.

B. Dramatic play—NO, this play is seen in preschoolers but involves imitating behaviors or enactment.

C. Solitary play—NO, this play is seen in the infant whose senses are stimulated but there is no engagement with another child.

D. Associative play—YES, this play is seen in the preschooler who enjoys cooperating with others.

Exercise 1-13: *Select all that apply*

Which of the following immunizations are recommended by the CDC for the 5-year-old school-age child?

☒ **Yearly seasonal influenza vaccine—YES**

☒ **Pertussis vaccine (Tdap)—YES**

❏ Human papillomavirus—NO, between 11 and 12 years.

☒ **Inactivated polio vaccine—YES, between 4 and 6 years.**

❏ Hepatitis B—NO, during infancy.

Exercise 1-14: *Multiple-choice question*

Which of the following assessments would indicate that the child is in the concrete operations stage of cognitive development?

A. The child is using formal logic to problem solve—NO, formal operations.

B. The child is able to set priorities based on problem solving—NO, formal operations.

C. The child is able to conserve mass—**YES, concrete operations.**

D. The child moves from egocentric thought and develops awareness of others—NO, preoperational thinking.

Exercise 1-15: *Ordering*

Order the steps of sexual maturation in females from 1 to 4, beginning with the first stage and ending with the last stage.

__4__	Menarche
__1__	Development of breast buds
__2__	Pubic hair growth
__3__	Axillary hair growth

Exercise 1-16: *Ordering*

Order the steps of sexual maturation in males (from 1 to 4) beginning with the first stage and ending with the last stage.

    4   Deepening of the voice

    3   Facial hair growth

    2   Pubic hair growth

    1   Enlargement of the testes

Exercise 1-17: *Multiple-choice question*

Also in the clinic is a 16-year-old female who has a history of heavy bleeding with her menstrual cycles. As a result, she is experiencing iron deficiency. Which of the following foods should be encouraged to increase her iron levels?

A. **Dark leafy green vegetables and citrus fruits—YES, iron-rich foods should be taken with vitamin C.**

B. Peanut butter, jelly, and bananas—NO, not iron-rich foods.

C. Seafood and yellow vegetables—NO, not iron-rich foods.

D. Beans and dairy products—NO, although beans are rich in iron, dairy is not.

Exercise 1-18: *Multiple-choice question*

Another patient, Andy, a 16-year-old boy, views himself as competitive, athletic, and masculine. This image of oneself is known as:

A. Gender schemes—NO, this refers to gender typing and the role of the environment and the child's cognitive status.

B. Androgyny—NO, this gender identity has equal masculine and feminine traits.

C. **Gender identity—YES, this is an image of either masculine or feminine traits.**

D. Gender stereotype—NO, a preconceived notion of expected behaviors based upon gender.

Exercise 1-19: *True or false*

True Prior to puberty, the child's bones are soft and flexible, which predisposes them to fractures.

Exercise 1-20: *Select all that apply*

Which findings would indicate that Frankie has met fine motor age-appropriate milestones?

☒ **Ties shoelace—YES, this behavior occurs at 5 to 6 years.**

☒ **Cuts with scissors—YES, this behavior occurs at 4 to 5 years.**

☒ **Prints first name—YES, this behavior occurs around 6 years.**

❑ Plays a musical instrument—NO, this behavior does not occur until school age.

❑ Weaves potholders on small looms—NO, this behavior does not occur until school age.

Exercise 1-21: *Select all that apply*

Which of the following strategies facilitate social development in the school-age child?

❑ Reinforce competitive behaviors in organized sports—NO, discourage competitive sports that focus on individual player's gains.

☒ **Encourage children to select activities based upon their own interests—YES, expose the child to a variety of activities so the child can determine what suits him or her best.**

☒ **Emphasize teamwork and fair play in organized sports—YES, emphasize collaborating with peers.**

❑ Limit involvement to one organized sport—NO, expose the child to a variety of activities so the child can determine what suits him or her best.

2

Pediatric Assessment and Nursing Care

Susan Parnell Scholtz

Unfolding Case Study #2-1 ▒ Lindsay

You are the nurse at a well baby clinic in an inner-city setting. A 1-year-old infant girl, Lindsay, is being seen next. The child weighed 8 pounds at birth and was 21 inches long. At this visit, the child weighed 16 pounds, 8 ounces.

Exercise 2-1: *Multiple-choice question*
Based on an understanding of growth and development, these findings indicate which of the following?

     A. This weight indicates normal weight gain for an infant.

     B. This weight indicates low weight gain for an infant.

     C. This weight indicates above-average weight gain for an infant.

     D. This weight indicates maternal deprivation.

 eResource 2-1: Consult your mobile device and open the World Health Organization's (WHO) STAT GrowthCharts™ (downloaded in Chapter 1): [Pathway: STAT GrowthChart™ → Enter weight into the appropriate field → View result at the bottom of the screen]

As you are doing your assessment of Lindsay, you answer questions about her growth and development for her 16-year-old mom and the baby's father. They ask you if Lindsay has gained enough weight because they sometimes have to "water down" her milk to "make ends meet."

Exercise 2-2: *Calculation*
Lindsay's present weight of 16 pounds, 8 ounces is converted to kilograms. What is her weight in kilograms?

 eResource 2-2: Utilize a Medical Calculator to verify your answer:
- Online, use MedCalc: [Pathway: www.medcalc.com → Select "General" → Select "Weights & Measures" and enter information into appropriate fields]
- On your mobile device, use:
  - QxMD Medical Calculator (downloaded from: goo.gl/mkiMev [Android] or goo.gl/TORcbQ [iOS]): [Pathway: QxMD → Select "weight conversion" → Enter Lindsay's weight into field]

■ Universal Converter by oWorld Software (downloaded from: goo.
gl/WWEGcX [Android] or goo.gl/d4wld5 [iOS]): [Pathway: Universal
Converter → Select "weight conversion" → Enter Lindsay's weight
into field]

Exercise 2-3: *Fill-in*

In order to assess Lindsay's weight-for-age percentile, her weight is plotted on the
Centers for Disease Control and Prevention's (CDC) "Birth to 36 Months Growth Chart."
Based on this calculation, Lindsay's weight is approximately in the _____ percentile.

eResource 2-3: In order to plot Lindsay's weight go to:
■ The CDC's website (www.cdc.gov.growthcharts) and download the
Birth to 36 Months: Length for Age and Weight for Age profiles. Plot
the appropriate weight and height to determine the percentile each
parameter falls within.
■ Utilize Online Child Growth Chart Calculators at:
  ■ Baby Center: [Pathway: goo.gl/6YtwJM → Enter child's sex, age,
  length, weight, and head circumference → View percentile each
  parameter falls within]
  ■ MedCalc Interactive Growth Chart: [Pathway: www.medcalc.com
  → Select "Pediatrics" → Select "Growth Charts" → Enter age, sex,
  height, weight, and head circumference → Select Combined HC-
  for-Age and Weight-for-Length Birth to 36 Months → Select "Create
  Growth Chart" to view results]

You discuss with Lindsay's family their qualifications for the Women, Infants, and
Children (WIC) program in order to assist them to obtain more food sources. The
WIC office is within walking distance of the well baby clinic so you make them an
appointment to go there this afternoon.

eResource 2-4: Lindsay's parents have a lot of questions about WIC, so
to supplement your teaching, you provide Lindsay's parents the following
information:
■ Nutrition Program Fact Sheet: goo.gl/U0iBu8
■ Frequently Asked Questions about WIC: goo.gl/wKtNRH
■ Article (with text to audio option), *Feeding Your 1–2 Year Old*:
goo.gl/gSTMVb

Exercise 2-4: *Select all that apply*

You plan to use the Denver Developmental Screening Test to assess Lindsay's fine motor skills. Based on this screening tool, the 1-year-old should be able to complete the
following fine motor skills:

❏ Builds a tower of two cubes

❏ Bangs two cubes held in hands

❏ Places blocks in a cup

❏ Demonstrates a pinscher grasp

❏ Throws a ball overhead

Answers to this chapter begin on page 28.

You discuss with the parents the activities that they do with Lindsay at home and make some play suggestions to them that are appropriate for 1-year-olds. You also ask them about living conditions and discuss safety issues now that Lindsay is mobile. The parents understand that stairways need to be blocked and that kitchen cabinets need to be secured.

 eResource 2-5: To reinforce your teaching, you show the following videos to Lindsay's parents:
- *Baby on the Move: Cruising:* goo.gl/ludYtJ
- *Baby on the Move: Walking:* goo.gl/DlYX3r
- *Child Proofing and Home Safety:* goo.gl/j6YFw8

Unfolding Case Study #2-2 José

José is brought to the well baby clinic for his 1-week check-up. José's mother speaks very little English but is pleasant and attentive. José's 8-year-old sister, Marta, interprets for her mother.

 eResource 2-6: You also use your mobile device to access English-to-Spanish Dictionary (downloaded from: goo.gl/io6eVZ [Android] or goo.gl/5VHcSv [iOS]) to look up key words and phrases.

You assess José systematically from head to toe.

Exercise 2-5: *Matching*
Match the assessment skill in column A with the correct term in column B.

Column A	Column B
_____ Through the use of a stethoscope, listening to the internal sounds of the body to ascertain any abnormalities.	A. Inspection
	B. Auscultation
_____ Through the use of the examiner's hands, tapping the patient's skin to determine density of the tissue being examined.	C. Palpation
	D. Percussion
_____ Through use of the examiner's hands, touching the patient to determine position and size of the organs.	
_____ Through use of the examiner's eyes, head-to-toe observation of the patient.	

Understanding the growth and development of infants is very important in order to interpret assessment findings and develop a plan of care.

 eResource 2-7: To reinforce your understanding of normal growth and development of infants, review the CDC's materials regarding developmental milestones: goo.gl/ccsYiX

Answers to this chapter begin on page 28.

Exercise 2-6: *True or false*

_____ The liver and spleen of an infant are poorly protected by the abdomen from trauma.

_____ Total body surface area of an infant is large, making it difficult for the child to conserve heat when exposed.

_____ Hyperthermia (greater than 100° F) in the infant from birth to 3 months is an expected finding.

_____ Palpation of an apical pulse is more accurate in infants than use of a stethoscope.

_____ Myelination of the spinal cord is mature at birth.

_____ An increased metabolic rate in the infant increases the infant's oxygen demands.

Infants, like José, often have findings that are not seen in older children.

Exercise 2-7: *Select all that apply*

During a newborn assessment, you, the neonatal nurse, document findings of the overall assessment. Identify findings that are considered normal variations.

❑ Epstein pearls

❑ Ptosis of the eyelid

❑ Purulent discharge from the lacrimal ducts

❑ Absence of the red reflex in the eye

❑ Upper third of the ear falls below the outer canthus of the eye

❑ Boggy mass under the scalp that does not cross suture lines

At 1 week old you do not expect to find any abnormalities in José's heart or lungs that were not diagnosed in the hospital of birth, but it is always prudent to understand that some newborn conditions manifest after discharge.

 eResource 2-8: To review a complete head-to-toe assessment of a neonate, please view the following videos:
  ■ *Head to Toe Examination of the Neonate:* goo.gl/ZExNSi
  ■ *Newborn Assessment:* goo.gl/yNzpsR

Exercise 2-8: *Multiple-choice question*

Which of the following assessment findings would indicate that the neonate may be in respiratory distress immediately after birth?

    A. Periodic respirations. Respiratory rate of 50 breaths per minute with occasional pauses of respirations (less than 20 seconds)

    B. Respiratory rate of 55 breaths per minute with apnea and bradycardia

    C. Diaphragmatic breathing and a rise in the abdomen during breathing

    D. Bronchovesicular breath

Answers to this chapter begin on page 28.

eResource 2-9: To review your understanding of respiratory assessment of the neonate, you watch the video, *Newborn Care Series: Breathing Problems*: goo.gl/F0YxIz

José's check-up for weight and his head-to-toe assessment are all within normal limits. José's mother is given a follow-up appointment for 1 month. She is also provided with infant development literature in Spanish and an emergency telephone number for the telemedicine line that can be accessed in English and Spanish 22 hours a day, should she need it.

Unfolding Case Study #2-3 Suzy

Suzy is brought to the well baby clinic for her routine 2-year-old check-up but her mother says she has been acting sick since last evening.

Exercise 2-9: *Ordering*
Two-year-old Suzy is brought to the clinic with a chief complaint of an earache and a fever. You plan to assess her middle ear. List the steps of an ear examination in the order in which they would occur.

_____ Place Suzy on her parent's lap and ask the parent to restrain Suzy's legs between his or her legs.

_____ Pull the lower pinna of the ear downward and backward.

_____ Ask the parent to restrain Suzy's arms and pull her face close to the parent's chest.

_____ Hold the otoscope and inflator in the examiner's dominant hand.

_____ Introduce air and then release to assess mobility.

 eResource 2-10: To learn more about the clinical manifestations of otitis media, access Medscape:
- Online: [Pathway: www.medscape.org → Under the tab "Reference," select "References & Tools" → Enter "otitis media" into the search field → Under the "Overview" tab, review "Practice Essentials" and "Background"; be sure to view the multimedia library]
- On your mobile device, you can access the same information: [Pathway: Medscape → Enter "otitis media" into the search field → Under the "Overview" tab, review "Background"; be sure to view images as well]

Suzy has a history of ear infections and you understand that chronic ear infections in a child can affect the child's hearing, which can, in turn, affect learning and comprehension. Screening for potential hearing loss is very important at any developmental stage.

Answers to this chapter begin on page 28.

Exercise 2-10: *Matching*

Match the diagnostic test in Column A with the correct term in Column B.

Column A	Column B
_____ Utilization of head phones to detect the quietest of sounds a child can hear.	A. Pneumonic otoscopy
_____ This test determines motility of the tympanic membrane and fluid within the tympanic membrane.	B. Rinne test C. Weber test
_____ Use of inflator to instill air into the middle ear of a child.	D. Tympanometry E. Audiogram
_____ Placement of a tuning fork midline on the child's head and asking the child where the sound originates.	
_____ Placement of a tuning fork behind the ear and asking the child to state when no vibrations are heard.	

Suzy is prescribed antibiotics and provided with a referral to an ENT (ear, nose, and throat) specialist for recurring ear infections (three in 1 year). You explain to the parents that the ENT specialist may recommend "tubes in her ears" to prevent further infections.

 eResource 2-11: To reinforce your teaching, refer to Medscape:
- Online: [Pathway: www.medscape.org → Under the tab "Reference," select "References & Tools" → Enter "otitis media" into the search field → Under the "Follow-up" tab, review "Outpatient Care," "Deterrence and Prevention," and "Patient Teaching"]
- On your mobile device, you can access the same information: [Pathway: Medscape → Enter "otitis media" into the search field → Under the "Follow-up" tab, review "Outpatient Care," "Deterrence and Prevention," and "Patient Teaching"]

Unfolding Case Study #2-4 ■ Michael

Michael is your next patient at the well baby clinic. Michael is 3 years old and is being prepared for preschool. You perform a head-to-toe assessment on him but concentrate on his abdominal assessment because his past health history reveals two umbilical hernia repairs.

 eResource 2-12: To learn more about this procedure, consult Medscape:
- Online: [Pathway: www.medscape.org → Under the tab "Reference," select "References & Tools" → Enter "umbilical hernia" into the search field → Select "umbilical hernia repair" and review content]

Answers to this chapter begin on page 28.

■ On your mobile device, you can access the same information: [Pathway: Medscape → Enter "umbilical hernia" into the search field → Select "umbilical hernia repair" and review content]

Exercise 2-11: *Matching*

Match the organ in Column A with the quadrant of the abdomen where it can be located in the child from Column B.

Column A	Column B
_____ Liver	A. Right upper quadrant (RUQ)
_____ Spleen	B. Left upper quadrant (LUQ)
_____ Stomach	C. Right lower quadrant (RLQ)
_____ Bladder if distended	D. Left lower quadrant (LLQ)
_____ Head of pancreas	
_____ Sigmoid colon	

Exercise 2-12: *Ordering*

You are about to assess Michael's abdomen. Identify the order of the assessment from 1 to 4 beginning with Step 1.

_____ Auscultation

_____ Palpation

_____ Percussion

_____ Inspection

e **eResource 2-13:** To learn more about umbilical hernias, consult Epocrates Online: [Pathway: online.epocrates.com → Select "Diseases" tab → Enter "hernia" into the search field → Select "Umbilical Hernia" and review content]

Exercise 2-13: *Fill-in*

To assess Michael's liver, you place your fingers over and under the costal margins. The liver is palpated as the child takes a deep breath. This technique is known as_____.

During the abdominal assessment you notice a significant finding.

Exercise 2-14: *Multiple-choice question*

You document that there is rebound tenderness over the abdomen. Which of the following best describes this finding?

A. The child, who is fearful, contracts the abdominal muscles when assessed.

B. The child complains of severe pain when pressure is released.

C. The child will be able to accurately point to the painful area.

D. The child will shield the area that is being examined.

This finding is reported to the nurse practitioner (NP) on duty at the clinic. The NP sends Michael's parents to the emergency department to have a diagnostic test to rule out abdominal obstruction or appendicitis.

Unfolding Case Study #2-5 Kristen

Kristen is a healthy, active 15-year-old who resents her mother bringing her to the clinic for her yearly check-up. Kristen's dad has recently lost his job and Kristen's mother is trying her best to hold the family together and provide what her three teenage children need. Kristen has been "on watch" for scoliosis since she was age 12.

eResource 2-14: To learn more about scoliosis, consult Epocrates Online: [Pathway: online.epocrates.com → Select "Diseases" tab → Enter "scoliosis" into the search field and review content]

Exercise 2-15: *Multiple-choice question*
You have just completed patient education with 15-year-old Kristen and her mother about scoliosis. Which statement, if made by her mother, indicates that additional teaching is needed?
   A. "My daughter will need to wear a corrective device 23 hours per day"
   B. "Exercise will be the only treatment needed to correct her scoliosis"
   C. "My daughter was referred for further evaluation because her curvature was greater than 7 degrees"
   D. "Kristen's curve seemed to decrease when she had her growth spurt, which is typical of scoliosis"

Kristen is referred to a physical therapist that comes to the clinic on Wednesday afternoons. Kristen is provided with a note so she can leave school early and take the bus to the clinic. Kristen is accepting of this and understands the rationale but has questions about what to expect.

eResource 2-15: To supplement your patient teaching, you show Kristen a couple of videos regarding nonsurgical treatment of scoliosis:
   ▪ *Scoliosis Non-Surgical Treatment: Reduction and Rehabilitation:* goo.gl/ozVFB0
   ▪ *Scoliosis Exercises:* goo.gl/uO0mYc

You suddenly realize that the waiting room at the clinic is full and there are many children to see before the day is over.

Answers to this chapter begin on page 28.

Unfolding Case Study #2-6 *"Triaging"*

It is evident that not all the children will be able to be seen today. Many have well baby appointments but others are walk-ins due to health care issues. As the charge nurse you assume a "triage role" and do a fast intake history on all the patients waiting in order to prioritize who is seen and refer any that need emergency department care or an appointment on a different day. The first parent you speak with has an appointment and is next so you bring her back to the examination room with her 3-year-old son, Marcus, and assign their care to an experienced staff nurse so you can continue to triage. You complete a cardiac assessment on Marcus and document, "Still a murmur auscultated at the left sternal border."

e   eResource 2-16: To review your understanding of murmurs, refer to:
- Online [Pathway: www.medscape.org → Under the tab "Reference," select "References & Tools" → Enter "Murmurs" into the search field → Under the content of "Heart Sounds," review content regarding "Murmurs"]
- On your mobile device, you can access the same information: [Pathway: Medscape → Enter "Murmurs" into the search field → Under the content of "Heart Sounds," review content regarding "Murmurs"]

Exercise 2-16: *Multiple-choice question*
Based on an understanding of cardiac murmurs in a child, you base patient education on which of the following factors?
- A. This murmur is benign and is often heard in the left lower sternal border when the child is lying supine.
- B. This is a serious murmur heard in the left upper sternal border during activity.
- C. This is a benign systolic ejection murmur heard in the clavicular region.
- D. This is a serious murmur that is audible without the stethoscope in direct contact with the chest.

The nurse assessing Marcus has years of experience with pediatric nursing. She knows that cardiac issues range from minor to life-threatening and has a good grasp of what disorders need to be assessed and referred immediately.

Exercise 2-17: *Fill-in*
Identify the cardiac disorder based on the definition presented.
_____ A disorder characterized by vasculitis in the small vessels and the potential for cardiac aneurysms.
_____ An acquired cardiac disease that typically follows an untreated streptococcal infection such as pharyngitis.
_____ A disorder manifested by cyanosis, cough, shortness of breath, and fatigue.
_____ Inflammation of the sac that surrounds the myocardium and may lead to heart failure.

Answers to this chapter begin on page 28.

_____ Cyanotic congenital heart disorder characterized by four structural defects.

_____ A structural disorder characterized by an opening or hole between the lower chambers of the heart.

_____ Often without symptoms, a ductus arteriosus does not immediately close after birth.

The next patient you interview is a 16-year-old female, Wendy, who was with her boyfriend. She presents to the clinic with a fever of 101° F, pain on voiding, and dark amber urine.

Exercise 2-18: *Select all that apply*

You should privately ask Wendy which of the following questions?

❑ "Have you recently taken a bubble bath or used bath gels?"

❑ "Have you recently engaged in sexual intercourse?"

❑ "Have you recently experienced bed-wetting?"

❑ "Do you wear cotton-lined underwear?"

❑ "Would you say your jeans are tight or loose fitting?"

You place Wendy at the top of the list to be seen due to her temperature and the potential for urinary tract infections (UTIs) to turn into severe kidney infections or *pyelonephritis*.

 eResource 2-17: To learn more about pyelonephritis, go to Epocrates Online: [Pathway: online.epocrates.com → Under the "Diseases" tab, enter "Pyelonephritis" in the search field → Select "Acute Pyelonephritis" → Review content under "Basics" and "Diagnosis"]

The next person to be seen for brief health history and current complaint is a 5-year-old boy. The skin assessment reveals areas of lightly pigmented, dry skin across his back. His mother states, "These areas become more pronounced during the summer months especially when he has been out in the sun." The skin does not appear to be itchy.

Exercise 2-19: *Multiple-choice question*

Based on this assessment, you suspect he has which of the following fungal infections?

A. Folliculitis

B. Tinea versicolor

C. Atopic dermatitis

D. Contact dermatitis

You see many skin lesions at the clinic and understand the common variations that present in this population.

Answers to this chapter begin on page 28.

Exercise 2-20: *Matching*

Match the skin finding/lesion description in Column A with the correct term in Column B.

Column A	Column B
_____ A lesion that is clearly demarcated with a pink ring and is often seen in ringworm.	A. Milia
_____ A generalized rash that is a characteristic sign of fifth disease.	B. Pustule
_____ A fluid-filled lesion that is manifested in varicella.	C. Wheal
_____ An irregular, raised lesion found in a positive response to an antigen.	D. Reticulated
_____ A fluid-filled lesion with purulent drainage such as impetigo.	E. Annular
_____ Tiny, white, palpable lesions that normally occur over the bridge of a newborn's nose.	F. Vesicle

Answers to this chapter begin on page 28.

Answers

Exercise 2-1: *Multiple-choice question*

Based on an understanding of growth and development, these findings indicate which of the following?

A. This weight indicates normal weight gain for an infant—NO, an infant generally doubles birth weight by 5 months and triples the birth weight by 1 year.

B. This weight indicates low weight gain for an infant—YES, an infant generally triples the birth weight by 1 year.

C. This weight indicates above-average weight gain for an infant—NO, an infant generally doubles birth weight by 5 months and triples birth weight by 1 year. This weight gain is low based on this parameter.

D. This weight indicates maternal deprivation—NO, although the weight gain is low, it does not mean the problem is related to poor maternal–child attachment.

Exercise 2-2: *Calculation*

Lindsay's present weight of 16 pounds, 8 ounces is converted to kilograms. What is her weight in kilograms?

<u>7.6 kilograms</u>

Exercise 2-3: *Fill-in*

In order to assess Lindsay's weight-for-age percentile, her weight is plotted on the Centers for Disease Control and Prevention's "Birth to 36 Months Growth Chart." Based on this calculation, Lindsay's weight is approximately in the **<u>10th</u>** percentile.

Exercise 2-4: *Select all that apply*

You plan to use the Denver Developmental Screening Test to assess Lindsay's fine motor skills. Based on this screening tool, the 1-year-old should be able to complete the following fine motor skills:

❑ Builds a tower of two cubes—NO, this skill occurs around 17 months.

☒ **Bangs two cubes held in hands—YES, this skill occurs before the first birthday.**

❑ Places blocks in a cup—NO, this skill may be present but is expected at 13 months.

☒ **Demonstrates a pinscher grasp—YES, this skill occurs around 9 to 10 months.**

❑ Throws a ball overhead—NO, this is a gross motor skill that occurs around 22 months.

Exercise 2-5: *Matching*

Match the assessment skill in column A with the correct term in column B.

Column A	Column B
__B__ Through the use of a stethoscope, listening to the internal sounds of the body to ascertain any abnormalities.	A. Inspection B. Auscultation C. Palpation D. Percussion
__D__ Through the use of the examiner's hands, tapping the patient's skin to determine density of the tissue being examined.	
__C__ Through use of the examiner's hands, touching the patient to determine position and size of the organs.	
__A__ Through use of the examiner's eyes, head-to-toe observation of the patient.	

Exercise 2-6: *True or false*

__True__ **The liver and spleen of an infant are poorly protected by the abdomen from trauma.—YES, during infancy, these organs lie more anteriorly and are not protected by ribs and developed muscles.**

__True__ **Total body surface area of an infant is large, making it difficult for the child to conserve heat when exposed.—YES, an infant who pulls the arms and legs toward the center of the body, decreases the total body surface area and is better able to conserve heat.**

__False__ Hyperthermia (greater than 100° F) in the infant from birth to 3 months is an expected finding.—NO, any temperature elevation above 100° F must be further evaluated for a serious illness such as sepsis.

__True__ **Palpation of an apical pulse is more accurate in infants than use of a stethoscope.—YES, since there are many fluctuations in the pulse due to crying, palpation of the pulse enables the examiner to detect the changes.**

___False___ Myelination of the spinal cord is mature at birth.—NO, although all brain cells are present at birth, myelination develops in the first year of life.

___True___ **An increased metabolic rate in the infant increases the infant's oxygen demands.—YES, as the child's metabolic rate increases, the infant will need more oxygen and calories to meet the body's needs.**

Exercise 2-7: *Select all that apply*

During a newborn assessment, you, the neonatal nurse, document findings of the overall assessment. Identify findings that are considered normal variations.

☒ **Epstein pearls—YES, benign white, firm nodules found on the palate.**

☒ **Ptosis of the eyelid—YES, drooping of the eyelids that disappears a few days after birth.**

❏ Purulent discharge from the lacrimal ducts.—NO, this may indicate a blocked lacrimal duct and infection.

❏ Absence of the red reflex in the eye.—NO, may be indicative of a cataract.

❏ Upper third of the ear falls below the outer canthus of the eye.—NO, low placement may indicate Down's syndrome.

❏ Boggy mass under the scalp that does not cross suture lines.—NO, may indicate cephalohematoma.

Exercise 2-8: *Multiple-choice question*

Which of the following assessment findings would indicate that the neonate may be in respiratory distress immediately after birth?

A. Periodic respirations. Respiratory rate of 50 breaths per minute with occasional pauses of respirations (less than 20 seconds)—NO, this is considered normal respirations for a newborn.

B. **Respiratory rate of 55 breaths per minute with apnea and bradycardia—YES, although the respiratory rate is within normal limits, periods of apnea greater than 20 seconds per minute and bradycardia are signs of respiratory distress.**

C. Diaphragmatic breathing and a rise in the abdomen during breathing—NO, this type of breathing is typically seen in the newborn period.

D. Bronchovesicular breath sounds—NO, these are soft breath sounds over the smaller airway passages in the newborn.

Exercise 2-9: *Ordering*

Two-year-old Suzy is brought to the clinic with a chief complaint of an earache and a fever. You plan to assess her middle ear. List the steps of an ear examination in the order in which they would occur.

___1___ Place Suzy on her parent's lap and ask the parent to restrain Suzy's legs between his or her legs. **This step is done first to properly restrain the child.**

___4___ Pull the lower pinna of the ear downward and backward. **The lower pinna is pulled downward in the young child to allow for proper visualization of the tympanic membrane.**

__2__ Ask the parent to restrain Suzy's arms and pull her face close to the parent's chest. **Once the child's legs are restrained, it is necessary to immobilize the child's face and upper extremities.**

__3__ Hold the otoscope and inflator in the examiner's dominant hand. **This step is done once immobilization and positioning of the child are complete.**

__5__ Introduce air and then release to assess mobility. **This step is the actual initiation of the visualization and assessment of the middle ear.**

Exercise 2-10: *Matching*

Match the diagnostic test in Column A with the correct term in Column B.

Column A	Column B
__E__ Utilization of head phones to detect the quietest of sounds a child can hear.	A. Pneumonic otoscopy
__D__ This test determines motility of the tympanic membrane and fluid within the ear and uses a probe to form a pressurized seal.	B. Rinne test C. Weber test D. Tympanometry
__A__ Use of inflator to instill air into the middle ear of a child.	E. Audiogram
__C__ Placement of a tuning fork midline on the child's head and asking the child where the sound originates.	
__B__ Placement of a tuning fork behind the ear and asking the child to state when no vibrations are heard.	

Exercise 2-11: *Matching*

Match the organ in Column A with the quadrant of the abdomen where it can be located in the child in Column B.

Column A	Column B
__A__ Liver	A. Right upper quadrant (RUQ)
__B__ Spleen	B. Left upper quadrant (LUQ)
__B__ Stomach	C. Right lower quadrant (RLQ)
__C or D__ Bladder if distended	D. Left lower quadrant (LLQ)
__A__ Head of pancreas	
__D__ Sigmoid colon	

Exercise 2-12: *Ordering*

You are about to assess Michael's abdomen. Identify the order of the assessment from 1 to 4 beginning with Step 1.

___**2**___ Auscultation

___**4**___ Palpation

___**3**___ Percussion

___**1**___ Inspection

(*Note:* This sequence is only used in the assessment of the abdomen to prevent disruption of the bowel sounds.)

Exercise 2-13: *Fill-in*

To assess of Michael's liver, you place your fingers over and under the costal margins. The liver is palpated as the child takes a deep breath. This technique is known as **hooking** technique.

Exercise 2-14: *Multiple-choice question*

You document that there is rebound tenderness over the abdomen. Which of the following best describes this finding?

A. The child, who is fearful, contracts the abdominal muscles when assessed—NO, this phenomenon occurs in relation to anxiety about the exam and does not necessary indicate pain.

B. The child complains of severe pain when pressure is released—YES, the child will experience sharp pain in cases of inflammation.

C. The child will be able to accurately point to the painful area—NO, young children often point to the area around the umbilicus even in instances when there is no pain.

D. The child will shield the area that is being examined—NO, this phenomenon is called guarding

Exercise 2-15: *Multiple-choice question*

You have just completed patient education with 15-year-old Kristen and her mother about scoliosis. Which statement, if made by her mother, indicates that additional teaching is needed?

A. "My daughter will need to wear a corrective device 23 hours per day."—NO, when a corrective device such as a Milwaukee brace is used, it can be taken off for a maximum of 1 hour so that correction is not lost.

B. "Exercise will be the only treatment needed to correct her scoliosis."—YES, exercise can be employed in combination with bracing.

C. "My daughter was referred for further evaluation because her curvature was greater than 7 degrees."—NO, a curvature of 7 degrees or greater requires further evaluation and treatment.

D. "Kristen's curve seemed to decrease when she had her growth spurt, which is typical of scoliosis.—NO, although programmed for this disorder at conception, it is typically present until prepubescence.

Exercise 2-16: *Multiple-choice question*

You complete a cardiac assessment on Marcus and document, "Murmur still auscultated at the left sternal border." Based on an understanding of cardiac murmurs in a child, you base patient education on which of the following factors?

A. This murmur is benign and is often heard in the left lower sternal border when the child is lying supine—YES, it is a common benign murmur in toddlers.

B. This is a serious murmur heard in the left upper sternal border during activity—NO, Stills murmur is not threatening and is heard in the left lower sternal border.

C. This is a benign systolic ejection murmur heard in the clavicular region—NO, murmurs found in the left infraclavicular area may indicate physiological peripheral pulmonic stenosis.

D. This is a serious murmur that is audible without the stethoscope in direct contact with the chest—NO, this is descriptive of a Grade V or Grade VI murmur.

Exercise 2-17: *Fill-in*

Identify the cardiac disorder based on the definition presented.

Kawasaki disease A disorder characterized by vasculitis in the small vessels and the potential for cardiac aneurysms.

Rheumatic fever An acquired cardiac disease that typically follows an untreated streptococcal infection such as pharyngitis.

Congestive heart failure A disorder manifested by cyanosis, cough, shortness of breath, and fatigue.

Pericarditis Inflammation of the sac that surrounds the myocardium and may lead to heart failure.

Tetralogy of Fallot Cyanotic congenital heart disorder characterized by four structural defects.

Ventricular septal defect A structural disorder characterized by an opening or hole between the lower chambers of the heart.

Patent ductus arteriosus Often without symptoms, a ductus arteriosus does not immediately close after birth.

Exercise 2-18: *Select all that apply*

You should privately ask Wendy which of the following questions?

☒ **"Have you recently taken a bubble bath or used bath gels?"—YES, bubble bath and gels change the pH of the vaginal secretions and can cause irritation, which predisposes the female to urinary tract infections.**

☒ **"Have you recently engaged in sexual intercourse?"—YES, sexual intercourse in addition to a full bladder can predispose the adolescent to a urinary tract infection.**

☐ "Have you recently experienced bed-wetting?"—NO, this would be an appropriate question for a younger child.

☒ **"Do you wear cotton-lined underwear?"—YES, nylon-lined underwear can cause irritation, which leads to infection.**

☒ **"Would you say your jeans are tight or loose fitting?"—YES, tight-fitting jeans prevent air movement and produce an environment conducive to infection.**

Exercise 2-19: *Multiple-choice question*
Based on this assessment, you suspect he has which of the following fungal infections?
  A. Folliculitis—NO, this disorder is typically caused by a *Staphilococcus aureus* infection and involves the hair follicles.
  B. Tinea versicolor—YES, this fungal infection typically presents on the trunk and is characterized by areas that have decreased pigmentation.
  C. Atopic dermatitis—NO, this disorder is not caused by a fungus and is inflammatory in nature.
  D. Contact dermatitis—NO, this disorder is not caused by a fungus and often develops as a response to an allergen.

Exercise 2-20: *Matching*
Match the skin finding/lesion description in Column A with the correct term in Column B.

Column A	Column B
__E__ A lesion that is clearly demarcated with a pink ring and is often seen in ringworm.	A. Milia
__D__ A generalized rash that is a characteristic sign of fifth disease.	B. Pustule
__F__ A fluid-filled lesion that is manifested in varicella.	C. Wheal
__C__ An irregular, raised lesion found in a positive response to an antigen.	D. Reticulated
__B__ A fluid-filled lesion with purulent drainage such as impetigo.	E. Annular
__A__ Tiny, white, palpable lesions that normally occur over the bridge of a newborn's nose.	F. Vesicle

3

Nutrition in the Child

Susan Parnell Scholtz

Unfolding Case Study #3-1 ▓ Marla

A pregnant woman, Marla, comes to the prenatal clinic for her 24-week check-up. Marla is doing well and can feel the fetus kicking on a daily basis. Marla states she is contemplating breastfeeding her newborn. Marla is a gravid II, para I. Her first child is now a toddler but she did not breastfeed him. You are the nurse in the prenatal clinic and want to give her facts about breastfeeding that may help her to make her decision.

Exercise 3-1: *Select all that apply*
Which of the following statements is accurate about breastfeeding?

❏ Breastfed babies have a greater ability to maintain a normal body temperature.

❏ Breastfed babies should begin solid foods within the first 2 months of life.

❏ Breastfed premature neonates may require the addition of human milk fortifiers.

❏ If neonates cannot maintain breastfeeding, bottle feeding should be started.

❏ Human milk fortifiers can be used in preterm and term neonates.

e **eResource 3-1:** You show Marla Medline's *Healthy Nutrition: Breastfeeding*, a brief video to supplement her teaching regarding the health benefits of breastfeeding: vimeo.com/9309036

e **eResource 3-2:** To further understand issues surrounding newborn nutrition, refer to MerckMedicus Online on your mobile device: [Pathway: www.merckmanuals.com → Select "Merck Manual of Diagnosis and Therapy" → Select "Merck Manual for Healthcare Professionals" → Enter "Newborn nutrition" into the search field → Review the following content "Breastfeeding" and "Breastfeeding techniques" and "Complications"]

Marla's sister, Paula, is with her for her visit and is excited to hear the baby's heatbeat with Marla. Paula has a 6-month-old boy named Hunter, who is with her along with Marla's toddler, Jeffrey. Paula has questions for you regarding progressing Hunter to solid foods. "How do I start introducing solid foods to Hunter?"

Answers to this chapter begin on page 40.

Exercise 3-2: *Multiple-choice question*

You prepare to teach Paula ways to introduce solids to Hunter. Which of the following instructions are appropriate?

    A. Begin with combination meals that have an appealing taste

    B. Introduce a commercially prepared rice cereal first

    C. Add small amounts of honey to increase flavor

    D. Introduce scrambled eggs as a finger food

Exercise 3-3: *Ordering*

Order the steps in the introduction of solids to an infant.

_____ Introduce beef, turkey, and chicken baby food

_____ Introduce fruits and vegetables

_____ Introduce whole cow's milk

_____ Introduce commercially prepared rice cereal

_____ Introduce eggs and strawberries

(e) **eResource 3-3:** You provide Paula with a copy of *Guide to Firsts: Feeding Your Baby Solid Food* teaching handout, to supplement the teaching: goo.gl/NxitQI

Exercise 3-4: *Fill-in*

Describe weaning to the parents of an infant.

_____

(e) **eResource 3-4:** You also show Paula a video tutorial, *Introducing Your Baby to Solid Foods*, to further reinforce her teaching: goo.gl/hoki4b

(e) **eResource 3-5:** To further understand issues surrounding weaning, refer to MerckMedicus Online on your mobile device: [Pathway: www .merckmanuals.com → Select "Merck Manual of Diagnosis and Therapy" → Select "Merck Manual for Healthcare Professionals" → Enter "Newborn nutrition" into the search field → Review "weaning"]

Marla tells you that Jeffrey, her 2-year-old toddler is a "picky" eater. "I know good nutrition is very important but I just can't get him to eat the foods that are good for him." You try to help Marla with the dilemma.

Exercise 3-5: *Select all that apply*

Marla asks you for advice about nutrition for her child. Which of the following statements is accurate patient education?

    ❏ Limit consumption of 100% fruit juice to 16 ounces daily

    ❏ Offer water in addition to whole fruits as snacks

    ❏ She can introduce 2% milk at 2 years

    ❏ Toddlers may appear to eat little (i.e., physiologic anorexia), but this is normal

    ❏ The child can be offered a nighttime bottle of milk

Answers to this chapter begin on page 40.

Exercise 3-6: *Calculation*

Jeffrey is 2 years old and weighs 30 pounds. Using the physical growth percentile for height, what percentile is he in?

You also tell Marla what to expect as Jeffrey grows out of the toddler stage and begins the preschool stage.

Exercise 3-7: *Multiple-choice question*

How do nutritional patterns differ between the toddler and the preschooler?

    A. Food jags are common but temporary

    B. Limit the amount of social interaction with peers during mealtime

    C. Introduce no-fat milk

    D. Parents continue to make all food choices for the preschooler

Exercise 3-8: *Matching*

Match the nutritional term in Column A with the definition that best defines the concept in Column B.

Column A	Column B
_____ Marasmus	A. A dietary deficiency due to a diet that is insufficient in proteins
_____ Kwashiorkor	
_____ Physiologic anorexia	B. A dietary deficiency due to inadequate intake of carbohydrates
_____ Idiopathic failure to thrive	C. Vitamin C deficiency
_____ Scurvy	D. Failure to gain weight without a physiological cause
	E. A normal occurrence when toddlers have a decreased interest in food

 eResource 3-6: To reinforce your understanding of these nutritional disorders, consult Medscape

  ■ Online: [Pathway: www.medscape.org → Under the tab "Reference," select "References & Tools" → Enter "Marasmus" into the search field → Under the "Overview" tab, review "Pathophysiology" and "Epidemiology." Repeat with kwashiorkor, physiologic anorexia, idiopathic failure to thrive, and scurvy]

  ■ On your mobile device, you can access the same information: [Pathway: Medscape → enter "Marasmus" into the search field → Under the "Overview" tab, review "Pathophysiology" and "Epidemiology." Repeat with kwashiorkor, physiologic anorexia, idiopathic failure to thrive, and scurvy]

Another child in the clinic that day is Mia who is 2½ years old. Her mother brings her in for a check-up with her adolescent sister, Joan.

Answers to this chapter begin on page 40.

Exercise 3-9: *Calculation*

Mia weighs 26.5 pounds and her height is 34.5 inches. Based on this information, what is the child's body mass index?

 eResource 3-7: To verify your calculations, refer to *Medscape* on your mobile device: [Pathway: Medscape → Select "Reference" → Select "Calculators" → Select "Pediatric and Neonatal" → Select "Body Mass Index (BMI) Percentiles for Girls (2–20 Years)" → Enter the data into the relevant fields]

Exercise 3-10: *Multiple-choice question*

Which of the following statements is accurate about Joan's, an adolescent, nutritional requirements?

    A. The need for calcium does not increase until menopause

    B. Adolescents have a heightened need for folic acid

    C. Sufficient vitamin D levels can be achieved by sun exposure

    D. Macronutrient deficiencies are typically a problem only in developing countries

Mia's older sister, Joan, is a thin adolescent girl but her BMI is within the lower percent of normal.

Exercise 3-11: *Select all that apply*

Identify factors that can predispose an adolescent girl to anorexia nervosa.

    ❑ The adolescent denies there is a problem with the low weight

    ❑ There typically is an underlying medical cause for the disorder

    ❑ There is a distorted body image

    ❑ It is a typical finding in the adolescent girl

    ❑ It is classified as a mental disorder in the *DSM–5*

Mia and Joan's mom is a single parent and she confides in you that it is difficult to make ends meet, especially since her job "let her go."

Exercise 3-12: *Fill-in*

Identify a community resource that would be appropriate for the family who cannot afford to buy nutritious foods for their children.

Exercise 3-13: *Multiple-choice question*

After doing a social assessment on Mia and Joan's family, you are concerned because they live in a 100-year-old building with peeling paint. Which of the following blood tests would most likely be ordered for a child who engages in pica?

    A. Lead levels

    B. Iron levels

    C. Platelets

    D. White blood count

Answers to this chapter begin on page 40.

e **eResource 3-8:** You provide initial teaching regarding lead and the associated health hazards related to lead and children. You also provide some educational materials to the mother:

- A short video, *Lead Awareness for Parents*: goo.gl/KA9Zmo
- The *Lead Safety Video*: goo.gl/O3GAqv
- A pamphlet from the Centers for Disease Control and Prevention (CDC), *Know the Facts:* A fact sheet with general lead poisoning prevention information: goo.gl/lDhSJ
- Additional educational materials from the CDC: goo.gl/QuVUg

You make follow-up appointments for Marla, Mia, and Joan. You also refer Mia and Joan's mom to social services for a home visit and assessment.

Answers to this chapter begin on page 40.

Answers

Exercise 3-1: *Select all that apply*

Which of the following statements is accurate about breastfeeding?

☒ **Breastfed babies have a greater ability to maintain a normal body temperature.—YES, breastfed babies have a better ability to maintain their temperature and oxygen levels.**

❑ Breastfed babies should begin solid foods within the first 2 months of life.—NO, it is recommended that solid food should not be given until 6 months.

☒ **Breastfed premature neonates may require the addition of human milk fortifiers.—YES, in infants less than 1,500 grams.**

❑ If neonates cannot maintain breastfeeding, bottle feeding should be started.—NO, additional support from a lactation counselor may be needed.

❑ Human milk fortifiers can be used in preterm and term neonates.—NO, human fortifies should only be used in babies weighing less than 1,800 grams.

Exercise 3-2: *Multiple-choice question*

You prepare to teach the mother of an infant ways to introduce solids. Which of the following instructions is appropriate?

A. Begin with combination meals that have an appealing taste—NO, these meals typically have a high sugar and salt content.

B. **Introduce a commercially prepared rice cereal first—YES, rice cereal is fortified with iron and easy to digest.**

C. Add small amounts of honey to increase flavor—NO, honey may cause botulism in the infant.

D. Introduce scrambled eggs as a finger food—NO, eggs are associated with food allergies.

Exercise 3-3: *Ordering*

Order the steps in the introduction of solids to an infant.

__3__	Introduce beef, turkey, and chicken baby food
__2__	Introduce fruits and vegetables
__4__	Introduce whole cow's milk
__1__	Introduce commercially prepared rice cereal
__5__	Introduce eggs and strawberries

Exercise 3-4: *Fill-in*
Describe weaning to the parents of an infant.
Weaning occurs with the child's change in a pattern of feeding, typically drinking from a bottle to drinking from a youth cup.

Exercise 3-5: *Select all that apply*
Marla asks you for advice about nutrition for her child. Which of the following statements is accurate patient education?

☐ Limit consumption of 100% fruit juice to 16 ounces daily—NO, the maximum intake of juice is 4 to 6 ounces.

☒ **Offer water in addition to whole fruits as snacks—YES, fruit adds fiber.**

☒ **She can introduce 2% milk at 2 years—YES, intake should not exceed 1 L.**

☒ **Toddlers may appear to eat little (i.e., physiologic anorexia), but this is normal—YES, physiologic anorexia is normal in the toddler.**

☐ The child can be offered a nighttime bottle of milk—NO, the child should be weaned by this age.

Exercise 3-6: *Calculation*
Jeffrey is 2 years old and weighs 30 pounds. Using the physical growth percentile for height, what percentile is he in?
75th percentile

Exercise 3-7: *Multiple-choice question*
How do nutritional patterns differ between the toddler and the preschooler?
A. Food jags are common but temporary—**YES, assess nutrition over 2 weeks.**
B. Limit the amount of social interaction with peers during mealtime—NO, meals become more social in nature.
C. Introduce no-fat milk—NO, children need a certain percentage of fat for brain growth.
D. Parents continue to make all food choices for the preschooler—NO, preschoolers are in the stage of initiative and should be given choices.

Exercise 3-8: *Matching*
Match the nutritional term in Column A with the definition that best defines the concept in Column B.

Column A	Column B
B Marasmus	A. A dietary deficiency due to a diet that is insufficient in proteins
A Kwashiorkor	
E Physiologic anorexia	B. A dietary deficiency due to inadequate intake of carbohydrates

Column A	Column B
__D__ Idiopathic failure to thrive	C. Vitamin C deficiency
	D. Failure to gain weight without a physiological cause
__C__ Scurvy	E. A normal occurrence when toddlers have a decreased interest in food

Exercise 3-9: *Calculate*

Mia weighs 26.5 pounds and her height is 34.5 inches. Based on this information, what is the child's body mass index?

body mass index = 15.63

Exercise 3-10: *Multiple-choice question*

Which of the following statements is accurate about Joan's, an adolescent, nutritional requirements?

A. The need for calcium does not increase until menopause—NO, adolescents need calcium for bone development.

B. Adolescents have a heightened need for folic acid—YES, adolescent females typically have low levels of folic acid.

C. Sufficient vitamin D levels can be achieved by sun exposure—NO, it is difficult to get the required amount of sunlight for synthesis.

D. Macronutrient deficiencies are typically a problem only in developing countries—NO, macronutrient deficiencies are a global problem

Exercise 3-11: *Select all that apply*

Identify factors that can predispose an adolescent girl to anorexia nervosa.

☒ **The adolescent denies there is a problem with the low weight—YES, there is a distorted image of one's weight.**

☐ There typically is an underlying medical cause for the disorder—NO, there is no organic cause for anorexia nervosa.

☒ **There is a distorted body image—YES, there is a distorted image of one's weight.**

☐ It is a typical finding in the adolescent girl—NO, it is classified as a mental disorder in the *DSM-5.*

☒ **It is classified as a mental disorder in the *DSM-5*—YES, it is classified as a mental disorder in the *DSM-5.***

Exercise 3-12: *Fill-in*

Identify a community resource that would be appropriate for the family who cannot afford to buy nutritious foods for their children?

Women, Infants, and Children (WIC)

Food stamps program

Community food banks

Parish nurse programs

Exercise 3-13: *Multiple-choice question*

Which of the following blood tests would most likely be ordered for a child who engages in pica?

A. Lead levels—**YES, children with pica often ingest lead-based paint chips.**

B. Ferritin levels—NO, this test would not be done initially.

C. Platelets—NO, platelets typically are not affected.

D. White blood count—NO, this blood test would not be done.

4

Health Promotion

Susan Parnell Scholtz

Unfolding Case Study #4-1 ▨ Elyse

Elyse is a 32-week-gestational-age neonate who was delivered via cesarean section. She is gaining weight and has no symptoms of respiratory distress. Her parents are receiving parent education regarding growth and development. Elyse's mother states to you, "My older daughter walked at age 8 months, which was early but she was full term."

Exercise 4-1: *Multiple-choice question*
Which of the following statements made by you, the nurse, is accurate relative to a preterm infant?

   A. "Since Elyse was 8 weeks premature, she will most likely achieve her developmental milestones 8 weeks later than full-term babies her age."
   B. "Elyse most likely will be developmentally delayed because of prematurity."
   C. "Although Elyse was premature, she will achieve her developmental milestones on time."
   D. "Premature infants never really catch up developmentally to children who were born full term."

You advise that, "You need to use the *corrected age* (also known as adjusted age) as your baby's age when watching how your baby develops."

 eResource 4-1: Using an online calculator for premature babies, you show the parents visually what Elyse's corrected age is and uses this information to respond to Elyse's mother's comment: [Pathway: goo.gl/4LfJh → Enter date of birth and number of weeks premature → View results]

Elyse's parents have many questions for you. You gladly spend time with them and patiently answer all their questions.

Answers to this chapter begin on page 52.

eResource 4-2: To reinforce the parents' education, you show the parents two videos:
- *Preemies in the ICU, How Parents Can Help:* goo.gl/uQjzWf
- The March of Dimes, *Developmental Milestones: Premature Babies:* bcove.me/wa2zoqok

After a 6-week stay in the neonatal intensive care unit (NICU), Elyse is discharged to her home.

Appropriate referrals have been made and Elyse's mother understands the importance of follow-up.

Exercise 4-2: *Multiple-choice question*

Which of the following assessments would indicate that the parent–child attachment process may be disturbed?

    A. Elyse's mother seems nervous when she changes the baby's diaper.
    B. Elyse's mother looks to you for validation that she is bathing the baby correctly.
    C. Elyse's mother is sending numerous text messages when she is feeding her baby.
    D. Elyse's mother states her mother will be a good source of support when Elyse is discharged.

Elyse's parents bring her to the clinic for her 2-month check-up. You plan education based on the American Academy of Pediatrics Recommendation for Preventive Care, a guideline for assessment during childhood.

Exercise 4-3: *Select all that apply*

Identify all of the assessments/interventions that are recommended for her 2-month check-up.

    ❑ Autism screening
    ❑ Physical examination
    ❑ Immunizations
    ❑ Tuberculosis screening
    ❑ Physical measurements
    ❑ Lead screening

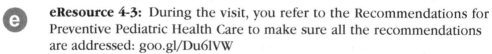 **eResource 4-3:** During the visit, you refer to the Recommendations for Preventive Pediatric Health Care to make sure all the recommendations are addressed: goo.gl/Du6lVW

The nurse weighs Elyse and finds that she weighs 7 pounds 7 ounces.

Answers to this chapter begin on page 52.

Exercise 4-4: *Calculation*

What is Elyse's weight in kilograms?

 eResource 4-4: To verify your conversion calculations, you refer to Skyscape's Archimedes medical calculator: [Pathway on device: Skyscape → Archimedes → Weight Conversion → Enter the weight into the input field and select units]

As Elyse's is about to be discharged from her appointment, you want to reinforce anticipatory guidance and inform her parents about the typical side effects that may be seen following immunizations.

Exercise 4-5: *Select all that apply*

Identify the immunizations that are typically given to a 2-month-old.

❑ Hib

❑ Rotovirus

❑ PCV

❑ DTaP

❑ Varicella

❑ Measles, mumps, and rubella

 eResource 4-5: To reinforce your understanding of the recommended immunizations for Elyse, refer to *Shots™ by STFM,* from the Group on Immunization Education of the Society of Teachers of Family Medicine on your mobile device. (Downloaded from goo.gl/HGS6W8 [Android] or goo.gl/nLHn8m [iTunes].) [Pathway: Shots™ → Select "Child" → View recommendations for 2-month-old → Tap on blue text to read more]

Elyse's mother makes the next follow-up appointment.

Unfolding Case Study #4-2 ▒ Francesca and Anthony

Fifteen-month-old Francesca is seen at the pediatrician's office for a well child visit. You are filling in for a nurse who is out on family leave.

Exercise 4-6: *Select all that apply*

Which of the following immunizations is typically administered between 12 and 18 months?

❑ Varicella

❑ Measles, mumps, and rubella

❑ Diptheria, pertussis, and tetanus

❑ Rotavirus vaccine

Answers to this chapter begin on page 52.

eResource 4-6: Again, refer to *Shots*™ on your mobile device: [Pathway: *Shots*™ → Select "Child" → View recommendations for 12 to 18 months → Tap on blue text to read more]

Exercise 4-7: *Multiple-choice question*

Which of the following gross motor skills should Francesca display during this visit?

    A. Walks up stairs

    B. Walks with a wide-based stance

    C. Jumps

    D. Rides a tricycle

Francesca's mother notes that she notices Francesca's amazement with turning the bathroom light fixture on and off. She states, "It seems as though Francesca knows that when she flips the light switch, the light will come on."

Exercise 4-8: *Multiple-choice question*

The toddler's awareness of a causal relationship between a light switch and a light is an example of:

    A. Sensorimotor phase of cognitive development

    B. Gross motor skill acquisition

    C. Preconceptual phase of development

    D. Magical thinking

You discuss normal development for toddlers Francesca's age with the mother.

 eResource 4-7: To reinforce parent teaching, you provide Francesca's mother a handout: goo.gl/qSXmVL

Francesca's mother states, "I am concerned that Francesca wants to take her favorite blanket everywhere! She seems to cling to it, especially when she must leave me. Do you think I should start to discourage this behavior?"

Exercise 4-9: *Multiple-choice question*

Based on an understanding of growth and development, your best response would be:

    A. "Yes. I would gradually start to make efforts to leave the blanket behind."

    B. "No. It sounds as though she may have some issues with regression."

    C. "Yes. This behavior is interfering with her ability to separate and individuate."

    D. "No. This is normal behavior because the blanket is a transitional object to the parents."

During this visit, Francesca's mother has some questions about her 4-year-old son's development. Anthony is able to feed himself as well as dress himself.

Answers to this chapter begin on page 52.

Exercise 4-10: *Select all that apply*

Based on an understanding of growth and development, you explain appropriate skills for a 4- to 5-year-old. Select behaviors that are appropriate for this age group.

❑ Sings "Row, Row, Row Your Boat" as he washes his hands

❑ Throws a ball overhand

❑ Shows evidence of conservation of mass

❑ States name correctly

❑ Begins to lose primary dentition (baby teeth)

Anthony likes to play in the preschool kitchen. He enjoys pretending to cook and serving his friends the "make believe" food he has made.

Exercise 4-11: *Multiple-choice question*

The 4-year-old, who plays chef in a preschool kitchen, is exemplifying _____ play.

    A. Parallel

    B. Associative

    C. Dramatic play

    D. Magical thinking

You spend a good amount of time with Francesca's mother answering her questions and it is clear that she is eager to learn more.

 eResource 4-8: You tell Francesca's mother about a mobile resource called *Healthy Children,* from the American Academy of Pediatrics (AAP) that has a lot of information that she can use. (Downloaded from goo.gl/FTPQLH [Android] or goo.gl/7b1Fwm [iTunes].) [Pathway: Healthy Children → Select "Age or Stage" → Browse content]

Exercise 4-12: *Fill-in*

Anthony, age 4 years, weighs 50 pounds and is 42 inches tall. Based on stature for age and weight for age, Anthony is in the _____ percentile for weight and _____ percentile for length.

Exercise 4-13: *Multiple-choice question*

Based on the findings related to Anthony's height and weight assessment, which of the following nursing interventions is appropriate?

    A. There is no need for intervention; the findings are normal

    B. Conduct a nutritional assessment

    C. Initiate a weight loss program

    D. Discuss the seriousness of the child's obesity with his mother

Answers to this chapter begin on page 52.

eResource 4-9: In order verify your calculations, utilize one of the Online Child Growth Chart Calculators at:
- Baby Center: [Pathway: goo.gl/6YtwJM → Enter child's sex, age, height, and weight → View percentile each parameter falls within]
- MedCalc Interactive Growth Chart: [Pathway: www.medcalc.com → Select "Pediatrics" → Select "Growth Charts" → Enter age, sex, height, and weight → Select Combined Length and Weight-for-Age 2 to 20 years → Select "Create Growth Chart" to view results]

Unfolding Case Study #4-3 James

James, a 6-year-old child, is living in an old house with his mother. He arrives at the well child clinic with his mother for his 6-year examination.

Exercise 4-14: *Select all that apply*
Which of the following tests/immunizations will be done during the 6-year visit?
- ❏ Lead levels to rule out plumbism
- ❏ Measles, mumps, and rubella booster vaccine
- ❏ Varicella booster vaccine
- ❏ Giardasil vaccine
- ❏ Rotavirus vaccine

James's mother states that he typically feels very irritable after his immunizations and asks how much Motrin she should administer. Based on his weight, James should receive 2 teaspoons of the medication.

Exercise 4-15: *Calculation*
How many mL should James receive if the ordered dose is 2 teaspoons?

 eResource 4-10: To verify your calculations, refer to the Weights and Measures conversion calculators you have on your mobile device:
- Skyscape's Archimedes: [Pathway: Archimedes → Enter "Conversion" into the search field → Enter patient data]
- Medcalc [Pathway: Medcalc → Enter "Cnversion" into search field → Select "Units Conversion (Physics)" → Select units and enter data → View results]

Unfolding Case Study #4-4 Amy

Fifteen-year-old Amy is instructed to increase folic acid in her diet because young women often have low levels.

Answers to this chapter begin on page 52.

Exercise 4-16: *Multiple-choice question*

Which of the following foods does not have a high amount of folate?

     A. Bread products

     B. Beans

     C. Poultry

     D. Green, leafy vegetables

 eResource 4-11: You provide Amy with several handouts that explain the importance of folic acid (vitamin B$_9$).
- *Folic Acid: Frequently Asked Questions:* goo.gl/4skJeX
- *Vitamin B$_9$ Benefits:* goo.gl/CGVRj1

Exercise 4-17: *Select all that apply*

During the annual examination, which of the following assessments must be performed for all female adolescents?

     ❑ Pelvic examination

     ❑ Lipid screening

     ❑ Lead screening

     ❑ Breast examination

     ❑ Scoliosis screening

 eResource 4-12: To learn more about folic acid and precautions, consult Skyscape's RxDrugs on your mobile device: [Pathway: Skyscape → Select "RxDrugs" → Enter "Folic Acid" into the search field → Scroll down to view "Warnings/Precautions"]

Answers to this chapter begin on page 52.

Answers

Exercise 4-1: *Multiple-choice question*

Which of the following statements made by you, the nurse, is accurate relative to a preterm infant?

A. "Since Elyse was 8 weeks premature, she will most likely achieve her developmental milestones 8 weeks later than full-term babies her age."—YES, when assessing the premature infant's developmental milestones, subtract the weeks of prematurity from the child's age and evaluate the child at this adjusted age.

B. "Elyse most likely will be developmentally delayed because of prematurity."—NO, there is not a cause-and-effect relationship between prematurity and developmental delays.

C. "Although Elyse was premature, she will achieve her developmental milestones on time."—NO, when assessing the premature infant's developmental milestones, subtract the weeks of prematurity from the infant's age and evaluate the child at this adjusted age.

D. "Premature infants never really catch up developmentally to children who were born full term."—NO, there is no evidence to support this statement.

Exercise 4-2: *Multiple-choice question*

Which of the following assessments would indicate that the parent–child attachment process may be disturbed?

A. Elyse's mother seems nervous when she changes the baby's diaper—NO, this is a normal response when initially performing such tasks on a small, premature infant. She wants to make sure that she is doing it correctly.

B. Elyse's mother looks to you for validation that she is bathing the baby correctly—NO, this is a normal response when initially performing such tasks on a small, premature infant. She wants to make sure that she is doing it correctly.

C. Elyse's mother is sending numerous text messages when she is feeding her baby—YES, this behavior distracts the mother from eye-to-eye contact with Elyse, which is an important mediator of attachment during the process of feeding a baby.

D. Elyse's mother states her mother will be a good source of support when Elyse is discharged—NO, a support system is important to all mothers.

Exercise 4-3: *Select all that apply*
Identify all of the assessments/interventions that are recommended for her 2-month check-up.

❑ Autism screening—NO, although attachment behaviors are noted, autism assessment does not occur until after the first birthday.

☒ **Physical examination—YES, the physical examination is done at each visit.**

☒ **Immunizations—YES, immunizations are scheduled for the 2-month visit.**

❑ Tuberculosis screening—NO, this screening is done at a later time.

☒ **Physical measurements—YES, head, chest, length, and weight are measured.**

❑ Lead screening—NO, lead screening is done later in childhood.

Exercise 4-4: *Calculation*
What is Elyse's weight in kilograms?
3.37 kg

Exercise 4-5: *Select all that apply*
Identify the immunizations that are typically given to a 2-month-old.

☒ **Hib—YES, this is given at 2, 4, and 6 months.**

☒ **Rotovirus—YES, this is given at 2, 4, and 6 months.**

☒ **PCV —YES, this is given at 2, 4, and 6 months.**

☒ **DTaP —YES, this is given at 2, 4, and 6 months.**

❑ Varicella—NO, the initial varicella is given at 12 to 15 months.

❑ Measles, mumps, and rubella—NO, the initial measles, mumps, and rubella vaccine is given between 12 and 15 months.

Exercise 4-6: *Select all that apply*
Which of the following immunizations is typically administered between 12 and 18 months?

☒ **Varicella—YES, the varicella vaccine #1 can be given between 12 and 18 months.**

☒ **Measles, mumps, and rubella—YES, measles, mumps, and rubella is typically given at 15 months.**

☒ **Diptheria, pertussis, and tetanus—YES, the diptheria, pertussis, and tetanus vaccine #4 can be given between 15 and 18 months.**

❑ Rotavirus vaccine—NO, the rotavirus can be given at 2, 4, and 6 months.

Exercise 4-7: *Multiple-choice question*

Which of the following gross motor skills should Francesca display during this visit?

A. Walks up stairs—NO, this occurs about 2 years of age.

B. Walks with a wide-based stance—YES, this occurs typically around the first birthday.

C. Jumps—NO, this occurs at approximately 30 months.

D. Rides a tricycle—NO, this occurs around age 3.

Exercise 4-8: *Multiple-choice question*

The toddler's awareness of a causal relationship between a light switch and a light is an example of:

A. Sensorimotor phase of cognitive development—YES, the child uses experimentation to learn about the world around her.

B. Gross motor skill acquisition—NO, this is an example of a fine motor skill and is an example of tertiary circular reactions.

C. Preconceptual phase of development—NO, this phase of cognitive development occurs between 2 and 4 years.

D. Magical thinking—NO, magical thinking happens between 2 and 4 years.

Exercise 4-9: *Multiple-choice question*

Based on an understanding of growth and development, your best response would be:

A. "Yes. I would gradually start to make efforts to leave the blanket behind."—NO, this is normal behavior for a toddler who finds the blanket a source of comfort in otherwise stressful situations.

B. "No. It sounds as though she may have some issues with regression."—NO, this is normal behavior for a toddler who finds the blanket a source of comfort in otherwise stressful situations.

C. "Yes. This behavior is interfering with her ability to separate and individuate."—NO, separation and individuation from a parent emerges as the child realizes she is unique and not fused with a parent.

D. "No. This is normal behavior because the blanket is a transitional object to the parents."—YES, a transitional object is a child's possession that serves as a linkage to the parent and often provides comfort in stressful situations.

Exercise 4-10: *Select all that apply*

Based on an understanding of growth and development, you explain appropriate skills for a 4- to 5-year-old. Select behaviors that are appropriate for this age group.

☒ **Sings "Row, Row, Row Your Boat" as he washes his hands—YES, the preschooler can sing songs and rhymes.**

☒ **Throws a ball overhand—YES, this is a gross motor milestone for the preschooler.**

❑ Shows evidence of conservation of mass—NO, this cognitive achievement does not typically occur until the school-age years.

☒ **States name correctly—YES, this is a language developmental milestone for the preschooler.**

❑ Begins to lose primary dentition (baby teeth)—NO, this does not occur until the school-age years.

Exercise 4-11: *Multiple-choice question*

The 4-year-old, who plays chef in a preschool kitchen, is exemplifying _____ play.

A. Parallel—NO, this type of play, typically observed in toddlers, is characterized by children playing side by side with little interaction

B. Associative—NO, although this is a type of play seen in the preschool years, it does not necessarily involve imaginative or fantasy play.

C. **Dramatic play—YES, preschoolers tend to re-enact activities they have seen in their own life in their fantasy play.**

D. Magical thinking—NO, magical thinking is not a type of play. The child believes that he is omnipotent and that his actions or thoughts can cause punitive consequences.

Exercise 4-12: *Fill-in*

Anthony, age 4 years, weighs 50 pounds and is 42 inches tall. Based on stature for age and weight for age, Anthony is in the **greater than 95th** percentile for weight and **greater than 75th** percentile for length.

Exercise 4-13: *Multiple-choice question*

Based on the findings related to Anthony's height and weight assessment, which of the following nursing interventions is appropriate?

A. There is no need for intervention, the findings are normal—NO, weight greater than the 95th percentile needs further assessment.

B. **Conduct a nutritional assessment—YES, weight greater than the 95th percentile needs further nutritional assessment prior to development of an intervention.**

C. Initiate a weight loss program—NO, a nutritional assessment is needed to determine factors that may be contributing to his weight gain.

D. Discuss the seriousness of the child's obesity with his mother—NO, weight greater than the 95th percentile needs further assessment.

Exercise 4-14: *Select all that apply*

Which of the following tests/immunizations will be done during the 6-year visit?

☒ **Lead levels to rule out plumbism—YES, this test is repeated in children at age 6, particularly in those living in houses with lead-based paint.**

☒ **Measles, mumps, and rubella booster vaccine—YES, this booster shot is given between 4 and 6 years of age.**

☒ **Varicella booster vaccine—YES, this booster shot is given between 4 and 6 years of age.**

❏ Giardasil vaccine—NO, this vaccine is administered to protect against HPV and is given during adolescence.

❏ Rotavirus vaccine—NO, this series is complete by 6 months of age.

Exercise 4-15: *Calculation*
How many mL should James receive if the ordered dose is 2 teaspoons?
10 mL

Exercise 4-16: *Multiple-choice question*
Which of the following foods does not have a high amount of folate?
  A. Bread products—NO, food with flour and yeast is high in folate.
  B. Beans—NO, legumes are high in folate.
  C. Poultry—YES, poultry is not high in folate.
  D. Green, leafy vegetables—NO, green leafy vegetables such as spinach and kale are high in folate.

Exercise 4-17: *Select all that apply*
❏ Pelvic examination—NO, a pelvic exam, Pap smear, and testing for sexually transmitted infections is only done in adolescents who are sexually active.

❏ Lipid screening—NO, this screening is done for adolescents whose family history is positive for hyperlipidemia.

❏ Lead screening—NO, this screening is done at 4 to 6 years for children in old housing.

☒ **Breast examination—YES, the breast examination is done and the adolescent girl is instructed on the correct way to conduct a breast self-exam.**

☒ **Scoliosis screening—YES, this screening begins in the school-age child and continues through adolescence.**

5

Nursing Care of the Hospitalized Pediatric Patient

Susan Parnell Scholtz

Unfolding Case Study #5-1 ▨ Alexis, RN

Alexis is a pediatric nurse who has 2 years' experience. Alexis is receiving report and her first patient is Cooper, age 2½ years, who is hospitalized with a diagnosis of "rule out meningitis." The orders state that he will receive a lumbar puncture as well as blood cultures. He is crying as Alexis approaches his bed. On admission, Alexis learns from his mother that he has recently been potty trained and has met all appropriate developmental milestones for his age.

Exercise 5-1: *Multiple-choice question*
Cooper's parents are concerned that he will become upset when they leave him. In order to help the parents deal with the issues related to separation when they leave their toddler at the hospital, Alexis makes the following suggestion:
- A. Place a clock at the child's bedside so the child can anticipate their return
- B. Quietly leave when the child is asleep
- C. Use associations such as "I will be back when *Sid the Science Kid* comes on television in the morning"
- D. Assure the parents that toddlers adapt well and it should not be a concern

 eResource 5-1: To supplement your understanding of the hospitalized preschooler, view the video: *Hospitalization of Children:* goo.gl/fyaGll

Exercise 5-2: *Multiple-choice question*
Cooper has been hospitalized for over a week and now has been urinating in the bed. Alexis addresses his mother's concerns, basing her response on her understanding of growth and development. This temporary loss of a developmental milestone in response to stress is due to:
- A. Regression
- B. Anger at the parent
- C. Self-assertion
- D. Detachment

eResource 5-2: To further understand normal childhood development, refer to MerckMedicus Online on your mobile device: [Pathway: www.merckmanuals.com → Select "Merck Manual of Diagnosis and Therapy" → Select "Merck Manual for Healthcare Professionals" → Enter "Childhood Development" into the search field → Review the following content "Cognitive Development" and "Emotional and Behavioral Development"]

Exercise 5-3: *Multiple-choice question*

A blood culture will be performed shortly on Cooper. Based on an understanding of toddler growth and development, Alexis should:

  A. Perform the procedure in the child's room to decrease anxiety.
  B. Give the child a choice in which arm to use.
  C. Give short explanations as the procedure is done.
  D. Prepare the child well in advance of the procedure.

Exercise 5-4: *Calculation*

Cooper weighs 30 pounds on admission. He is ordered to receive the following IV medication: Ceftriaxone 50 mg/kg/day every 12 hours. What dose would be administered every 12 hours?

---

 eResource 5-3: Use one of the following calculators to verify your answer:
  ▪ MedCalc: A free online medication calculator: [Pathway: www.medcalc.com → Tap on "Pediatrics" → Select "Dosing Calc" to access the calculator → Enter the data into the relevant fields]
  ▪ Or download it to your mobile device to access the same information: (www.medscape.com/public/mobileapp). Once you have the app downloaded onto your device: [Pathway: Medscape → Select "Reference" → Select "Calculators" → Select "Medication Protocols" → Select "Weight-Based Dose Calculator" → Enter the data into the relevant fields]

 eResource 5-4: To learn more about Ceftriaxone and the nursing considerations when administering this drug:
  ▪ Access Medscape to find information about this drug:
    ▪ Online: [Pathway: www.medscape.com → Click on the tab "Reference" → Enter "Ceftriaxone" into the search field → Select "Ceftriaxone" → Select the "Pediatric" tab and review content]
    ▪ Or use your mobile device to access the same information: [Pathway: Medscape → Enter "Ceftriaxone" into the search field → Select the "Pediatric" tab and review content]

Answers to this chapter begin on page 69.

■ Download RxDrugs™, a free drug resource from Skyscape.com onto your mobile device: [Pathway: Skyscape → Select "RxDrugs™" → Enter "Ceftriaxone" into the search field → Select "Use and Dosing" → Scroll down to "Pediatric Dosing" and review content. Pay particular attention to "Warnings/Precautions"]

Exercise 5-5: *Multiple-choice question*

Alexis wants to utilize play therapy to explain the application of a cast to a preschool child. Which of the following interventions would meet the developmental needs of the preschooler?

    A. Use a doll to demonstrate the casting procedure

    B. Offer a tape recording that describes the procedure

    C. Utilize a diagram to explain the procedure

    D. Simply explain the procedure as it is performed

 eResource 5-5: To learn more about the value of creative play therapy activities for the hospitalized child:
■ View Child Life: Healing Through Play: goo.gl/YpwGLE
■ Visit Pinterest to view some Play Therapy Ideas: pinterest.com/taliahdz34/some-play-therapy-ideas

Exercise 5-6: *Multiple-choice question*

Which of the following interventions is most appropriate for the needs of a 7-year-old child who is hospitalized for an extended period of time?

    A. Bring security items such as a blanket

    B. Provide play activities that foster industry

    C. Allow the child to make all decisions in treatment

    D. Complete all treatments in the play room

Exercise 5-7: *Multiple-choice question*

The toddler, who has been hospitalized for 1 week, cries each time his mother leaves his bedside. Based on an understanding of growth and development, Alexis realizes this behavior is typical of:

    A. Stranger anxiety

    B. Despair

    C. Regression

    D. Protest

 eResource 5-6: To further understand normal childhood development:
■ View Child Growth and Development: goo.gl/DBHRzy
■ Review Child Development content on MerckMedicus Online: [Pathway: www.merckmanuals.com → Select "Merck Manual of Diagnosis and Therapy" → Select "Merck Manual for Healthcare Professionals" → Enter "Childhood Development" into the search field → Review the following content "Cognitive Development" and "Emotional and Behavioral Development"]

Answers to this chapter begin on page 69.

Exercise 5-8: *Select all that apply*

Alexis is assigned to a 2-year-old child who must receive an intramuscular injection of ampicillin. Alexis would complete which of the following steps in the administration of this medication:

❑ Cleanse a site in the anterolateral aspect of the thigh

❑ Select a 7/8 inch- to 1-inch, 23- to 25-gauge needle

❑ Insert needle at a 45-degree angle into the vastus lateralis

❑ Inject the medication slowly into the deltoid muscle

❑ Restrain the child to avoid dislodging of the needle

 eResource 5-7: To review the proper technique for administration of an intramuscular injection:
- ▪ View the video demonstration: *IVs and Injections for Pediatric Patients*, goo.gl/y0W4AM
- ▪ Read: *How to Administer IM (Intramuscular) Injections:* goo.gl/qFtNqn

Unfolding Case Study #5-2 ▬ Leah

Leah, age 2 years, presents at the emergency department (ED) with an earache and fever and is diagnosed with otitis media.

Exercise 5-9: *Fill-in*

The health care provider orders amoxicillin 40 mg/kg/day orally three times a day. Leah weighs 28 pounds. What dosage should be administered every 8 hours?

_____

 eResource 5-8: To verify proper dosage, consult one of the following medical calculators:
- ▪ MedCalc: [Pathway: www.medcalc.com → Tap on "Pediatrics" → Select "Dosing Calc" to access the calculator → Enter the data into the relevant fields]
- ▪ Medscape on your mobile device: [Pathway: Medscape → Select "Reference" → Select "Calculators" → Select "Medication Protocols" → Select "Weight-Based Dose Calculator" → Enter the data into the relevant fields]

To learn more about standard practice guidelines for the care of the child with otitis media, the ED nurse decides to visit the National Guidelines Clearinghouse to review Practice Guidelines to review the standards.

eResource 5-9: To access this very important resource for practice, visit the Agency for Healthcare Research Quality (AHRQ) National Guidelines Clearinghouse: [Pathway www.guideline.gov → Enter "Otitis Media" into the search field → Review relevant guidelines as they pertain to treatment of otitis media]

Prior to administering the first dose, the ED nurse wants to provide patient teaching to Leah's mother, who has questions regarding the diagnosis and prescribed medication. In particular, she wants to know about side effects of the medication.

 eResource 5-10: You decide to consult several resources to learn about the medication and the diagnosis:

- RxDrugs™ on your mobile device: [Pathway: → Enter "Amoxicillin" into the search field → Select "ID" or "C" to obtain information about Indications and Dosages or Warnings/Precautions]
- Epocrates online: [Pathway: online.epocrates.com → Tap on the "Online Products" tab → Select "Drugs" → Enter "Ceftriaxone" in the search field to view content → Select "Peds Dosing," "Safety/Monitoring," and "Patient Education"]

Exercise 5-10: *Multiple-choice question*
All of the following techniques for oral medication administration to an infant are acceptable except:

A. Adding the medication to the infant's bottle of formula

B. Allowing the infant to sit in the parent's lap during administration

C. Encouraging the infant to suck the medication from an empty nipple

D. Inserting a needleless syringe into the side of the mouth for the infant to suck

 eResource 5-11: To supplement patient teaching, you provide the following handouts:

- Merck Medicus Online: [Pathway: www.merckmedicus.com → Select "Patient Handouts" tab → Enter "Otitis Media" into the keyword search field → Select "Ear Infection (Otitis Media) pediatric"]
- Epocrates online, *Acute Otitis Media* (*JAMA Patient Page*), a patient education handout: goo.gl/E1pmc7

Exercise 5-11: *Ordering*
Order the steps in the intervention of administering ear drops into the ear canal of an infant.

_____ Straighten ear canal by gently pulling the earlobe down and back.

_____ Complete the Five Rights for the child.

_____ Warm the medication by rolling between hands. Shake as indicated.

_____ Administer drops into the ear canal but not directly into the ear.

_____ Lie infant on his or her side so affected ear is accessible.

_____ Keep infant on unaffected side for a few minutes.

Answers to this chapter begin on page 69.

eResource 5-12: To verify your understanding of the proper administration, you refer to WebMD on your mobile device: [Pathway: WebMD → Enter "Otitis Media" into the search field → Select "Ear Infection Facts" to read an overview about the etiology, pathology, and administration of medication into the child's ear canal]

Leah's mother still has more questions and asks you "What causes otitis media?"

 eResource 5-13: To reinforce your patient teaching, you open up *Medscape* on your mobile device: [Pathway: Medscape → Select "Conditions" → Enter "Otitis Media" into the search field → Read "Practice Essentials," "Background," and "Pathophysiology"]

Exercise 5-12: *Matching*
List the developmental stage (infant, toddler, preschooler, school-age child, and adolescent) that coincides with typical stressors of hospitalization.

_____ Body mutilation fears

_____ Associates pain with punishment for poor behaviors

_____ Separation anxiety

_____ Begins awareness of finality of death

_____ Loss of identity and privacy

_____ Maternal separation/deprivation

Unfolding Case Study #5-3 ▬ Jack

Jack, a 4-month-old infant, is hospitalized with a diagnosis of "rule out respiratory syncytial virus (RSV)."

 eResource 5-14: To learn more about RSV; visit Medscape:
- Online: [Pathway: www.medscape.org → Under the tab "Reference, select "References & Tools" → Enter "Respiratory Syncytial Virus" into the search field → Under the "Overview" tab, review "Pathophysiology" and "Etiology"]
- On your mobile device, you can access the same information: [Pathway: Medscape → Enter "Respiratory Syncytial Virus" into the search field → Under the "Overview" tab, review "Pathophysiology" and "Etiology"]

Jack's parents are present during the admission; however, since both parents work during the day there will be periods of time when he will be alone.

Exercise 5-13: *Select all that apply*
You want to minimize stressors to the infant during his hospitalization. Which of the following interventions would be appropriate?

❑ Assign the same nurse to Jack every day when possible

❑ Encourage his parents to bring his favorite toy from home

❑ Reassure his parents that he is too young to realize they are not present

❑ Offer the parents a flexible visiting schedule to meet their needs

❑ Encourage the parents to leave when he is asleep

❑ Hold and rock the infant frequently

❑ Minimize prolonged stimuli

Exercise 5-14: *Multiple-choice question*
A nasopharyngeal swab will be done to determine if the respiratory syncytial virus is the causative organism of Jack's illness. Which of the following interventions is most important when performing this procedure on the child?

A. Explain the procedure to the child immediately prior to the procedure

B. Ask his parents to restrain him during the procedure

C. Complete the procedure in the infant's crib

D. Immobilize the child securely but gently

Exercise 5-15: *Multiple-choice question*
Which of the following play therapy activities would encourage growth and development in the hospitalized infant?

A. Explain techniques using a puppet

B. Place a brightly colored mobile over the crib

C. Suspend brightly colored latex balloons over the crib

D. Allow the child to play with hospital equipment

Unfolding Case Study #5-4 ▨ Alexis, RN

Exercise 5-16: *Multiple-choice question*
On admission of the 1-year-old infant, Alexis obtains a weight of 22 pounds. In order to calculate the correct dosage of medication for this infant, she must convert the weight to kilograms. What is his weight in kilograms? _____

eResource 5-15: To verify your mental math calculations, consult one of these resources:

▣ MedCalc: [Pathway: www.medcalc.com → Tap on "Pediatrics" → Select "Dosing Calc" to access the calculator → Enter the date into the relevant fields]

▣ Medscape on your mobile device: [Pathway: Medscape → Select "Reference" → Select "Calculators" → Select "Medication Protocols" → Select "Weight-Based Dose Calculator" → Enter the data into the relevant fields]

You want to assess growth and development so you decide to consult some additional resources.

Answers to this chapter begin on page 69.

eResource 5-16: You know that there are several resources to choose from:
■ Online Interactive Growth Charts:
   ■ Infant Chart: www.infantchart.com
   ■ MedCalc: www.medcalc.com/growth
■ On your mobile device, you can use STAT GrowthCharts™ (downloaded from goo.gl/yZn1zx [iTunes] or goo.gl/ChaXJe [Android]): [Pathway: STAT GrowthCharts™ → Enter age, gender and weight → View results]
■ Download a growth chart handout from the Centers for Disease Control and Prevention (CDC) or the World Health Organization (WHO): goo.gl/WqFbwu

Exercise 5-17: *Multiple-choice question*
Francesca, a preschooler, recently underwent chelating therapy for lead poisoning. Her play therapist wants to gain insight into her reaction to the experience. Which of the following interventions would be helpful to meet this goal?
    A. Ask the child to explain how she felt after the treatment
    B. Engage the child in an interactive skit using puppets
    C. Ask her parents about her reaction to the chelating treatment
    D. Tell the child to draw a picture of her receiving the chelating agent

Exercise 5-18: *Multiple-choice question*
Louise, age 4, received an intramuscular injection in her vastus lateralis. Although it did not bleed, she insists that she "needs a Band-Aid." Based on an understanding of growth and development, Alexis should:
    A. Show her the injection site to reinforce there is no active bleeding
    B. Apply a brightly colored Band-Aid on the injection site
    C. Try to distract her with her favorite toy
    D. Explain to her that a Band-Aid is unnecessary following injections

Exercise 5-19: *Select all that apply*
A 4-year-old is scheduled to have a tonsillectomy and needs preoperative teaching. Select all instructions that would be appropriate for this child.
    ❑ Offer the child and parent a tour of the operating room and holding area
    ❑ Use nonthreatening terms such as "remove your tonsils"
    ❑ Begin preoperative teaching at least 1 week prior to surgery
    ❑ Teach the child coughing and deep breathing exercises
    ❑ Work with the child without the parents in attendance to gain trust
    ❑ Encourage the child to play with surgical masks and caps

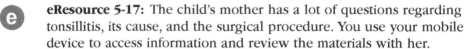 **eResource 5-17:** The child's mother has a lot of questions regarding tonsillitis, its cause, and the surgical procedure. You use your mobile device to access information and review the materials with her.
■ Merck Medicus Online: [Pathway: www.merckmedicus.com → Select "Patient Handouts" tab → Enter "tonsillitis" into the keyword search field → Select "Tonsil and Adenoid Surgery Pediatric"]

Answers to this chapter begin on page 69.

■ WebMD: [Pathway: WebMD → Select "Conditions" → Enter "Tonsillitis" into the search field → Read "Overview" and select articles]

Exercise 5-20: *Multiple-choice question*
Which of the following nursing diagnoses is the priority for a child who has just been admitted to the postanesthesia care unit following a tonsillectomy?

    A. Risk for fluid volume deficit: Related to decreased intake because of pain while swallowing

    B. Acute pain: Related to surgical procedure

    C. Gas exchange impaired: Related to anesthetics and pain

    D. Bleeding: At risk for a decrease in blood volume that may compromise health

 eResource 5-18: To better understand the postoperative care for this child and the priorities for care, consult Medscape on your mobile device: [Pathway: Medscape → Select "Conditions" → Enter "Tonsillectomy" into the search field → Select "Treatment and Management" → Read "Postoperative Details," "Follow-up," and "Complications"]

Exercise 5-21: *Multiple-choice question*
Alexis is called to assist with a 6-year-old girl who has just been admitted to the postanesthesia recovery room following an appendectomy. She is crying and guarding the right lower quadrant of her abdomen in the area of her surgical site. Which of the following measures would be most useful to determine the severity of her pain?

    A. Assess her behavioral cues such as guarding, crying, and immobilization of the operative site

    B. Utilize an age-appropriate pain assessment tool to rate her pain

    C. Ask her to rate her pain on a 5 to 10 Likert scale

    D. Ask her parents if this is her typical response to severe pain

 eResource 5-19: To learn more about pain scales utilized in children:
■ Read *Pain Assessment and Management—Pediatric:* goo.gl/Edm1ad
■ View the Wong-Baker FACES Pain Rating Scale typically used to assess pain in children under 8: goo.gl/Edm1ad

Exercise 5-22: *Calculation*
The 6-year-old girl was moved to the pediatric unit and is 3 days postoperative appendectomy and requests medication for pain. The doctor orders Tylenol 15 mg/kg orally every 4 to 6 hours, as needed. Her morning weight was 53 pounds. How much should she receive per dose? _____ mg

 eResource 5-20: To verify your dosage calculation, use one of the following dosage calculators:
■ MedCalc: [Pathway: www.medcalc.com → Tap on "Pediatrics" → Select "Dosing Calc" to access the calculator → Enter the data into the relevant fields]
■ Medscape: [Pathway: Medscape → Select "Reference" → Select "Calculators" → Select "Medication Protocols" → Select "Weight-Based Dose Calculator" → Enter the data into the relevant fields]

Answers to this chapter begin on page 69.

eResource 5-21: To learn more about Tylenol and the nursing considerations when administering this drug, use your mobile device to access information:
- Medscape: [Pathway: Medscape → Enter "Tylenol" into the search field → Select the "Pediatric" tab and review content]
- RxDrugs™: [Pathway: Skyscape → Select "RxDrugs™" → Enter "Tylenol" into the search field → Select "Use and Dosing" → Scroll down to "Pediatric Dosing" and review content. Pay particular attention to "Warnings/Precautions"]

Exercise 5-23: *Calculation*
Alexis is also caring for a child who is receiving maintenance intravenous therapy during her hospitalization. Her weight is documented at 63 pounds. What is her maintenance rate? _____

 eResource 5-22: To verify the calculation of the maintenance fluid calculation, consult the following tools on your mobile device:
- Medscape: [Pathway: Medscape → Tap on "Reference" → Select "Calculators" → Select "Fluids" → Select "Maintenance Fluid Calculation for Children" → Enter child's weight in pounds to determine maintenance fluids]
- MedCalc: [Pathway: MedCalc → Enter "Maintenance Fluids" → Select "Maintenance Fluid (Children)" → Enter child's weight in pounds to determine maintenance fluids]

Exercise 5-24: *Multiple-choice question*
An 8-year-old child is about to be discharged following application of a cast to a fractured femur. Which behavior by the child's parent would be a good indicator that cast care is understood?

    A. The parent states, "I had a cast about a year ago and know how to take care of it."

    B. The parent signs the discharge instruction sheet which states, "I understand all instructions as documented."

    C. The parent satisfactorily demonstrates cast care to you.

    D. The parent reassures you he will "call the doctor if any problems arise."

Exercise 5-25: *Select all that apply*
The child's nursing diagnosis is "Constipation: Risk for related to appendectomy and anesthetics." Which of the following nursing interventions would be appropriate for this child on the first postoperative day?

❑ Auscultate bowel sounds every shift

❑ Offer liquids when bowel sounds are present

❑ Restrict oral fluids to avoid distention when peristalsis is not normal

❑ Limit activity until peristalsis has returned

❑ Notify the physician if the child has not had a bowel movement

Answers to this chapter begin on page 69.

Exercise 5-26: *Ordering*
The preschool child has returned to the unit following a tonsillectomy. Prioritize the following nursing diagnoses in the order of their importance.

_____ Pain related to the surgical procedure

_____ Gas exchange related to anesthetics and increased oral secretions

_____ Anxiety related to change in health status

_____ Fluid volume: Potential for imbalance related to postoperative bleeding

_____ Knowledge deficit related to postoperative care at home

Exercise 5-27: *True or false*
Identify if the following statements regarding preoperative care of the child are true or false:

_____ Infants can have breast milk until 4 hours prior to surgery.

_____ Check and document if there are loose teeth or tongue piercings.

_____ Administer preoperative medications in the child's room.

_____ Allow parental presence during anesthesia when able.

_____ Utilize play therapy to familiarize the child with hospital gowns and masks.

_____ Visit the intensive care unit if the child will be transported there postoperatively.

_____ Encourage the parent to accompany the child to the holding area when possible.

_____ Preoperative teaching is not necessary until the school-age years.

Exercise 5-28: *Multiple-choice question*
Which of the following strategies would be most effective in the nursing care of the hospitalized adolescent?

    A. Use age-appropriate crafts to provide diversion and a sense of industry.

    B. Encourage interactions with other hospitalized adolescents to prevent isolation.

    C. Use projective techniques such as "Draw Me a Person."

    D. Encourage the parent to be present during all nursing care.

Exercise 5-29: *Select all that apply*
Identify nursing interventions that will facilitate self-care in the child who has repeated hospitalizations for a chronic illness.

    ❑ Instruct the school-age child on one self-care skill such as use of an inhaler.

    ❑ Ask the toddler to select a site to use for insulin injections.

    ❑ Teach the preschooler a simple task such as hand washing.

    ❑ Encourage the adolescent to become the manager of his or her daily care.

    ❑ Recognize the needs of the siblings of chronically ill children.

    ❑ Encourage parents to use support groups to manage caregiver burden.

Answers to this chapter begin on page 69.

Exercise 5-30: *True or false*

An emergency admission to the hospital may be traumatic to a child. Identify the following statements related to the hospitalized child as either true or false.

_____ Hospitalized infants are at risk for impaired parent–child attachment.

_____ Children who have been cared for in an intensive care unit may be predisposed to posttraumatic stress disorder (PTSD).

_____ Young children who are patients in an intensive care unit may experience sensory overload.

_____ Lack of parental interaction can lead to maternal deprivation.

_____ Infants and toddlers are not at risk for post-hospitalization emotional problems.

_____ Parental presence at the bedside promotes a sense of security in the child.

_____ Continuity of nurses assigned to the child promotes trust.

Answers to this chapter begin on page 69.

Answers

Exercise 5-1: *Multiple-choice question*

Cooper's parents are concerned that he will become upset when they leave him. In order to help the parents deal with the issues related to separation when they leave their toddler at the hospital, Alexis should make the following suggestion:

A. Place a clock at the child's bedside so the child can anticipate their return—NO, developmentally, the child is too young to tell time using a clock.

B. Quietly leave when the child is asleep—NO, this practice may create sleep disturbances because the child realizes every time he or she falls asleep, parents leave.

C. Use associations such as "I will be back when *Sid the Science Kid* comes on television in the morning"—YES

D. Assure the parents that toddlers adapt well and it should not be a concern—NO, toddlers experience separation anxiety.

Exercise 5-2: *Multiple-choice question*

Cooper has been hospitalized for over a week and now has been urinating in the bed. Alexis addresses his mother's concerns, basing her response on her understanding of growth and development. This temporary loss of a developmental milestone in response to stress is due to:

A. Regression—YES

B. Anger at the parent—NO, the child may be temporarily angry at this situation but this is not a developmental delay.

C. Self-assertion—NO, the child will voice his wants as a result of a sense of autonomy but this is not a manifestation of a developmental delay.

D. Detachment—NO, this behavior manifests itself as a break in the bond between parent and child and typically occurs after a prolonged separation.

Exercise 5-3: *Multiple-choice question*

A blood culture will be performed shortly on Cooper. Based on an understanding of a toddler's growth and development, Alexis should:

A. Perform the procedure in the child's room to decrease anxiety—NO, the child's hospital room and the play room should be safe havens from invasive or intrusive treatments.

B. Give the child a choice in which arm to use—NO, although fostering a sense of autonomy is important, choices related to painful procedures are unrealistic.

C. **Give short explanations as the procedure is done—YES**

D. Prepare the child well in advance of the procedure—NO, a toddler's cognitive skills enable the child to understand steps immediately before the procedure.

Exercise 5-4: *Calculation*

Cooper weighs 30 pounds on admission. He is ordered to receive the following IV medication: Ceftriaxone 50 mg/kg/day every 12 hours. What dose should be administered every 12 hours?

40 mg every 12 hours

Exercise 5-5: *Multiple-choice question*

Alexis wants to utilize play therapy to explain application of a cast to a preschool child. Which of the following interventions would meet the developmental needs of the preschooler?

A. **Use a doll to demonstrate the casting procedure—YES**

B. Offer a tape recording that describes the procedure—NO, play therapy using a visual doll enables the child to see that the procedure is not harmful.

C. Utilize a diagram to explain the procedure—NO, this mode of instruction is more appropriate to the learning needs of the school-age child.

D. Simply explain the procedure as it is performed—NO, the opportunity to see the procedure will minimize any fears of body mutilation or loss of body integrity, which is common during this period of development.

Exercise 5-6: *Multiple-choice question*

Which of the following interventions is most appropriate for the needs of a 7-year-old child who is hospitalized for an extended period of time?

A. Bring security items such as a blanket—NO, this measure is more appropriate to meet the psychosocial needs of the infant who is developing a sense of trust.

B. **Provide play activities that foster industry—YES**

C. Allow the child to make all decisions in treatment—NO, this technique would be more appropriate for the adolescent who is a formal operational thinker.

D. Complete all treatments in the play room—NO, the play room is considered a safe haven for a child and should not be associated with painful procedures. Intrusive procedures should be done in the treatment room.

Exercise 5-7: *Multiple-choice question*

The toddler, who has been hospitalized for 1 week, cries each time his mother leaves his bedside. Based on an understanding of growth and development, Alexis realizes this behavior is typical of:

A. Stranger anxiety—NO, this behavior occurs in the infant at approximately 8 months and is a developmental milestone. The infant reacts by crying whenever an unfamiliar person approaches the child.

B. Despair—NO, despair follows the protest phase and is characterized by quiet disorganization. Misses the parent but does not protest.

C. Regression—NO, regression is manifested by a temporary loss of a developmental milestone and this is not a developmental milestone; rather, it is a reaction to prolonged hospitalization characterized by quiet disorganization. Misses the parent but does not protest.

D. Protest—YES

Exercise 5-8: *Select all that apply*

You are assigned to a 2-year-old child who must receive an intramuscular injection of ampicillin. You would complete which of the following steps in the administration of this medication:

☒ **Cleanse a site in the anterolateral aspect of the thigh—YES**

☒ **Select a 7/8 inch- to 1-inch, 23- to 25-gauge needle—YES**

❑ Insert needle at a 45-degree angle into the vastus lateralis—NO, the needle should be inserted at a 90-degree angle.

❑ Inject the medication slowly into the deltoid muscle—NO, the medication should be injected in the vastus lateralis of an infant.

☒ **Restrain the child to avoid dislodging of the needle—YES**

Exercise 5-9: *Fill-in*

Leah, age 2 years, presents at the emergency department (ED) with an earache and fever and is diagnosed with otitis media. The health care provider orders amoxicillin 40 mg/kg/day orally, three times a day. She weighs 28 pounds. What dosage should be administered every 8 hours?

170 mg three times a day

Exercise 5-10: *Multiple-choice question*

All of the following techniques for oral medication administration to an infant are acceptable except:

A. Adding the medication to the infant's bottle of formula—YES

B. Allowing the infant to sit in the parent's lap during administration—NO, this is an acceptable mode of administration and helps decrease anxiety.

C. Encouraging the infant to suck the medication from an empty nipple—NO, this is an acceptable mode of administration and enables you to see if the entire dose has been swallowed.

D. Inserting a needleless syringe into the side of the mouth for the infant to suck— NO, this is a safe mode of administration and you can see if the entire dose has been swallowed.

Exercise 5-11: *Ordering*

Order the steps in the intervention of administering ear drops into the ear canal of an infant.

__4__	Straighten ear canal by gently pulling the earlobe down and back.
__1__	Complete the Five Rights for the child.
__2__	Warm the medication by rolling between hands. Shake as indicated.
__5__	Administer drops into the ear canal but not directly into the ear.
__3__	Lie infant on his or her side so affected ear is accessible.
__6__	Keep infant on unaffected side for a few minutes.

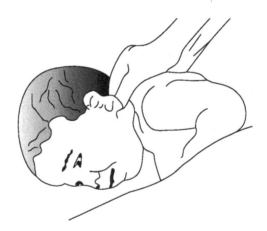

Exercise 5-12: *Matching*

List the developmental stage (infant, toddler, preschooler, school-age child, and adolescent) that coincides with a typical stressors of hospitalization.

Preschooler	Body mutilation fears
Toddler	Associates pain with punishment for poor behaviors
Infant, Toddler	Separation anxiety
School-age	Begins awareness of finality of death
Adolescent	Loss of identity and privacy
Infant	Maternal separation/deprivation

Exercise 5-13: *Select all that apply*

You want to minimize stressors to the infant during his hospitalization. Which of the following interventions would be appropriate?

☒ **Assign the same nurse to Jack every day when possible—YES, continuity of care promotes a sense of trust in the newborn.**

☒ **Encourage his parents to bring his favorite toy from home—YES, a transitional object is a link between parent and child and promotes attachment when the parent cannot always be present.**

☐ Reassure his parents that he is too young to realize they are not present—NO, infants, who experience significant periods of separation from the parents are at risk for maternal deprivation.

☒ **Offer the parents a flexible visiting schedule to meet their needs—YES, parents should be encouraged to room in whenever possible; however, if not possible, they should be able to visit their child as their schedule permits.**

☐ Encourage the parents to leave when he is asleep.—NO, leaving the child during periods of sleep can cause sleep disorders. The infant learns that every time he or she sleeps, parents will leave, which is distressing.

☒ **Hold and rock the infant frequently—YES, this measure is comforting to the child and promotes a sense of security.**

☒ **Minimize prolonged stimuli—YES, sensory overload can cause a disturbance in sleep.**

Exercise 5-14: *Multiple-choice question*

A nasopharyngeal swab will be done to determine if the respiratory syncytial virus is the causative organism of Jack's illness. Which of the following interventions is most important when performing this procedure on the child?

A. Explain the procedure to the child immediately prior to the procedure—NO, an infant does not have the cognitive abilities to understand a procedure.

B. Ask his parents to restrain him during the procedure—NO, although the parents may be present during the procedure, for safety purposes, you should restrain. Also, it can be very distressing for the parents to hold the child for this procedure.

C. Complete the procedure in the infant's crib—NO, all procedures should be performed in the treatment room.

D. Immobilize the child securely but gently—YES

Exercise 5-15: *Multiple-choice question*
Which of the following play therapy activities would encourage growth and development in the hospitalized infant?
  A. Explain techniques using a puppet—NO, although the infant would enjoy the movement and color of the puppet, the child is too young cognitively to understand any explanations.
  B. Place a brightly colored mobile over the crib—YES
  C. Suspend brightly colored latex balloons over the crib—NO, latex balloons should never be left with an infant because they pose a choking safety risk.
  D. Allow the child to play with hospital equipment—NO, the infant is not cognitively able to perform this type of play therapy.

Exercise 5-16: *Multiple-choice question*
On admission of the 1-year-old infant, Alexis obtains a weight of 22 pounds. In order to calculate the correct dosage of medication for this infant, you must convert the weight to kilograms. What is his weight in kilograms?
9.97 kg; Conversion: 1 kilogram = 2.2 pounds

Exercise 5-17: *Multiple-choice question*
Francesca, a preschooler, recently underwent chelating therapy for lead poisoning. Her play therapist wants to gain insight into her reaction to the experience. Which of the following interventions would be helpful to meet this goal?
  A. Ask the child to explain how she felt after the treatment—NO, the child may be too stressed to relive the experience and may become upset.
  B. Engage the child in an interactive skit using puppets—YES
  C. Ask her parents about her reaction to the chelating treatment—NO, although the parents may have insight into the child's reaction, the use of a projective technique will help the child to process the stressful event.
  D. Tell the child to draw a picture of herself receiving the chelating agent—NO, the child may be too young to express her feelings in this manner. Also, if a play therapist wanted to use drawings, the child would be asked to "Draw a Picture of a Person," which is less threatening.

Exercise 5-18: *Multiple-choice question*
Louise, age 4, received an intramuscular injection in her vastus lateralis. Although it did not bleed, she insists that she "needs a Band-Aid." Based on an understanding of growth and development, Alexis should:
  A. Show her the injection site to reinforce there is no active bleeding—NO, This measure would deny the fact that there is a developmental concern for body integrity.
  B. Apply a brightly colored Band-Aid on the injection site—YES

C. Try to distract her with her favorite toy—NO, this measure would deny the fact that there is a developmental concern for body integrity.

D. Explain to her that a Band-Aid is unnecessary following injections—NO, her request is based upon the fact that she fears loss of body integrity and body mutilation.

Exercise 5-19: *Select all that apply*

A 4-year-old is scheduled to have a tonsillectomy and needs preoperative teaching. Select all instructions that would be appropriate for this child.

☒ **Offer the child and parent a tour of the operating room and holding area— YES, this enables the child and parent to view the area when there is no accompanying stressor.**

☒ **Use nonthreatening terms such as "remove your tonsils"—YES, terms such as "cut out" reinforce fears of body mutilation.**

❑ Begin preoperative teaching at least 1 week prior to surgery—NO, based on the preschooler's cognitive capacity, the teaching should be done close to the time of the procedure.

❑ Teach the child coughing and deep breathing exercises—NO, this activity could cause bleeding in the postoperative tonsillectomy patient.

❑ Work with the child without parents in attendance to gain trust—NO, since this is a traumatic experience for the child, it is important to have the parents involved to promote a sense of security.

☒ **Encourage the child to play with surgical masks and caps—YES, this form of play therapy helps familiarize the child with appearances in the surgical suite.**

Exercise 5-20: *Multiple-choice question*

Which of the following nursing diagnoses is the priority for a child who has just been admitted to the postanesthesia care unit following a tonsillectomy?

A. Risk for fluid volume deficit: Related to decreased intake because of pain while swallowing—NO, although this diagnosis is vital, in terms of priority, an open airway in always the main priority.

B. Acute pain: Related to surgical procedure—NO, although pain management is important, in terms of priority, an open airway is always the main priority.

C. **Gas exchange impaired: Related to anesthetics and pain—YES, this is the priority concern.**

D. Bleeding: At risk for a decrease in blood volume that may compromise health— NO, although circulation is an important nursing diagnosis, in terms of priority, an open airway is always the main priority.

Exercise 5-21: *Multiple-choice question*
Alexis is called to assist with a 6-year-old girl who has just been admitted to the post-anesthesia recovery room following an appendectomy. She is crying and guarding the right lower quadrant of her abdomen in the area of her surgical site. Which of the following measures would be most useful to determine the severity of her pain?
A. Assess her behavioral cues such as guarding, crying, and immobilization of the operative site—NO, although these are important cues, each child reacts uniquely to pain and behavioral cues may not be the most accurate indicators.
B. Utilize an age-appropriate pain assessment tool to rate her pain—YES, an age-appropriate tool should be used.
C. Ask her to rate her pain on a 5 to 10 Likert scale—NO, because of the age of the child and her cognitive abilities, she may not be able to accurately rate her pain.
D. Ask her parents if this is her typical response to severe pain—NO, although the parents' input is important, pain is a unique experience and the child can be the best judge of the intensity of pain experienced.

Exercise 5-22: *Calculation*
The 6-year-old girl was moved to the pediatric unit and is 3 days postoperative appendectomy and requests medication for pain. The doctor orders Tylenol 15 mg/kg orally every 4 to 6 hours, as needed. Her morning weight was 53 pounds. How much should she receive per dose?
360 mg every 4 to 6 hours

Exercise 5-23: *Calculation*
Alexis is also caring for a child who is receiving maintenance intravenous therapy during her hospitalization. Her weight is documented at 63 pounds. What is her maintenance rate?
69.6 mL/hr

Exercise 5-24: *Multiple-choice question*
An 8-year-old child is about to be discharged following application of a cast to a fractured femur. Which behavior by the child's parent would be a good indicator that cast care is understood?
A. The parent states, "I had a cast about a year ago and know how to take care of it."—NO, It is important to have the parent demonstrate on the child that the correct cast care procedure is maintained.
B. The parent signs the discharge instruction sheet which states, "I understand all instructions as documented."—NO, although the parent states he understands cast care, it is important for the parent to demonstrate the care to ensure that correct cast care procedure is implemented.
C. The parent satisfactorily demonstrates cast care to you—YES, return demonstration validates the knowledge.
D. The parent reassures you he will "call the doctor if any problems arise."—NO, In order to prevent any complications that may arise from improper cast care, it is important to have the parent demonstrate correct cast care protocol.

Exercise 5-25: *Select all that apply*

The child's nursing diagnosis is "Constipation: Risk for related to appendectomy and anesthetics." Which of the following nursing interventions would be appropriate for this child on the first postoperative day?

☐ Auscultate bowel sounds every shift—NO, bowel sounds should be assessed at a minimum of every 4 hours.

☒ **Offer liquids when bowel sounds are present—YES, this means that peristalsis has resumed and there is no paralytic ileus.**

☒ **Restrict oral fluids to avoid distention when peristalsis is not normal—YES, the oral intake of fluids will cause abdominal distention if the bowels are not functioning normally.**

☐ Limit activity until peristalsis has returned—NO, activity should be increased as tolerated to promote gastric motility.

☐ Notify the physician if the child has not had a bowel movement—NO, the physician should be notified if the child has not had a bowel movement 3 to 4 days postoperatively.

Exercise 5-26: *Ordering*

The preschool child has returned to the unit following a tonsillectomy. Prioritize the following nursing diagnoses in the order of their importance.

3	Pain related to the surgical procedure
1	Gas exchange related to anesthetics and increased oral secretions
4	Anxiety related to change in health status
2	Fluid volume: Potential for imbalance related to postoperative bleeding
5	Knowledge deficit related to postoperative care at home

Exercise 5-27: *True or false*

Identify if the following statements regarding preoperative care of the child are true or false:

True   **Infants can have breast milk until 4 hours prior to surgery—YES, infants have difficulty conserving fluids and may dehydrate if fluids (breast milk) are withheld greater than 4 hours preoperatively. Infant formula may be given up to 6 hours preoperatively.**

True   **Check and document if there are loose teeth or tongue piercings—YES, they could dislodge and be aspirated during intubation or surgery.**

False   Administer preoperative medications in the child's room—NO, all intramuscular injections should be given in the treatment room or holding area since the child's room is considered a safe haven from invasive procedures.

False   Allow parental presence during anesthesia induction when able—NO, the parents may accompany the child to the holding room but are not allowed within the sterile environment of the operating room.

True Utilize play therapy to familiarize the child with hospital gowns and masks—YES, this form of play therapy enables the child to become familiar with the surgical attire of the surgical team and decreases anxiety.

True Visit the intensive care unit if the child will be transported there post-operatively—YES, the child can become familiar with the environment in a situation that is not stress laden or frightening.

True Encourage the parent to accompany the child to the holding area when possible—YES, parents in attendance help the child to accommodate to the new setting with a sense of security.

False Preoperative teaching is not necessary until the school-age years—NO, children as young as toddlers have the capacity to understand information about the setting and should receive developmentally appropriate patient preoperative education.

Exercise 5-28: *Multiple-choice question*
Which of the following strategies would be most effective in the nursing care of the hospitalized adolescent?

A. Use age-appropriate crafts to provide diversion and a sense of industry—NO, This type of therapeutic play would be appropriate for the psychosocial development of the school-age child to develop a sense of industry.

B. Encourage interactions with other hospitalized adolescents to prevent isolation—YES

C. Use projective techniques such as "Draw Me a Person"—NO, this type of thera-peutic play would be appropriate for the psychosocial development of the school-age child.

D. Encourage the parent to be present during all nursing care—NO, adolescents need periods of time by themselves when they can privately discuss health care concerns.

Exercise 5-29: *Select all that apply*
Identify nursing interventions that will facilitate self-care in the child who has repeated hospitalizations for a chronic illness.

☒ **Instruct the school-age child on one self-care skill such as use of an inhaler—YES, the school-age child can cognitively master a simply self-care skill using concrete thought.**

❑ Ask the toddler to select a site to use for insulin injections—NO, although the toddler should be developing a sense of autonomy, this choice may be too stressful to make because of the pain associated with the procedure.

☒ **Teach the preschooler a simple task such as hand washing—YES, preschoolers can learn simple tasks such as hand washing.**

☒ Encourage the adolescent to become the manager of his or her daily care—YES, adolescents, who have reached the formal operations of cognitive thinking, have the ability to manage their daily self-care.

☒ Recognize the needs of the siblings of chronically ill children—YES, the siblings of children who are chronically ill have unique needs related to the stressors associated with frequent hospitalizations of their sibling.

☒ Encourage parents to use support groups to manage caregiver burden—YES, parents of the chronically ill child can benefit from sharing experiences and fears with parents who have similar concerns.

Exercise 5-30: *True or false*

An emergency admission to the hospital may be traumatic to a child. Identify the following statements related to the hospitalized child as either true or false.

__True__ Hospitalized infants are at risk for impaired parent–child attachment.— YES, infants hospitalized for prolonged periods of time are at risk for maternal deprivation.

__True__ Children who have been cared for in an intensive care unit may be predisposed to posttraumatic stress disorder (PTSD).—YES, because of the intensity of these units and the complexity of the care, the child is at a greater risk for PTSD.

__True__ Young children who are patients in an intensive care unit may experience sensory overload.—YES, sensory stimulation occurs in the intensive care unit because of heightened stimuli.

__True__ Lack of parental interaction can lead to maternal deprivation in infants.—YES, the child who is separated from the parents for prolonged periods of times is at risk for a sense of mistrust and maternal deprivation.

__False__ Infants and toddlers are not at risk for post-hospitalization emotional problems.—NO, all children are at risk for problems due to the multidimensional stressors of hospitalization.

__False__ Parental presence at the bedside promotes a sense of dependency in the child.—NO, parental presence at the bedside promotes a sense of security and familiarity.

__True__ Continuity of nurses assigned to the child promotes trust.—YES, continuity of care promotes a sense of security and a familiarity in an environment associated with unfamiliar caregivers.

6

Nursing Care of the Pediatric Patient With a Compromised Immunological System

Vicki A. Martin

Unfolding Case Study #6-1 ▓ Logan

Logan is a 5-year-old boy who contracted HIV from his mother while she was pregnant with him. His mother contracted HIV after receiving a blood transfusion following a motor vehicle accident when she developed disseminated intravascular coagulation (DIC). His mother died when he was 2 years old from complications of AIDS. Logan's father and older sibling were tested for HIV and were negative. Logan's father remarried and his stepmother was accommodating in meeting Logan's needs for a chronic illness.

 eResource 6-1: To supplement your understanding of HIV as a chronic illness, refer to:
- Medscape:
  - Online: [Pathway: www.medscape.org → Under the tab "Reference," enter "HIV" into the search field → Review content under "Overview" focusing particularly on "Practice Essentials," Epidemiology," and "Prognosis"]
  - On your mobile device, you can access the same information: [Pathway: Medscape → Select "Reference" → Select "Conditions" → Enter "HIV" into the search field → Review content under "Overview" focusing particularly on "Practice Essentials," Epidemiology," and "Prognosis"]
- Epocrates Online: [Pathway: online.epocrates.com → Under the "Diseases" tab, enter "HIV" in the search field → Select "HIV Overview" → Review content]

They have a large supportive family. Early on in Logan's care, the family had a lot of questions about HIV.

e **eResource 6-2:** The health care professionals caring for Logan, provided a lot of patient education materials to Logan's family: goo.gl/2szTBf

You are following Logan as the home health nurse. During a home health visit, you note Logan has skin lesions on his chest and back, a nonproductive cough, crackles in all lung fields upon auscultation, white patches in his mouth, and complaints of being fatigued and thirsty.

His vital signs are:

- Temperature: 39.0° C (102.2° F)
- Pulse: 120
- Respirations: 30
- Blood pressure: 134/84

e **eResource 6-3:** To review lung sounds, go to:

- Crackles—Early Inspiratory (Rales): goo.gl/gUx17
- Crackles—Fine (Rales): goo.gl/vBr2h
- Crackles—Coarse (Rales): goo.gl/e2FR1

e **eResource 6-4:** To reinforce your understanding of opportunistic infections in HIV/AIDS, refer to Epocrates Online: [Pathway: online. epocrates.com → Under the "Diseases" tab, enter "HIV" in the search field → Select "HIV-related opportunistic infections" → Review content]

You notify the health care provider of the assessment findings and a complete blood count (CBC) and CD4+ lymphocyte count is ordered. The laboratory results reveal:

- Hemoglobin: 8.0 g/dL
- Hematocrit: 25%
- Leukocyte—white blood cell (WBC): 1,300
- Platelet: 100,000
- CD4+: 190

e **eResource 6-5:** To reinforce your understanding of normal serum levels, refer to GlobalRPh's Common Laboratory Values: [Pathway: goo.gl/0F1J15 → Select "C" → Select "Complete Blood Count" → Review content; repeat by selecting "L" → Select "Lymphocyte surface markers" → Review content]

Exercise 6-1: *Select all that apply*

You identify which clinical manifestations as being associated with HIV/AIDS:

- ❏ Iron deficiency anemia
- ❏ Lymphadenopathy
- ❏ Failure to thrive
- ❏ Bacterial infections
- ❏ Recurrent candidiasis

Answers to this chapter begin on page 92.

eResource 6-6: To reinforce your understanding of the clinical manifestations associated with HIV/AIDS, consult:
- Medscape
  - Online: [Pathway: www.medscape.org → Under the tab "Reference," select "References & Tools" → Enter "HIV" into the search field → Select "HIV Disease" → Under the "Clinical Presentation" tab, review "History" and "Physical Examination"]
  - On your mobile device, you can access the same information: [Pathway: Medscape → Enter "HIV" into the search field → Select "HIV Disease" → Under the "Clinical Presentation" tab, review "History" and "Physical Examination"]
- Epocrates Online: [Pathway: online.epocrates.com → Under the "Diseases" tab, enter "HIV" in the search field → Select "HIV Infection" and review content focusing particularly on "Highlights"]

You complete Logan's health history. Logan weighs 13.7 kg or 30 pounds. He has lost 10 pounds in the last month and his CD4+ lymphocyte count has decreased from the previous reading of 400.

 eResource 6-7: You open your mobile device to check what weight percentile Logan falls in currently: [Pathway: STAT GrowthChart™ → Enter gender, age, length and weight into the appropriate fields]

Exercise 6-2: *Fill-in*

Logan has high-risk factors for HIV, which can result in a poor prognosis. Identify three of Logan's risk factors: _____, _____, and _____.

You are also interested in learning more about standards of practice for caring for this population so you decide to do an internet search for practice guidelines to supplement your understanding of standards of care.

 eResource 6-8: On your mobile device, you access the following information:
- National Institute of Health's (NIH) Guidelines for the Prevention and Treatment of Opportunistic Infections in HIV-Exposed and HIV-Infected Children: Review the National Institute of Health's AIDS guidelines: goo.gl/9B2fI0
- National Guideline Clearinghouse (NGC): [Pathway: www.guideline.gov → Enter "HIV opportunistic infections" into the search field → Select and review the relevant content presented]

Exercise 6-3: *Fill-in*

You inform Logan's father and stepmother the treatment for his HIV requires the health care provider to change his Highly Active Antiretroviral Therapy (HAART). The goal is to prevent further _____ and to keep his CD4+ lymphocyte count at a desirable level of _____.

Answers to this chapter begin on page 92.

eResource 6-9: To learn more about HAART treatment, refer to Epocrates Online: [Pathway: online.epocrates.com → Under the "Diseases" tab, enter "HIV" in the search field → Select "HIV Infection" → Select "Treatment" tab and review content]

After Logan is seen by the health care provider, you review the treatment regimen with Logan's family, which includes: (a) regaining weight, (b) adopting a high-calorie, high-protein diet, (c) maintaining optimal weight for height and age, (d) healing of skin without further breakdown, (e) managing opportunistic infections, (f) verbalizing feelings and concerns of chronic illness, and (g) demonstrating understanding of home care and the importance of medical follow-up.

Exercise 6-4: *Multiple-choice question*
When educating them about nutrient-rich meals and snacks, which foods should you recommend to Logan's family?
    A. Increase intake of fruits, vegetables, and lean protein products.
    B. Increase intake of sweetened beverages, sodium, and low-fat foods.
    C. Decrease intake of fruits, vegetables, and whole grains.
    D. Decrease intake of fruits, vegetables, and meat products.

 eResource 6-10: To learn more about Practice Guidelines associated with nutritional support of children with HIV, visit the National Guidelines Clearinghouse (NGC): [Pathway: www.guideline.gov → Enter "nutrition and HIV children" into the search field → Review list of guidelines → Select "A.S.P.E.N. clinical guidelines: nutrition support of children with human immunodeficiency virus infection" → Scroll down to "Recommendations" and review content; repeat with "HIV/ AIDS evidence-based nutrition practice guideline"→ Scroll down to "Recommendations" and review content]

 eResource 6-11: To supplement your understanding of nutritional considerations and management of individuals with HIV, refer to Medscape
    ■ Online [Pathway: www.medscape.org → Under the tab "Reference" enter "HIV" into the search field → Select "HIV and Nutrition" → Review content]
    ■ On your mobile device, you can access the same information: [Pathway: Medscape → Select "Reference" → Select "Conditions" → Enter "HIV" into the search field → Select "HIV and Nutrition" → Review content]

At Logan's next monthly visit, you draw a CBC and CD4+ lymphocyte count. The results are as follows:
■ Hemoglobin: 10.5 g/dL
■ Hematocrit: 32%
■ WBC: 5,000
■ Platelet: 20,000
■ CD4+ lymphocyte

Answers to this chapter begin on page 92.

Exercise 6-5: *Matching*

Match the lab test in Column A to its normal numerical value in Column B.

Column A	Column B
A. Hemoglobin	_____ 35 to 45%
B. Hematocrit	_____ 5,500 to 15,500/mm³
C. WBC	_____ 150 to 400/mm³
D. Platelet	_____ 200 or greater/mcL
E. CD4+	_____ 11.5 to 15.5 g/dcL

eResource 6-12: Don't forget: To supplement your understanding about normal blood values, go to GlobalRPh"s Common Laboratory Values: [Pathway: goo.gl/0F1J15 → Select "C" → Select "Complete Blood Count" → Review content; repeat by selecting "L" → Select "Lymphocyte surface markers" → Review content]

Exercise 6-6: *Select all that apply*

What are the most common opportunistic infections of HIV/AIDS?

❑ *Pneumocystic carinii* pneumonia
❑ *Escherichia coli* infections
❑ Herpes simplex and herpes zoster
❑ Toxoplasmosis and cytomegalovirus (CMV)

eResource 6-13: To learn more about strategies to help Logan maintain optimal levels of health, refer to Medscape:

■ Online: [Pathway: www.medscape.org → Under the tab "Reference," select "References & Tools" → Enter "opportunistic" into the search field → Select "Preventing Opportunistic Infections in Patients With HIV" → Review content focusing in particular on "General Guidelines" and "Exposure Avoidance"]

■ On your mobile device, you can access the same information: [Pathway: Medscape → Enter "opportunistic" into the search field → Select "Preventing Opportunistic Infections in Patients With HIV" → Review content focusing in particular on "General Guidelines" and "Exposure Avoidance"]

Logan is rescheduled to visit the health care provider in 1 month to evaluate whether his dietary and medication regimen are effective for his HIV illness.

Unfolding Case Study #6-2 Tiffany

Tiffany is a 10-year-old female born with spina bifida who requires daily in and out catheterization due to a neurogenic bladder.

Exercise 6-7: *Fill-in*

Based on medical information about spina bifida, you understand vitamins containing
_____ _____ could have prevented this neural tube defect during her mother's
pregnancy.

e **eResource 6-14:** To reinforce your understanding of the risk factors
contributing to neural tube defects, consult Epocrates Online: [Pathway:
online.epocrates.com → Under the "Diseases" tab, enter "Spina bifida"
in the search field → Select "Spina bifida and neural tube defects" →
Select "Diagnosis" → Select "Risk Factors" and review content]

e **eResources 6-15:** To learn more about Tiffany's diagnosis, refer to:
- Epocrates Online: [Pathway: online.epocrates.com → Under the
  "Diseases" tab, enter "Spina bifida" in the search field → Select
  "Spina bifida and neural tube defects" → Review content, focusing
  on "Highlights" and "Basics"]
- Medscape:
  - Online: [Pathway: www.medscape.org → Under the tab "Reference,"
    select "References & Tools" → Enter "neurogenic bladder" into
    the search field → Select "neurogenic bladder" → Review content
    focusing in particular on "Treatment and Management" and
    "Medications Used to Treat Neurogenic Bladder"]
  - On your mobile device, you can access the same information:
    [Pathway: Medscape → Enter "neurogenic bladder" into the search
    field → Select "neurogenic bladder" → Review content focusing in
    particular on "Treatment and Management" and "Medications Used
    to Treat Neurogenic Bladder"]

Tiffany has become immunocompromised and developed latex allergies after
years of being exposed to numerous medical supplies and rubber products in her
environment. The health care provider has written the family a prescription for an
Epi-pen to have available with them at all times in case Tiffany ever develops any
type of anaphylactic reaction.

e **eResource 6-16:** To learn more about Epi-pen, consult Skyscape's
RxDrugs on your mobile device: [Pathway: Skyscape → Select "RxDrugs"
→ Enter "EpiPen" into the search field → Select "Epi-Pen" to review
content, focusing on "Warnings/Precautions" and "Adverse Reactions"]

Exercise 6-8: *Select all that apply*

Symptoms that define anaphylaxis include:
- ❏ Lip and tongue edema
- ❏ Urticaria and pruritus
- ❏ Shortness of breath
- ❏ Nonadventitious lung sounds

Answers to this chapter begin on page 92.

❑ Hypertension

❑ Stridor

❑ Wheezing

e **eResource 6-17:** To expand your understanding of management of anaphylaxis, refer to Epocrates Online: [Pathway: online.epocrates.com → Under the "Diseases" tab, enter "anaphylaxis" in the search field → Review content]

During a health care provider visit, you check Tiffany's head circumference and note she has an increased head circumference from her previous office visit 3 months ago. You speak with the health care provider and determine she has hydrocephalus requiring placement of a ventriculoperitoneal (VP) shunt. The parents have questions about this new diagnosis and the procedure.

e **eResource 6-18:** You want to provide patient education materials to the parents so you visit MerckMedicus Online: [Pathway: www.merckmedicus.com → Select "Patient Handouts" → Enter "Hydrocephalus" into the search field → Review content]

e **eResource 6-19:** Before continuing your preoperative teaching, you want to refresh your memory regarding this procedure so you refer to Medscape on your mobile device: [Pathway: Medscape → Select "Procedures" → Enter "shunt" into the search field → Select "ventriculoperitoneal shunt placement" → Review content focusing in particular on "Periprocedural Care"]

Exercise 6-9: *Multiple-choice question*
When a pediatric patient has a ventriculoperitoneal shunt, when should you become concerned the shunt may be malfunctioning?

    A. When the child's blood pressure decreases

    B. When the child starts having febrile seizures

    C. When the child has lethargy and a low-grade temperature

    D. When the child becomes nauseated and begins vomiting

Exercise 6-10: *Matching*
Match the immunoglobulin in Column A to its specific action in Column B

Column A	Column B
A. IgG	_____ Binds antigen to lymphocyte surface
B. IgA	_____ Activates phagocytosis
C. IgM	_____ Associated with allergic reactions
D. IgE	_____ Prevents infections
E. IgD	_____ Agglutinates antigen

Answers to this chapter begin on page 92.

Exercise 6-11: *Fill-in*

Identify at least four foods with a known cross-reactivity to latex:

1. _____
2. _____
3. _____
4. _____

Tiffany is scheduled for a follow-up appointment in 3 months. You educate the family on complications associated with shunt malfunction and anaphylaxis. The parents verbalize an understanding of the patient education.

Unfolding Case Study #6-3 ▨ Jessica

Jessica is a 3-year-old female brought to the emergency department by her parents for being irritable, inconsolable, and refusing to ambulate. Her parents had been medicating her with acetaminophen (Tylenol) every 4 hours with no relief of symptoms. She cried when flexing or extending her knees and ankles. She had previously been walking but was unable to ambulate without experiencing severe pain. Upon assessment, you noted pain, stiffness, loss of motion, and swelling in bilateral knees and ankles. The health care provider ordered an antinuclear antibody (ANA) and an erythrocyte sedimentation rate (ESR). The ANA was positive and the ESR was elevated. The child was admitted to the pediatric floor.

Exercise 6-12: *Fill-in*

Based on Jessica's emergency department admission assessment, she is exhibiting clinical manifestations of: _____ _____ _____.

Exercise 6-13: *Select all that apply*

The goals for treatment of arthritis include:

❑ Manage pain
❑ Control inflammation
❑ Manage systemic complications
❑ Preserve joint function and mobility
❑ Promote normal growth and development

Exercise 6-14: *True or false*

Juvenile idiopathic arthritis affects girls more than boys.

_____ True

_____ False

e **eResource 6-20:** To learn more about the etiology and pathophysiology of juvenile idiopathic arthritis, refer to Medscape on your mobile device:

Answers to this chapter begin on page 92.

[Pathway: Medscape → Select "conditions" → Enter "arthritis" into the search field → Select "juvenile idiopathic arthritis" → Review content focusing in particular on "etiology and pathophysiology"]

Exercise 6-15: *True or false*

Acetaminophen (Tylenol) is the drug of choice for treatment of juvenile idiopathic arthritis.

_____ True

_____ False

Exercise 6-16: *Calculation*

Order: Give naproxen 5 to 10 mg/kg orally, twice a day. The child weighs 30 pounds. Calculate how many mg of naproxen to administer per dose: _____

Exercise 6-17: *Multiple-choice question*

The parents of a child with juvenile idiopathic arthritis ask you to recommend an exercise activity. Which activity should you recommend?

    A. Softball

    B. Football

    C. Swimming

    D. Running

 eResource 6-21: You want to provide additional patient education material to the parents, so you refer to MerckMedicus Online: [Pathway: www.merckmedicus.com → Select "Patient Handouts" → Enter "juvenile arthritis" into the search field → Select "Juvenile Rheumatoid Arthritis" and "Juvenile Rheumatoid Arthritis: Resource List" to give to the parents]

Jessica is discharged from the hospital feeling better and is to return to the health care provider in 2 weeks for reevaluation of the ANA and ESR. She was immunized for varicella (chicken pox) when she was younger. This will help prevent her from acquiring Reye syndrome while being on high doses of aspirin in managing the pain and inflammation associated with juvenile idiopathic arthritis.

Unfolding Case Study #6-4 ▨ Chad

Chad is a 2-month-old infant being seen in the pediatrician's office for fever, vomiting, poor feeding, and fussiness. Upon assessment, the office nurse notes an ill-appearing, febrile male infant and performs the ordered blood and urine tests to determine the illness. The pediatrician suspects Chad may have urosepsis. Chad's history reveals he was a normal newborn with no problems during delivery but he was born with bladder exstrophy. He required genitourinary surgery with a repair of the bladder within the first week of life. His surgery was completed in one session and was successful. He did not suffer any complications postoperatively and was discharged home when he was 2 weeks old.

 eResource 6-22: To reinforce your understanding of bladder exstrophy, you refer to MerckMedicus: [Pathway: www.merckmedicus.com → Enter "Bladder Anomalies" into the search field → Scroll down to "Exstrophy" and review content]

His mother states he has been doing very well until last night when he became fretful. His stent is patent and in proper placement.

The urinalysis and complete blood count (CBC) reveal:

- Urine culture and sensitivity (C&S): Positive with bacteria
- CBC/white blood cell (WBC): Elevated
- Blood C&S: Positive for septicemia and bacteremia

Chad is admitted to the pediatric intensive care unit (PICU) at the Children's Hospital. He was started on intravenous (IV) therapy of D5 ½ NS, Cefepime antibiotics, and antipyretics.

Exercise 6-18: *Select all that apply*

Which clinical manifestations are exhibited in infants with septicemia?

- ❑ Hypothermia
- ❑ Hypotonia
- ❑ Lethargy
- ❑ Gram-negative bacteria
- ❑ Decreased urine output

Sepsis results in the systemic inflammatory response syndrome (SIRS) due to the overwhelming infection in the bloodstream. The pathophysiology of sepsis is complex and complicated.

Exercise 6-19: *Fill-in*

Sepsis results from the effects of circulating _____ _____ and is mediated by release of _____.

Exercise 6-20: *Multiple-choice question*

Sepsis has a systemic effect on the body. Identify which organs may become impaired with sepsis.

A. Bowels, kidneys, and lungs

B. Lungs, liver, and kidneys

C. Gallbladder and appendix

D. Heart and spleen

Answers to this chapter begin on page 92.

eResource 6-23: To reinforce your understanding of management of the patient with sepsis, refer to Skyscape's Outline in Clinical Medicine on your mobile device (available for download from Skyscape.com): [Pathway: Outline of Clinical Medicine → Enter "sepsis" into the search field → Select "sepsis"→ Review content focusing particularly on "Overview," "Treatment," and "Follow-up"]

Exercise 6-21: *True or false*

If final culture reports are negative and symptoms have subsided, antibiotics may be discontinued after 72 hours of treatment.

_____ True

_____ False

Chad demonstrates an overall improvement in his health status and remains in the PICU for 2 weeks. Prior to discharge, the urinary stent was removed and he is voiding clear, yellow urine in adequate amounts for an infant. The pediatrician reassures the parents that he has a good prognosis.

Answers to this chapter begin on page 92.

Answers

Exercise 6-1: *Select all that apply*

You identify which clinical manifestations as being associated with HIV/AIDS:

☒ **Iron deficiency anemia**

☒ **Lymphadenopathy**

☒ **Failure to thrive**

☒ **Bacterial infections**

☒ **Recurrent candidiasis**

Exercise 6-2: *Fill-in*

Logan has high-risk factors for HIV, which can result in a poor prognosis. Identify three of Logan's risk factors: **maternal diagnosis**, **failure to thrive presentation**, and **history of recurrent bacterial infections**

Exercise 6-3: *Fill-in*

The nurse informs Logan's father and stepmother the treatment for his HIV requires the health care provider to change his highly active antiretroviral therapy (HAART). The goal is to prevent further **complications** and to keep his CD4+ lymphocyte count at a desirable level of **200 or greater**.

Exercise 6-4: *Multiple-choice question*

When educating them about nutrient-rich meals and snacks, which foods should you recommend to Logan's family?

A. Increase intake of fruits, vegetables, and lean protein products—YES

B. Increase intake of sweetened beverages, sodium, and low-fat foods—NO, these provide glucose and sodium.

C. Decrease intake of fruits, vegetables, and whole grains—NO, these are needed.

D. Decrease intake of fruits, vegetables, and meat products—NO, these are needed.

Exercise 6-5: *Matching*
Match the lab test in Column A to its normal numerical value in Column B.

Column A	Column B
A. Hemoglobin	__B__ 35 to 45%
B. Hematocrit	__C__ 5,500 to 15,500/mm³
C. WBC	__D__ 150 to 400/mm³
D. Platelet	__E__ 200 or greater/mcL
E. CD4+	__A__ 11.5 to 15.5 g/dL

Exercise 6-6: *Select all that apply*
What are the most common opportunistic infections of HIV/AIDS?

☒ *Pneumocystic carinii* **pneumonia (PCP)**

❑ *Escherichia coli* infections

☒ **Herpes simplex and herpes zoster**

☒ **Toxoplasmosis and cytomegalovirus (CMV)**

Exercise 6-7: *Fill-in*
Based on medical information about spina bifida, you understand vitamins containing **folic acid** could have prevented this neural tube defect during her mother's pregnancy.

Exercise 6-8: *Select all that apply*
Symptoms that define anaphylaxis include:

☒ **Lip and tongue edema**

☒ **Urticaria and pruritus**

☒ **Shortness of breath**

❑ Nonadventitious lung sounds

❑ Hypertension

☒ **Stridor**

☒ **Wheezing**

Exercise 6-9: *Multiple-choice question*
When a pediatric patient has a ventriculoperitoneal shunt, when should you become concerned the shunt may be malfunctioning?

A. When the child's blood pressure decreases—NO

B. When the child starts having febrile seizures—NO

C. When the child has lethargy and a low-grade temperature—NO

D. **When the child becomes nauseated and begins vomiting—YES**

Exercise 6-10: *Matching*

Match the immunoglobulin in Column A to its specific action in Column B.

Column A	Column B
A. IgG	__E__ Binds antigen to lymphocyte surface
B. IgA	__A__ Activates phagocytosis
C. IgM	__D__ Associated with allergic reactions
D. IgE	__B__ Prevents infections
E. IgD	__C__ Agglutinates antigen

Exercise 6-11: *Fill-in*

Identify at least four foods with a known cross-reactivity to latex:

1. **Peaches**
2. **Grapes**
3. **Potatoes**
4. **Carrots**

Exercise 6-12: *Fill-in*

Based on Jessica's emergency department admission assessment, she is exhibiting clinical manifestations of: **juvenile idiopathic arthritis**.

Exercise 6-13: *Select all that apply*

The goals for treatment of arthritis include:

☒ **Manage pain**
☒ **Control inflammation**
☒ **Manage systemic complications**
☒ **Preserve joint function and mobility**
☒ **Promote normal growth and development**

Exercise 6-14: *True or false*

Juvenile idiopathic arthritis affects girls more than boys.

___X___ True

_____ False

Exercise 6-15: *True or false*

Acetaminophen (Tylenol) is the drug of choice for treatment of juvenile idiopathic arthritis.

_____ True

___X___ **False**

Exercise 6-16: *Calculation*
Order: Give naproxen 5 to 10 mg/kg orally, twice a day. The child weighs 30 pounds. Calculate how many mg of naproxen to administer per dose: **68 mg to 136 mg**

Exercise 6-17: *Multiple-choice question*
The parents of a child with juvenile idiopathic arthritis ask you to recommend an exercise activity. Which activity should you recommend?
A. Softball—NO
B. Football—NO
C. Swimming—YES
D. Running—NO

Exercise 6-18: *Select all that apply*
Which clinical manifestations are exhibited in infants with septicemia?
☒ **Hypothermia**
☒ **Hypotonia**
☒ **Lethargy**
☒ **Gram-negative bacteria**
☒ **Decreased urine output**

Exercise 6-19: *Fill-in*
Sepsis results from the effects of circulating **bacterial toxins** and is mediated by release of **cytokines**.

Exercise 6-20: *Multiple-choice question*
Sepsis has a systemic effect on the body. Identify which organs may become impaired with sepsis.
A. Bowels, kidneys, and lungs—NO
B. Lungs, liver, and kidneys—YES
C. Gallbladder and appendix—NO
D. Heart and spleen—NO

Exercise 6-21: *True or false*
If final culture reports are negative and symptoms have subsided, antibiotics may be discontinued after 72 hours of treatment.
___**X**___ **True—If asymptomatic with negative cultures, antibiotics are not necessary.**
_____ False

Nursing Care of the Pediatric Patient With Fluid and Electrolyte Imbalances

Vicki A. Martin

Unfolding Case Study #7-1 ▨ Luke

Luke is a 2-week-old Hispanic male infant brought to the hospital emergency department by his mother. His father is at work and his mother speaks minimal English. His mother is young, anxious, and unable to communicate the child's current problems. The hospital obtains a translator. The translator reports the infant has been breastfeeding but is not feeding on each breast as long and frequently as before. The mother states he is sleeping all the time, is spitting up after eating, will not eat unless awakened, and she thinks he has lost weight. He appears fussy and irritable. The mother is concerned. The infant's birth weight was 7 pounds and 2 ounces. Upon assessment, the infant's current weight is 6 pounds and 2 ounces. Using the translator, you ask the mother how many times she has changed the infant's diapers today.

Exercise 7-1: *Fill-in*
A well-nourished infant should have _____ wet diapers per day as a daily expected occurrence.

Exercise 7-2: *Select all that apply*
Imbalances involving fluid and electrolyte disorders in growing children include:
- ❏ Sodium (Na)
- ❏ Potassium (K)
- ❏ Chloride (Cl)
- ❏ Magnesium (Mg)
- ❏ Calcium (Ca)

Exercise 7-3: *True or false*
Shock or hypovolemia is the greatest threat to life in isotonic dehydration.
_____ True
_____ False

Answers to this chapter begin on page 103.

Exercise 7-4: *Calculation*

Fluid loss can be calculated according to weight loss. Use this formula to calculate Luke's weight loss (1 kilogram of weight loss is equal to 1,000 mL of fluid loss).

Calculate how many mL of fluid loss the infant has experienced: _____

Exercise 7-5: *Multiple-choice question*

Which clinical manifestations are expected in dehydration of infants and young children?

    A. Bulging fontanels

    B. Flushed skin

    C. Reduction or lack of tears

    D. Moist mucous membranes

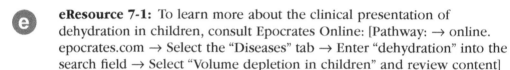 **eResource 7-1:** To learn more about the clinical presentation of dehydration in children, consult Epocrates Online: [Pathway: → online. epocrates.com → Select the "Diseases" tab → Enter "dehydration" into the search field → Select "Volume depletion in children" and review content]

Exercise 7-6: *Fill-in*

_____ _____ acid–base imbalance occurs as a result of bicarbonate retention and hydrogen ions and is commonly seen in children with prolonged vomiting and emesis of acidic stomach content.

 eResource 7-2: To learn more about acid-base imbalance and the treatment, refer to *MerckMedicus Online* on your mobile device:

    ■ [Pathway: www.merckmedicus.com → Select "Merck Manual" → Select "Merck Manual for Healthcare Professionals" → Enter "Acid-Base Regulation" into the search field → Select "acid base physiology" and "acid base balance" and review content]

    ■ [Pathway: www.merckmedicus.com → Select "Merck Manual" → Select "Merck Manual for Healthcare Professionals" → Enter "dehydration" into the search field → Select "Dehydration in children" → Select "Treatment" and review content]

Exercise 7-7: *Matching*

Match the diagnostic laboratory values in Column A to the type of dehydration in Column B.

Column A	Column B
A. Elevated serum sodium (Na+)	_____ Isotonic (isonatremic) dehydration
B. Normal serum sodium (Na+)	_____ Hypotonic (hyponatremic) dehydration
C. Decreased serum sodium (Na+)	_____ Hypertonic (hypernatremic) dehydration

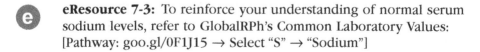 **eResource 7-3:** To reinforce your understanding of normal serum sodium levels, refer to GlobalRPh's Common Laboratory Values: [Pathway: goo.gl/0F1J15 → Select "S" → "Sodium"]

Answers to this chapter begin on page 103.

Luke was on the pediatric unit for 1 week. He started to gain weight and tolerate breast milk but required supplemental formula feedings in-between breastfeeding to meet his caloric needs. The lactation specialist and registered dietician were successful in working with Luke's mother regarding patient education with infants on breastfeeding and adequate nutrition. He was scheduled to have a follow-up appointment with the pediatrician in 1 week and was discharged with weight gain while weighing 7 pounds and 13 ounces.

eResource 7-4: Prior to discharge, you consult the following resources to ensure discharge teaching standards for Luke's mother have been met.

- National Guideline Clearinghouse (NGC) to view Practice Guidelines: www.guideline.gov: [Pathway: NGC → Enter "newborn" into the search field → Review "Postpartum maternal and newborn discharge" and other available newborn discharge guidelines]
- Go to the National Guideline Clearinghouse (NGC) to view Practice Guidelines: www.guideline.gov: [Pathway: NGC → Enter "routine preventable services infants" into the search field → Select and review the "Routine preventive services for infants and children (birth—24 months)" guideline]

Unfolding Case Study #7-2 Cassidy

Cassidy is a 1-year-old who was born with Down syndrome (trisomy 21). She resides with both parents in a middle-class home. She was born prematurely at 36 weeks gestation and was diagnosed with a heart murmur and atrial septal defect (ASD) in the neonatal intensive care unit (NICU).

eResource 7-5: To reinforce your understanding of Cassidy's diagnosis, refer to *Medscape:*

- Online: [Pathway: www.medscape.org → Under the tab "Reference" enter "Down syndrome" into the search field → Review content under "Overview." Next, enter "Atrial septal defect" into the search field → Review content]
- On your mobile device, you can access the same information: [Pathway: Medscape → Under the tab "Reference" enter "Down syndrome" into the search field → Review content under "Overview." Next, enter "Atrial septal defect" into the search field → Review content]

Cassidy has been seen regularly by the pediatrician and cardiologist for her medical issues. She has been receiving digoxin 100 mcg and furosemide 10 mg daily without any complications.

eResource 7-6: To learn more about these drugs and precautions, consult Skyscape's RxDrugs™ on your mobile device: [Pathway: Skyscape → Select "RxDrugs" → Enter "digoxin" into the search field → Scroll down to view Warnings/precautions; repeat with "Furosemide"]

Answers to this chapter begin on page 103.

Cassidy passed the Denver II developmental screening for her age but takes more time to perform the expected milestones than her counterparts. Her mother reports she has been doing well up until a few days ago when they were out of town and they did not have her furosemide with them. She started wheezing and looking swollen. In the cardiologist office, she has become slightly edematous and has gained about 1 pound in excess fluid.

 eResource 7-7: To learn more about respiratory wheezing, listen to The Merck Manual of Patient Symptoms Podcast: *Wheezing*: goo.gl/BA2cb

Exercise 7-8: *Fill-in*

Regarding medications in pharmacology, you understand furosemide is considered to be a _____ diuretic that is potassium wasting and digoxin is considered a _____ _____ that acts as an antiarrhythmic.

Exercise 7-9: *Select all that apply*

Symptoms that define fluid volume excess or edema include:
- ❑ Hypotension
- ❑ Bounding pulse
- ❑ Pitting edema
- ❑ Neck vein distention
- ❑ Venous congestion

Exercise 7-10: *Multiple-choice question*

What is the best diagnostic test for diagnosing a heart murmur and ASD?
- A. Cardiac auscultation
- B. Chest radiograph
- C. Cardiac catheterization
- D. Echocardiogram

 eResource 7-8: To reinforce your understanding of ASD, refer to MerckMedicus Online on your mobile device: [Pathway: www .merckmedicus.com → Select "Merck Manual" → Select "Merck Manual for Healthcare Professionals" → Enter "Atrial septal defect" into the search field → Select "diagnosis" and review content]

Exercise 7-11: *Matching*

Match the five-point scale rating in Column A to the degree of edema in Column B.

Column A	Column B
A. +0	_____ ¼ inch mild indentation
B. +1	_____ Greater than 1 inch very severe indentation
C. +2	_____ ½ to 1 inch severe indentation
D. +3	_____ ¼ to ½ inch moderate indentation
E. +4	_____ No persisting indentation

Answers to this chapter begin on page 103.

eResource 7-9: To learn more about assessment of edema, review Pitting edema grading: goo.gl/47Vk0I

Exercise 7-12: *Fill-in*

Identify at least four dietary foods known to be high in sodium that contribute to edema:

1. _____
2. _____
3. _____
4. _____

Exercise 7-13: *Fill-in*

Identify at least four dietary foods known to be potassium rich and aid in preventing hypokalemia:

1. _____
2. _____
3. _____
4. _____

Exercise 7-14: *Select all that apply*

Nursing management/interventions for the patient with fluid volume excess or edema include:

- ❏ Monitor daily weights
- ❏ Monitor vital signs every 4 hours
- ❏ Turn patient every 2 hours
- ❏ Assess for edema every shift
- ❏ Administer digoxin if pulse is less than 70
- ❏ Withhold furosemide if potassium is greater than 5

Exercise 7-15: *Matching*

Match the acid–base imbalance in Column A with the correct description in Column B.

Column A	Column B
A. Respiratory alkalosis	_____ Increased pH, increased HCO_3
B. Respiratory acidosis	_____ Decreased pH, decreased HCO_3
C. Metabolic alkalosis	_____ Increased pH, decreased pCO_2
D. Metabolic acidosis	_____ Decreased pH, increased pCO_2

eResource 7-10: To learn more about metabolic and respiratory acidosis and alkalosis, view the following video tutorial: goo.gl/SqzYdF

Answers to this chapter begin on page 103.

The mother administered 5 mg extra of furosemide in the cardiology office as ordered and the child was monitored in the office for 4 hours. After receiving the furosemide, the child lost ½ pound in weight and the edema and wheezing subsided. The mother was to return to the cardiology office if the child presented with any more edematous or cardiac issues. The mother verbalized an understanding of the home instructions and made an appointment to return in 1 month if the child did not experience any complications.

Answers to this chapter begin on page 103.

Answers

Exercise 7-1: *Fill-in*

A well-nourished infant should have **8 to 10** wet diapers per day as a daily expected occurrence.

Exercise 7-2: *Select all that apply*

Imbalances involving fluid and electrolyte disorders in growing children include:

☒ **Sodium (Na)**

☒ **Potassium (K)**

☐ Chloride (Cl)

☒ **Magnesium (Mg)**

☒ **Calcium (Ca)**

Exercise 7-3: *True or false*

Shock or hypovolemia is the greatest threat to life in isotonic dehydration.

___**X**___ **True**

_____ False

Exercise 7-4: *Calculation*

Fluid loss can be calculated according to weight lost. Use this formula to calculate Luke's weight loss (1 kilogram of weight loss is equal to 1,000 mL of fluid loss). Calculate how many mL of fluid loss the infant has experienced: **2,200 mL***

*Child lost 1 pound = 2.2 kg; 2.2 × 1,000 = 2,200 mL

Exercise 7-5: *Multiple-choice question*

Which clinical manifestations are expected in dehydration of infants and young children?

A. Bulging fontanels—NO, this is overhydration.

B. Flushed skin—NO, this is not a sign of dehydration.

C. **Reduction or lack of tears—YES, this is common in children with dehydration.**

D. Moist mucous membranes—NO, this is a sign of appropriate hydration.

Exercise 7-6: *Fill-in*

Metabolic alkalosis acid–base imbalance occurs as a result of bicarbonate retention or hydrogen ion loss and is commonly seen in children with prolonged vomiting as emesis is acidic stomach content.

Exercise 7-7: *Matching*

Match the diagnostic laboratory values in Column A to the type of dehydration in Column B.

Column A	Column B
A. Elevated serum sodium (Na+)	__B__ Isotonic (isonatremic) dehydration
B. Normal serum sodium (Na+)	__C__ Hypotonic (hyponatremic) dehydration
C. Decreased serum sodium (Na+)	__A__ Hypertonic (hypernatremic) dehydration

Exercise 7-8: *Fill-in*

Regarding medications in pharmacology, you understand furosemide is considered to be a **loop** diuretic that is potassium wasting and digoxin is considered a **digitalis glycoside** that acts as an antiarrhythmic.

Exercise 7-9: *Select all that apply*

Symptoms that define fluid volume excess or edema include:

☐ Hypotension

☒ **Bounding pulse**

☒ **Pitting edema**

☒ **Neck vein distention**

☒ **Venous congestion**

Exercise 7-10: *Multiple-choice question*

What is the best diagnostic test for diagnosing a heart murmur and ASD?

A. Cardiac auscultation—NO, this is not the best diagnostic test.

B. Chest radiograph—NO, a chest x-ray may not show the defect.

C. Cardiac catheterization—NO, this is not the first diagnostic test.

D. Echocardiogram—YES, this is the best diagnostic test for an ASD.

Exercise 7-11: *Matching*

Match the five-point scale rating in Column A to the degree of edema in Column B.

Column A	Column B
A. +0	__B__ ¼ inch mild indentation
B. +1	__E__ Greater than 1 inch very severe indentation
C. +2	__D__ ½ to 1 inch severe indentation
D. +3	__C__ ¼ to ½ inch moderate indentation
E. +4	__A__ No persisting indentation

Exercise 7-12: *Fill-in*

Identify at least four dietary foods known to be high in sodium that contribute to edema:

1. **Pickles**
2. **Potato chips**
3. **Canned foods**
4. **Regular colas**

Exercise 7-13: *Fill-in*

Identify at least four dietary foods known to be potassium rich and aid in preventing hypokalemia:

1. **Bananas**
2. **Orange juice**
3. **Raisins**
4. **Potatoes**

Exercise 7-14: *Select all that apply*

Nursing management/interventions for the patient with fluid volume excess or edema include:

☒ **Monitor daily weights**

☒ **Monitor vital signs every 4 hours**

☒ **Turn patient every 2 hours**

☒ **Assess for edema every shift**

❑ Administer digoxin if pulse is less than 70

❑ Withhold furosemide if potassium is greater than 5

Exercise 7-15: *Matching*

Match the acid–base imbalance in Column A with the correct description in Column B.

Column A	Column B
A. Respiratory alkalosis	__C__ Increased pH, increased HCO_3
B. Respiratory acidosis	__D__ Decreased pH, decreased HCO_3
C. Metabolic alkalosis	__A__ Increased pH, decreased pCO_2
D. Metabolic acidosis	__B__ Decreased pH, increased pCO_2

8

Children With Integumentary Health Care Needs

Vicki A. Martin

Unfolding Case Study #8-1 ▨ Paul

Paul is a 14-year-old adolescent with severe acne all over his face. He comes into the pediatrician's office for treatment of facial infections and pustules. His mother is concerned he will have permanent scarring on his face, which will cause him to have low self-esteem as a teenager. She explains to the nurse that he eats chocolate, drinks colas, and eats greasy, spicy foods. She feels his diet is a major contributor to the acne. They both want to get the acne under control with a manageable treatment plan.

Exercise 8-1: *Fill-in*
The health care provider informs Paul's mother that the type of acne he has is _____ _____, which is the most common form of acne and is estimated to affect 85% to 95% of adolescents.

Exercise 8-2: *Select all that apply*
The nurse identifies which clinical manifestations as being associated with acne lesions:
- ❏ Macules
- ❏ Nodules
- ❏ Comedones
- ❏ Pustules
- ❏ Papules

ⓔ **eResource 8-1:** To understand the pathophysiology of acne, refer to Medscape:
- ▨ MerckMedicus Online on your mobile device: [Pathway: www .merckmedicus.com → Select "Merck Manual" → Select "Merck Manual for Healthcare Professionals" → Enter "acne" into the search field → Select "acne vulgaris" → Review content, focusing on "pathophysiology" and "etiology"]

Answers to this chapter begin on page 123.

- Medscape:
  - Online: [Pathway: www.medscape.org → Select "Reference" → Enter "acne" into the search field → Select "acne vulgaris" → Under the "Overview" tab, review "practice essentials," "pathophysiology," and "etiology"]
  - On your mobile device, you can access the same information: [Pathway: Medscape → Select "Reference" → Enter "acne" into the search field → Select "acne vulgaris" → Under the "Overview" tab, review "practice essentials," "pathophysiology," and "etiology"]

Exercise 8-3: *True or false*

Research has proven that dietary factors are inconclusive in causing acne lesions.

_____ True

_____ False

Exercise 8-4: *Matching*

Match the acne lesion classification in Column A to the type of acne lesion in Column B.

Column A	Column B
A. Closed comedones	_____ Keloids
B. Open comedones	_____ Whiteheads
C. Pustules	_____ Blackheads
D. Nodules	_____ Papules with purulent material
E. Scarring	_____ Tender and greater than 5 mm in diameter

 eResource 8-2: To learn more about the clinical presentation and causes of acne, refer again to the following resources:
- MerckMedicus Online on your mobile device: [Pathway: www .merckmedicus.com → Select "Merck Manual" → Select "Merck Manual for Healthcare Professionals" → Enter "acne" into the search field → Select "acne vulgaris" → Select "signs and symptoms"; be sure to look at the images]
- Medscape:
  - Online: [Pathway: www.medscape.org → Select "Reference" → Enter "acne" into the search field → Select "acne vulgaris" → Under the "Clinical Presentation" tab, review "physical examination" and "causes"; be sure to look at the images]
  - On your mobile device, you can access the same information: [Pathway: Medscape → Select "Reference" → Enter "acne" into the search field → Select "acne vulgaris" → Under the "Clinical Presentation" tab, review "physical examination" and "causes"; be sure to look at the images]

Paul's treatment plan includes daily application of both topical and oral prescription medications such as cleansing the face with benzoyl peroxide, applying topical antibiotics, and taking oral isotretinoin (Accutane).

Answers to this chapter begin on page 123.

eResource 8-3: To learn more about how acne is treated and how various drugs work in treating acne, refer to MerckMedicus Online on your mobile device: [Pathway: www.merckmedicus.com → Select "Merck Manual" → Select "Merck Manual for Healthcare Professionals" → Enter "acne" into the search field → Select "acne vulgaris" → Select "treatment"]

Paul and his mother understand this treatment plan requires compliance and could take up to 8 to 10 weeks to resolve his acne problems. He is to discontinue the treatment once the acne has completely healed and resolved.

Unfolding Case Study #8-2 ▄ Ruth

Ruth is a 9-year-old girl who recently had an upper respiratory infection during the beginning of the summer. Her father reports she had a runny nose and was constantly scratching her nose. It has been 2 weeks since she was sick. Today she woke up with a honey-colored lesion around her nose and mouth. She is complaining of pain and refuses to eat or drink. Her father is babysitting while her mother is at work. He calls into the outpatient clinic inquiring about what he should do for her. The nurse instructs him to bring her to the clinic. Upon examination, it was determined she has impetigo. The father asks what impetigo is since he is not familiar with that medical term.

Exercise 8-5: *Multiple-choice question*
What is the best explanation by the nurse to explain impetigo to the father?

    A. It is not contagious nor is it a skin infection of concern.

    B. It is a highly contagious, superficial bacterial skin infection.

    C. It is a skin irritation most prevalent in the winter months.

    D. It is caused by bacteria known as *Staphylococcus pyogenes.*

 eResource 8-4: To supplement your teaching, you show Ruth's father a video, *What Is Impetigo?:* goo.gl/bOFXLJ

Exercise 8-6: *Matching*
Match the type of impetigo lesion in Column A to its specific description in Column B.

Column A	Column B
A. Macules	_____ Small blisters
B. Papules	_____ Small flat lesions
C. Vesicles	_____ Large blisters
D. Bullae	_____ Small raised lesions

Exercise 8-7: *Fill-in*
Most pediatric bacterial skin infections are caused by _____ and/or _____ _____.

Answers to this chapter begin on page 123.

eResource 8-5: To learn more about the causes and clinical presentation of impetigo, refer to Medscape:

- Online: [Pathway: www.medscape.org → Select "Reference" → Enter "impetigo" into the search field → Select "impetigo" → Review content under "Overview and "Clinical Presentation"; be sure to look at the images]
- On your mobile device, you can access the same information: [Pathway: Medscape → Select "Reference" → Enter "impetigo" into the search field → Select "impetigo" → Review content under "Overview and "Clinical Presentation"; be sure to look at the images]

Exercise 8-8: *Select all that apply*

Interventions used for treating impetigo include:

❑ Perform proper handwashing with antibacterial soap
❑ Encourage no sharing of towels, clothing, or other personal items
❑ Keep nails cut short or mittens on hands to prevent scratching
❑ Cleanse facial lesions daily with soap and warm water
❑ Remove honey-colored encrustations around nose and mouth
❑ Apply topical antibiotic ointment three or four times daily
❑ When participating in sports, can leave lesions open to air

Exercise 8-9: *True or false*

Impetigo is a not a self-limiting skin condition and requires immediate medical attention.

_____ True

_____ False

 eResource 8-6: To reinforce the teaching provided to Ruth's father, you tell him about HealthyChildren.org and direct him specifically to:

- Online: [Pathway: www.healthychildren.org → Enter "impetigo" into the search field → Select the following patient teaching materials "Impetigo," "Impetigo Care," and "Impetigo—Infected Sores" to view or listen to content]
- Mobile App (download for Android [goo.gl/FTPQLH] or iOS [goo .gl/7b1Fwm]): [Pathway: HealthyChildren → On the Home Page enter "impetigo" into the search field → Select the following patient teaching materials "Impetigo," "Impetigo Care," and "Impetigo— Infected Sores" to view or listen to content]

Unfolding Case Study #8-3 ▨ Bruce

Bruce is a very active 8-year-old boy who loves to play outdoors around his grandparents' old barn on the farm. His grandfather has interesting farm equipment, which Bruce is constantly investigating. He was playing on the tractor and jumped off, stepping onto a rusty nail. His immunizations were updated but his grandparents called his parents to inform them about the injury. His grandmother cleansed the wound with hydrogen peroxide, applied antibiotic ointment, and covered it with a Band-Aid. Two weeks had passed and Bruce was doing fine. After playing outside at home he came in to take a bath. He started yelling to his mother his left foot felt strange and hurt. The left foot had red streaks in it and it was warm to touch. His mother took him to the emergency department to have his foot checked. The nurse documented the left foot was edematous, had red streaking with erythema, and the child reported pain of 7 to 8 on a 0 to 10 pain scale. The health care provider told Bruce and his mother he had cellulitis and questioned them about any recent injuries. The two reported the rusty-nail injury. The treatment plan included intravenous antibiotics to be administered on the pediatric unit. Bruce was admitted to the pediatric floor of the hospital.

 eResource 8-7: To learn more about cellulitis and its treatment, refer to Epocrates Online: [Pathway: online.epocrates.com → Under the "Diseases" tab, enter "cellulitis" in the search field → Select "cellulitis" → Review content under "Treatment" starting with "Approach"]

Exercise 8-10: *Fill-in*
Identify the three most common systemic intravenous antibiotics essential for treating cellulitis in children:

1. _____
2. _____
3. _____

Exercise 8-11: *True or false*
Priorities for nursing management of cellulitis include eradication of the infection, comfort measures, preventing the spread of infection, and reducing complications.

_____ True

_____ False

Exercise 8-12: *Multiple-choice question*
When assessing pain for children who are 8 years old, the best communication tool for assessing pain (fifth vital sign) is which technique?

    A. Ask the parent's opinion

    B. Observe the child's behavior

    C. Use Wong-Baker Pain Rating Scale

    D. Assess by Pain Scale Rating of 0 to10

Exercise 8-13: *Select all that apply*
The classic clinical manifestations associated with cellulitis include:

    ❑ Erythema

    ❑ Lymphangitis

Answers to this chapter begin on page 123.

❑ Edema and pain
❑ Fever and chills
❑ Lethargy

Exercise 8-14: *Fill-in*

List the two most common oral medications used effectively with children in reducing fever and relieving pain:

1. _____

2. _____

 eResource 8-8: Bruce's parents have questions about cellulitis. You provide a patient education handout on *Cellulitis*: goo.gl/ukEKlV

After 7 days in the pediatric unit, the cellulitis symptoms resolve. Bruce is ambulatory and has no complaints of pain. He is discharged home with his parents with orders to take oral antibiotics until completely gone. He can return to school the next day. Bruce does not have to return to the health care provider unless he experiences any complications with his left foot or other illness symptoms.

Unfolding Case Study #8-4 ▨ Teresa

Teresa is a 1-year-old female who has had numerous otitis media (OM) middle ear infections. She has been on oral antibiotics intermittently the first year of her life. She has become fussy and irritable while being fed her bottle at the day care center. The caregiver notices she has white spots all over her tongue and mouth that appear to be bleeding. The director of the day care center contacts Teresa's mother at work. Teresa's mother contacts the nurse at the pediatrician's office. Teresa just completed the last round of oral antibiotics 4 days ago. The nurse instructs the mother to scrape the infant's tongue and call her back if there is bleeding. The mother calls the nurse back and reports the white spots do bleed when scraped. The nurse speaks with the pediatrician and the infant is diagnosed with thrush (candidiasis) from chronic antibiotic use for OM treatment. The next diaper change also reveals white plaque areas on both buttocks. The pediatrician is called for the second time. The diagnosis continues to be candidiasis for the buttocks rash, too. The health care provider orders Nystatin suspension for the thrush in the mouth and Nystatin topical for the buttocks.

Exercise 8-15: *Select all that apply*

Clinical manifestations associated with candidiasis include:
❑ White plaque lesions on the buttocks
❑ Satellite lesions in the mouth
❑ Pruritis
❑ Intertrigo
❑ Beefy erythema

Answers to this chapter begin on page 123.

e **eResource 8-9:** To learn more about thrush, review the following in Medscape: [Pathway: Medscape → Enter "Thrush" in the search field → Select "Thrush" → Review content, focusing on "Clinical Presentation." Be sure to view images under "Physical."]

Exercise 8-16: *Fill-in*

Many childhood infectious diseases involving skin conditions have the presence of a skin rash known as _____.

Exercise 8-17: *Fill-in*

List the most common nursing interventions in protecting skin integrity and preventing infants and young children from scratching pruritic skin lesions.

1. _____
2. _____
3. _____
4. _____

Exercise 8-18: *Multiple-choice question*

Which of the following is not a risk for a child's developing candidiasis?

 A. Taking oral antibiotics
 B. Being immunocompromised
 C. Using a steroid inhaler
 D. Having a female gender status

Exercise 8-19: *True or false*

The skin is the largest organ of the body.

_____ True

_____ False

Exercise 8-20: *Matching*

Match the following terms in Column A to the correct definition in Column B.

Column A	Column B
A. Miliaria	_____ Chafing in skin folds
B. Intertrigo	_____ Prickly heat
C. Pruritis	_____ Skin hives
D. Urticaria	_____ Itching of skin

Answers to this chapter begin on page 123.

Unfolding Case Study #8-5 ▨ Avery

Avery, a 2-month-old male infant, is brought to the after-hours pediatric clinic for being irritable and crying with diaper changes. His mother reports he has a rash on his buttocks and his head. On examination, it was determined the child has a severe diaper dermatitis and seborrheic dermatitis.

Exercise 8-21: *Fill-in*
_____ _____ is another name for seborrheic dermatitis.

Exercise 8-22: *Fill-in*
List the four common types of childhood dermatitis.

1. _____
2. _____
3. _____
4. _____

Exercise 8-23: *True or false*
Baby wipes are a good alternative for skin cleansing during diaper changes for infants with diaper dermatitis.

_____ True

_____ False

Exercise 8-24: *Multiple-choice question*
When instructing parents about preventing irritant diaper dermatitis, which patient education should be included in the plan of care?
  A. Use zinc oxide barrier cream to protect the skin.
  B. Use baby wipes with alcohol to keep the skin dry.
  C. Decrease the frequency of diaper changes to prevent irritation.
  D. Avoid using disposable diapers and apply cloth diapers instead.

Exercise 8-25: *Matching*
Match the following skin dermatitis in Column A to the correct definition in Column B.

Column A	Column B
A. Contact	_____ Thick, scaly scalp or face lesions
B. Diaper	_____ Asymmetric linear distributed lesions
C. Atopic	_____ Dry scaly lesions or weepy papules
D. Seborrheic	_____ Bright red rash with satellite lesions

Answers to this chapter begin on page 123.

Exercise 8-26: *Select all that apply*

Methods for promoting skin hydration for integumentary issues with children include:

❑ Use unscented soap

❑ Avoid hot water with baths

❑ Apply fragrance-free moisturizer

❑ Dry affected areas with a towel

❑ Leave the skin moist

e **eResource 8-10:** To reinforce the teaching provided to the parents, you tell them about HealthyChildren.org and direct them specifically to:

◼ Online: [Pathway: www.healthychildren.org → Enter "rash" into the search field → Select the following patient teaching materials "Diaper Rash," "Diaper Rash Solution," "Diaper Rash and Your Baby," and "When Diaper Rash Strikes" to view or listen to content]

◼ Mobile App: [Pathway: HealthyChildren → On the Home Page → Enter "rash" into the search field → Select the following patient teaching materials "Diaper Rash," "Diaper Rash Solution," "Diaper Rash and Your Baby," and "When Diaper Rash Strikes" to view or listen to content]

Exercise 8-27: *Multiple-choice question*

Pediatric atopic dermatitis is commonly known as childhood eczema. Which factors appear to play a role in the etiology of atopic dermatitis?

A. Being of male gender and living in a large family

B. Having a poor socioeconomic status and no family history

C. Having a genetic predisposition and a positive family history

D. Having a pet-free family and living in a rural environment

Unfolding Case Study #8-6 ▒ Brianna

Brianna is a 7-year-old first grader. She was sent to the school nurse's office by the teacher for a history of scratching her head intensely in class all week and complaining of her head hurting. The assessment reveals she has red, irritated areas, several scratch marks, a few open sores, and sesame-seed sized, yellow and silvery white masses adhered to the hair shafts. A diagnosis of pediculosis capitis was determined.

Exercise 8-28: *True or false*

Pediculosis capitis or head lice is very uncommon among school-aged children.

_____ True

_____ False

Answers to this chapter begin on page 123.

Exercise 8-29: *Select all that apply*

Clinical manifestations associated with head lice include:

❑ Smooth, teardrop-shaped masses

❑ Masses adhered to hair shafts

❑ Silvery-white or dark brown color

❑ Measure 0.5 to 0.8 mm in size

❑ Common on occipital and postauricular scalp

The nurse provides educational material to the parents to help them understand how to manage and prevent lice outbreaks.

e **eResource 8-11:** To reinforce the teaching provided to the parents, you tell them about HealthyChildren.org and direct them specifically to:

■ Online: [Pathway: www.healthychildren.org → Enter "lice" into the search field → Select the following patient teaching materials "Head Lice: What Parents Need to Know," "AAP Updated Guidelines on Treating Head Lice," "Healthy Children Radio podcast: Head Lice," and "Head Lice" to view or listen to content]

■ Mobile App: [Pathway: HealthyChildren → On the Home Page → Enter "lice" into the search field → Select the following patient teaching materials "Head Lice: What Parents Need to Know," "AAP Updated Guidelines on Treating Head Lice," "Healthy Children Radio podcast: Head Lice," and "Head Lice" to view or listen to content]

Exercise 8-30: *Fill-in*

List three of the psychosocial sequelae commonly experienced by the child with head lice.

1. _____

2. _____

3. _____

Exercise 8-31: *Multiple-choice question*

When providing patient education to the family about head lice treatment, which product should the nurse recommend as a first-line treatment option for children?

A. Lindane

B. Petroleum jelly

C. Permethrin

D. Cetaphil

Exercise 8-32: *True or false*

The only known physical complication of head lice is secondary bacterial infection causing localized lymph node enlargement.

_____ True

_____ False

Answers to this chapter begin on page 123.

Exercise 8-33: *Fill-in*

List examples of each type of skin disorder.

1. A macule is a _____.
2. A vesicle is a _____.
3. A crust is a _____.
4. An ecchymosis is a _____.
5. A papule is a _____.
6. A pustule is _____.
7. A wheal is a _____.

Unfolding Case Study #8-7 ▨ Jeff

Jeff is a fourth grader at an elementary school. He is sent to the school nurse for a rash on his head with spots of alopecia on his scalp. The school nurse assesses the child and determines he has several boggy, tender kerion lesions with sporadic patches of scaly dandruff and alopecia areas. She contacts his mother to take him to the health care provider. The school nurse questions whether he has a fungal infection and requests a note from the health care provider before Jeff can return to school.

Exercise 8-34: *Fill-in*

Tineas are the most common fungal infections of children under the age of 12. List the three types of tinea fungal infections involving the head, body, and feet.

1. _____.
2. _____.
3. _____.

Exercise 8-35: *True or false*

Griseofulvin is the only systemic antifungal medication approved for treating tinea capitis or ringworm of the scalp.

_____ True

_____ False

Exercise 8-36: *Select all that apply*

Children presenting with tinea capitis have clinical manifestations that include:

❑ Patches of alopecia
❑ Inflammatory kerions
❑ Dandruff-like scaling
❑ Pustules with pruritis
❑ Cervical lymphadenopathy

Answers to this chapter begin on page 123.

Exercise 8-37: *Matching*

Match the following fungal infections in Column A to the correct definition in Column B.

Column A	Column B
A. Tinea capitis	_____ Ringworm of the nails
B. Tinea corporis	_____ Ringworm of the feet
C. Tinea cruris	_____ Ringworm of the scalp
D. Tinea pedis	_____ Ringworm of the body
E. Tinea unguium	_____ Ringworm of the scrotum

 eResource 8-12: To reinforce your understanding of tinea capitis, refer to Medscape:
- Online: [Pathway: www.medscape.org → Select "Reference" → Enter "tinea" into the search field → Select "tinea capitis" → Review content]
- On your mobile device, you can access the same information: [Pathway: Medscape → Select "Reference" → Enter "tinea" into the search field → Select "tinea capitis" → Review content]

Exercise 8-38: *Multiple-choice question*

When providing patient education to the parents of a child diagnosed with tinea corporis, which explanation should be included in the teaching?

    A. It requires no treatment at this time.

    B. It can be passed human to human.

    C. It should be exposed to sunlight.

    D. It is a malignant skin condition.

eResource 8-13: To reinforce the teaching provided to the parents, you provide the following handout, *Ringworm on Body*: goo.gl/GbuWQJ

Unfolding Case Study #8-8 ▒ Lucy

Lucy is a busy and energetic 9-year-old who loves playing outdoors. One summer day she is outside playing on the swing set and is stung by an arthropod. Her mother is unsure of the type of insect bite she received. She takes Lucy into the house, cleans the bite with soap and water, and applies Benadryl topical ointment to the bite. Lucy appears to be fine and requests to go back outside to play. One hour after being outside, Lucy comes into the house with complaints of increased pain at the area of the bite. Her mother notices edema and erythema at the site. She is concerned and takes her to the local outpatient health clinic. Lucy had an allergic reaction to the insect bite and it was determined to be either a bee or wasp sting. She is given injections with diphenhydramine and adrenalin, and monitored for 2 hours at the clinic. Her chart has documentation of this allergy and the health care provider instructs Lucy's mother to purchase a medic alert bracelet for constant wear. She is given a prescription for an adrenalin injection to carry with her at all times. The pharmacist is to instruct the family on the administration of the injection.

Answers to this chapter begin on page 123.

eResource 8-14: To reinforce the instruction, the pharmacist shows the following video tutorial, *How to Use an Epinephrine Autoinjector*: youtu .be/YheJhyQ168Y

Exercise 8-39: *Multiple-choice question*
What is the drug of choice for treating children experiencing anaphylaxis from a bee or wasp sting?
- A. Prednisone (corticosteroid)
- B. Benadryl (diphenhydramine)
- C. Claritin (loratadine)
- D. Epinephrine (adrenalin)

Exercise 8-40: *Fill-in*
List the five immunoglobulins associated with the body's immune function.
1. _____
2. _____
3. _____
4. _____
5. _____

Exercise 8-41: *True or false*
In allergic children, generalized anaphylactic reactions usually develop within 1 to 2 hours after the bite.

_____ True

_____ False

Exercise 8-42: *Select all that apply*
Clinical manifestations exhibited during an anaphylactic reaction include:
- ❏ Urticaria or hives
- ❏ Edema of the airway
- ❏ Shortness of breath
- ❏ Wheezing and rales
- ❏ Severe headaches

 eResource 8-15: To reinforce your teaching, you also provide the parents with the following information from HealthyChildren:
- ■ Online: [Pathway: www.healthychildren.org → Enter "Anaphylaxis" into the search field → Select "Anaphylaxis" and view or listen to content]
- ■ Mobile App: [Pathway: HealthyChildren → Enter "Anaphylaxis" into the search field → Select "Anaphylaxis" and view or listen to content]

Answers to this chapter begin on page 123.

Unfolding Case Study #8-9 Peyton

Peyton is a 30-month-old toddler. His mother is a stay-at-home mom while his father works outside the home as the primary provider for the family. Peyton is an only child and his mother has very little support. Lately, the child has been getting on his mother's nerves. He is very curious and getting into everything. The mother is getting the bath water ready one evening and forgets to check the temperature since she was talking on the phone. She puts him into the bathtub and he starts screaming. When she checks the water temperature, she realizes it was turned toward the hot water dial on the faucet. She immediately puts his feet and legs into cool water to stop the burn. She gets upset and starts crying about her negligence. She contacts his father as he is pulling into the driveway from work. Both parents take him to the local emergency department. Peyton suffered second-degree burns from the bath water and has to be admitted to the pediatric intensive care unit (PICU).

Exercise 8-43: *True or false*
Second-degree burns in children are known as partial-thickness burns and involve the epidermis, superficial dermis, and/or deeper dermis.

_____ True

_____ False

eResource 8-16: To learn more about grading of burns, refer to Skyscape's Outline in Clinical Medication on your mobile device: [Pathway: Outline in Clinical Medication → Enter "Burn Injury" → Review content, focusing on "Grading of Burns," "Complications," and "Overview of Treatment"]

Exercise 8-44: *Fill-in*
After burns and the surrounding areas are cleaned, an antimicrobial cream, such as _____, is applied to minimize bacterial proliferation and prevent infection.

Exercise 8-45: *Multiple-choice question*
Evidence-based practice recommends which intervention as being appropriate for the first aid of burns?

    A. Immediately apply hot water to the burn site.

    B. Immediately apply ice to the burn site.

    C. Immediately apply butter to the burn site.

    D. Immediately apply cool water to the burn site.

Answers to this chapter begin on page 123.

Exercise 8-46: *Matching*

Match the following terms regarding burns in Column A to the definition in Column B.

Column A	Column B
A. Total body surface area	_____ Calcium alginate (seaweed) dressing
B. Parkland formula	_____ IV fluid for restoring fluid volume
C. Ringer's lactate	_____ Painful removal of dead tissue
D. Kaltostat	_____ Chart for estimating childhood burns
E. Debridement	_____ Method for calculating pediatric fluid needs

e **eResource 8-17:** To calculate the required fluid replacement for burn victims, refer to Skyscape's Archimedes on your mobile device: [Pathway: Archimedes → Enter "burn" into the search field → Select and review the following calculation tools: "Brooke-Modified," "Galveston," "Parkland," and "Slater"; enter patient data and compare your results among the calculators]

Exercise 8-47: *Select all that apply*

Signs of child abuse–induced burns include:

❑ Consistent history of caregivers
❑ Delay in seeking medical treatment
❑ Uniform appearance of burns
❑ Stocking/glove pattern on hands or feet
❑ Flexor-sparing burns
❑ Burns involving dorsum of hands

e **eResource 8-18:** To reinforce your understanding of assessment of suspected child abuse, refer to

■ Merck MerckMedicus Online on your mobile device: [Pathway: www .merckmedicus.com → Select "Merck Manual" → Select "Merck Manual for Healthcare Professionals" → Enter "child abuse" into the search field → Select "Overview of Child Maltreatment" → Access and review content] Medscape:

 ■ Online [Pathway: www.medscape.org → Select "Reference" → Enter "abuse" into the search field → Select "child abuse" → Review content; repeat with "physical child abuse"] under the "Overview" tab; review "Vaso-Occlusive Crisis Management"]

 ■ On your mobile device: [Pathway: Medscape → select "Reference" → Enter "abuse" into the search field → Select "child abuse" → Review content; repeat with "physical child abuse"]

After being in the hospital for 1 week, Peyton's burns healed without any significant scarring. His mother was not proven to be abusing him. He was discharged with orders to follow-up with the health care provider in 2 weeks. His parents were to perform daily dressing changes with wound cleanser and apply Silvadene dressings until the next health care appointment.

Answers to this chapter begin on page 123.

eResource 8-19: Among the other discharge materials you provide Peyton's parents, you also give them some additional parent teaching materials from:

- Centers for Disease Control and Prevention's (CDC) Podcast, *Protect the Ones You Love From Burns*: goo.gl/ar2yZh
- Kidshealth.org: [Pathway: kidshealth.org → Select "Parents" tab → Enter "burns" into the search field → View and listen to related materials]
  - *Household Safety, Preventing Burns, Shock and Fires*: goo.gl/aHkpHF
  - *Burns Instruction Sheet*: goo.gl/uHkCVy
  - *A to Z: Burns, Second Degree*: goo.gl/qDHNgQ

Answers to this chapter begin on page 123.

Answers

Exercise 8-1: *Fill-in*

The health care provider informs Paul's mother that the type of acne he has is **acne vulgaris**, which is the most common form of acne and is estimated to affect 85% to 95% of adolescents.

Exercise 8-2: *Select all that apply*

The nurse identifies which clinical manifestations as being associated with acne lesions:

☐ Macules

☒ **Nodules**

☒ **Comedones**

☒ **Pustules**

☒ **Papules**

Exercise 8-3: *True or false*

Research has proven that dietary factors are inconclusive in causing acne lesions.

___**X**___ True

_____ False

Exercise 8-4: *Matching*

Match the acne lesion classification in Column A to the type of acne lesion in Column B.

Column A		Column B
A. Closed comedones	__E__	Keloids
B. Open comedones	__A__	Whiteheads
C. Pustules	__B__	Blackheads
D. Nodules	__C__	Papules with purulent material
E. Scarring	__D__	Tender and greater than 5 mm in diameter

Exercise 8-5: *Multiple-choice question*

What is the best explanation by the nurse to explain impetigo to the father?

A. It is not contagious nor is it a skin infection of concern—NO, it is contagious.

B. It is a highly contagious, superficial bacterial skin infection—YES

C. It is a skin irritation most prevalent in the winter months—NO, it is most prevalent in the summer.

D. It is caused by bacteria known as *Staphylococcus pyogenes*—NO, it is caused by *Staphylococcus aureus*.

Exercise 8-6: *Matching*

Match the type of impetigo lesion in Column A to its specific description in Column B.

Column A		Column B
A. Macules	**C**	Small blisters
B. Papules	**A**	Small flat lesions
C. Vesicles	**D**	Large blisters
D. Bullae	**B**	Small raised lesions

Exercise 8-7: *Fill-in*

Most pediatric bacterial skin infections are caused by ***Staphylococcus aureus*** and/or ***Streptococcus pyogenes***.

Exercise 8-8: *Select all that apply*

Interventions used for treating impetigo include:

☒ **Perform proper handwashing with antibacterial soap**

☒ **Encourage no sharing of towels, clothing, or other personal items**

☒ **Keep nails cut short or mittens on hands to prevent scratching**

☒ **Cleanse facial lesions daily with soap and warm water**

☒ **Remove honey-colored encrustations around nose and mouth**

☒ **Apply topical antibiotic ointment three or four times daily**

❏ When participating in sports, can leave lesions open to air

Exercise 8-9: *True or false*

Impetigo is a not a self-limiting skin condition and requires immediate medical attention.

_____ True

__**X**__ False

Exercise 8-10: *Fill-in*

Identify the three most common systemic intravenous antibiotics essential for treating cellulitis in children:

1. **Dicloxacillin**

2. **Cephalexin**

3. **Clindamycin**

Exercise 8-11: *True or false*
Priorities for nursing management of cellulitis include eradication of the infection, comfort measures, preventing the spread of infection, and reducing complications.
___**X**___ True
_____ False

Exercise 8-12: *Multiple-choice question*
When assessing pain for children who are 8 years old, the best communication tool for assessing pain (fifth vital sign) is which technique?
   A. Ask the parent's opinion—NO, the parent's may not understand the difference in scales and cannot speak for the child's pain because it is subjective.
   B. Observe the child's behavior—NO, this may not always indicate the severity of pain in a child.
   C. Use Wong-Baker Pain Rating Scale—NO, this is for a younger child.
   D. Assess by Pain Scale Rating of 0 to 10—YES, an 8-year-old can do this.

Exercise 8-13: *Select all that apply*
The clinical manifestations associated with cellulitis include:
☒ **Erythema**
☒ **Lymphangitis**
☒ **Edema and pain**
☒ **Fever and chills**
☒ **Lethargy**

Exercise 8-14: *Fill-in*
List the two most common oral medications used effectively with children in reducing fever and relieving pain:
   1. **Ibuprofen (Motrin)**
   2. **Acetaminophen (Tylenol)**

Exercise 8-15: *Select all that apply*
Clinical manifestations associated with candidiasis include:
❑ White plaque lesion on buttocks
❑ Satellite lesions in the mouth
☒ **Pruritis**
☒ **Intertrigo**
☒ **Beefy erythema**

Exercise 8-16: *Fill-in*
Many childhood infectious diseases involving skin conditions have the presence of a skin rash known as **exanthem**.

Exercise 8-17: *Fill-in*

List the most common nursing interventions in protecting skin integrity and preventing infants and young children from scratching pruritic skin lesions.

1. **Provide oatmeal baths for soothing skin**.

2. **Apply topical emollients for skin lubrication**.

3. **Allow short, daily baths in lukewarm water**.

4. **Pat the skin dry with a towel**.

Exercise 8-18: *Multiple-choice question*

Which of the following is not a risk for a child's developing candidiasis?

A. Taking oral antibiotics—NO, this is a cause and risk factor.

B. Being immunocompromised—NO, this is a cause and risk factor.

C. Using a steroid inhaler—NO, this is a cause and risk factor because steroids decrease immunity.

D. **Having a female gender status—YES, it happens to both genders.**

Exercise 8-19: *True or false*

The skin is the largest organ of the body.

___**X**___ True

_____ False

Exercise 8-20: *Matching*

Match the following terms in Column A to the correct definition in Column B.

Column A	Column B	
A. Miliaria	__B__	Chafing in skin folds
B. Intertrigo	__A__	Prickly heat
C. Pruritis	__D__	Skin hives
D. Urticaria	__C__	Itching of skin

Exercise 8-21: *Fill-in*

Cradle cap is another name for seborrheic dermatitis.

Exercise 8-22: *Fill-in*

List the four common types of childhood dermatitis.

1. **Diaper dermatitis**

2. **Contact dermatitis**

3. **Seborrheic dermatitis**

4. **Atopic dermatitis**

Exercise 8-23: *True or false*
Baby wipes are a good alternative for skin cleansing during diaper changes for infants with diaper dermatitis.
_____ True
___**X**___ False

Exercise 8-24: *Multiple-choice question*
When instructing parents about preventing irritant diaper dermatitis, which patient education should be included in the plan of care?
A. **Use zinc oxide barrier cream to protect the skin—YES, this provides the best protection against moisture in the area.**
B. Use baby wipes with alcohol to keep the skin dry—NO, often these contain chemicals and are irritating.
C. Decrease the frequency of diaper changes to prevent irritation—NO, the increased moisture of sitting in a wet diaper will increase the rash.
D. Avoid using disposable diapers and apply cloth diapers instead—NO, there is no evidence that cloth diapers decrease moisture.

Exercise 8-25: *Matching*
Match the following skin dermatitis in Column A to the correct definition in Column B.

Column A	Column B
A. Contact	__**D**__ Thick, scaly scalp or face lesions
B. Diaper	__**A**__ Asymmetric linear distributed lesions
C. Atopic	__**C**__ Dry scaly lesions or weepy papules
D. Seborrheic	__**B**__ Bright red rash with satellite lesions

Exercise 8-26: *Select all that apply*
Methods for promoting skin hydration for integumentary issues with children include:
☒ **Use unscented soap**
☒ **Avoid hot water with baths**
☒ **Apply fragrance-free moisturizer**
☒ **Pat dry affected areas with a towel**
☒ **Leave the skin moist**

Exercise 8-27: *Multiple-choice question*
Pediatric atopic dermatitis is commonly known as childhood eczema. Which factors appear to play a role in the etiology of atopic dermatitis?
A. Being of male gender and living in a large family—NO, these are not risk factors.
B. Having a poor socioeconomic status and no family history—NO, these are not risk factors.

C. **Having a genetic predisposition and a positive family history—YES, these are known risk factors.**

D. Having a pet-free family and living in a rural environment—NO, these are not risk factors.

Exercise 8-28: *True or false*

Pediculosis capitis or head lice is very uncommon among school-aged children.

___**X**___ **True**

_____ False

Exercise 8-29: *Select all that apply*

Clinical manifestations associated with head lice include:

☒ **Smooth, teardrop-shaped masses**

☒ **Masses adhered to hair shafts**

☒ **Silvery-white or dark brown color**

☒ **Measure 0.5 to 0.8 mm in size**

☒ **Common on occipital and postauricular scalp**

Exercise 8-30: *Fill-in*

List three of the psychosocial sequelae commonly experienced by the child with head lice.

1. **Embarrassment**

2. **Low self-esteem**

3. **Teasing by peers**

Exercise 8-31: *Multiple-choice question*

When providing patient education to the family about head lice treatment, which product should the nurse recommend as a first-line treatment option for children?

A. Lindane—NO

B. Petroleum jelly—NO

C. **Permethrin—YES, this is the appropriate medication**

D. Cetaphil—NO

Exercise 8-32: *True or false*

The only known physical complication of head lice is secondary bacterial infection causing localized lymph node enlargement.

___**X**___ **True**

_____ False

Exercise 8-33: *Fill-in*
List examples of each type of skin disorder.

1. A macule is a **freckle**.

2. A vesicle is a **cold sore or chickenpox**.

3. A crust is a **scab**.

4. An ecchymosis is a **bruise**.

5. A papule is a **pimple**.

6. A pustule is **acne or impetigo**.

7. A wheal is a **mosquito bite or allergic reaction**.

Exercise 8-34: *Fill-in*
Tineas are the most common fungal infections of children under the age of 12. List the three types of tinea fungal infections involving the scalp, body, and feet.

1. **Tinea capitis**

2. **Tinea corporis**

3. **Tinea pedis**

Exercise 8-35: *True or false*
Griseofulvin is the only systemic antifungal medication approved for treating tinea capitis.

___**X**___ True

_____ False

Exercise 8-36: *Select all that apply*
Children presenting with tinea capitis have clinical manifestations that include:

☒ **Patches of alopecia**

☒ **Inflammatory kerions**

☒ **Dandruff-like scaling**

☒ **Pustules with pruritis**

☒ **Cervical lymphadenopathy**

Exercise 8-37: *Matching*
Match the following fungal infections in Column A to the correct definition in Column B.

Column A	Column B	
A. Tinea capitis	**E**	Ringworm of the nails
B. Tinea corporis	**D**	Ringworm of the feet
C. Tinea cruris	**B**	Ringworm of the body
D. Tinea pedis	**A**	Ringworm of the scalp
E. Tinea unguium	**C**	Ringworm of the scrotum

Exercise 8-38: *Multiple-choice question*

When providing patient education to the parents of a child diagnosed with tinea corporis, which explanation should be included in the teaching?

A. It requires no treatment at this time—NO, it does need to be treated.

B. It can be passed human to human—YES, it is contagious.

C. It should be exposed to sunlight—NO, sunlight increases the irritation.

D. It is a malignant skin condition—NO, it is benign.

Exercise 8-39: *Multiple-choice question*

What is the drug of choice for treating children experiencing anaphylaxis from a bee or wasp sting?

A. Prednisone (corticosteroid)—NO, this is not the drug of choice.

B. Benadryl (diphenhydramine)—NO, this is not the drug of choice because it is too slow.

C. Claritin (loratadine)—NO, this is not the drug of choice.

D. Epinephrine (adrenalin)—YES, this is fast acting.

Exercise 8-40: *Fill-in*

List the five immunoglobulins associated with the body's immune function.

1. **IgG**

2. **IgA**

3. **IgM**

4. **IgE**

5. **IgD**

Exercise 8-41: *True or false*

In allergic children, generalized anaphylactic reactions usually develop within 1 to 2 hours after the bite.

_____ True

___**X**___ False

Exercise 8-42: *Select all that apply*

Clinical manifestations exhibited during an anaphylactic reaction include:

☒ **Urticaria or hives**

☒ **Edema of the airway**

☒ **Shortness of breath**

☒ **Wheezing and rales**

❑ Severe headaches

Exercise 8-43: *True or false*

Second-degree burns in children are known as partial-thickness burns and involve the epidermis, superficial dermis, and/or deeper dermis.

___X___ True

_____ False

Exercise 8-44: *Fill-in*

After burns and the surrounding areas are cleaned, an antimicrobial cream, such as **Silvadene**, is applied to minimize bacterial proliferation and prevent infection.

Exercise 8-45: *Multiple-choice question*

Evidence-based practice recommends which intervention as being appropriate for the first aid of burns?

A. Immediately apply hot water to the burn site—NO, this will add to the burn.

B. Immediately apply ice to the burn site—NO, this may cause an ice burn.

C. Immediately apply butter to the burn site—NO, this will hold in the heat.

D. Immediately apply cool water to the burn site—YES, this will decrease the pain and decrease the burning.

Exercise 8-46: *Matching*

Match the following terms regarding burns in Column A to the definition in Column B.

Column A		Column B
A. Total body surface area	___D___	Calcium alginate (seaweed) dressing
B. Parkland formula	___C___	IV fluid for restoring fluid volume
C. Ringer's lactate crystalloid	___E___	Painful removal of dead tissue
D. Kaltostat	___A___	Chart for estimating childhood burns
E. Debridement	___B___	Method for calculating pediatric fluid needs

Exercise 8-47: *Select all that apply*

Signs of child abuse–induced burns include:

☐ Consistent history of caregivers

☒ **Delay in seeking medical treatment**

☒ **Uniform appearance of burns**

☒ **Stocking/glove pattern on hands or feet**

☒ **Flexor-sparing burns**

☒ **Burns involving dorsum of hands**

9

Children With Eyes, Ears, Nose, and Throat Health Care Needs

Vicki A. Martin

Unfolding Case Study #9-1 ▨ Gracie

Gracie is a 4-year-old with numerous allergies. Every fall season she comes down with an upper respiratory infection (URI). She has been coughing, sneezing, has nasal stuffiness, and a sore throat. The pediatrician has instructed the family that she has a cold and not to bring her into the office unless she develops a fever of 100° F or greater. The pediatrician has recommended using saline nasal spray, vapor baths, a room humidifier, over-the-counter nonaspirin analgesics, and drinking plenty of fluids.

Exercise 9-1: *True or false*
Antibiotics have been proven to be effective in treating viral infections such as the common cold.

_____ True

_____ False

Exercise 9-2: *Fill-in*
The common cold is also known as _____ and is responsible for making children sick with an estimated six to ten colds per year.

Exercise 9-3: *Select all that apply*
Clinical manifestations associated with the common cold include:

❑ Irritability

❑ Nasal discharge

❑ Headache

❑ Fever

❑ Rhinitis

❑ Muscle aches

❑ Afebrile seizures

Answers to this chapter begin on page 141.

Exercise 9-4: *Multiple-choice question*

Which intervention is a priority in preventing the spread of nasopharyngitis?

    A. It is contagious and requires strict handwashing.

    B. It is not contagious and is not a concern for others.

    C. It does not produce fever so others are not at risk of infection.

    D. It does cause fever but others are not at risk of infection.

 eResource 9-1: To reinforce your teaching with the parents, you share a comprehensive resource from HealthyChildren.org, and direct them specifically to the "symptom checker" resource and the information regarding "colds":

- Online: [Pathway: www.healthychildren.org → Select "Tips and Tools" from tool bar → Select "Symptom Checker" → Select "A-Z" tab → Select "C" → Scroll down to select "colds" → Tab to view or listen to content]
- Mobile App (downloaded for Android [goo.gl/FTPQLH] or iOS [goo.gl/7b1Fwm]): [Pathway: HealthyChildren → On the Home Page, scroll down to select "Conditions" under the "Health Issues" section → Select "C" → Scroll down to select "colds" → Tab to view or listen to content]

After 1 week of being managed at home, Gracie develops a severe sore throat, her temperature increases to 102° F, and she starts to have excessive drooling. Both parents take her to the emergency department for an assessment. She was diagnosed with tonsillitis. Since this is her third episode in 1 year, the pediatrician consults an ear, nose, and throat (ENT) specialist.

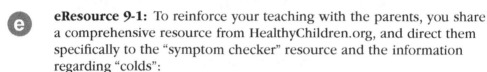 **eResource 9-2:** To review your understanding of tonsil and adenoid anatomy, refer to Medscape:

- Online: [Pathway: www.medscape.org → Under the tab "Reference", select "References & Tools" → Enter "Tonsil" into the search field → Select "Tonsil and Adenoid Anatomy" → Review content, including images and media files]
- On your mobile device, you can access the same information: [Pathway: Medscape → Enter "Tonsil" into the search field → Select "Tonsil and Adenoid Anatomy" → Review content, including images and media files]

The ENT physician will schedule a tonsillectomy and adenoidectomy (T&A) in a few days when Gracie is showing improvement and feeling better from penicillin (PCN) antibiotic therapy.

 eResource 9-3: To prepare for your preoperative teaching, review the following in Medscape:

- Online: [Pathway: www.medscape.org → Under the tab "Reference," select "References & Tools" → Enter "Tonsillectomy" into the search field → Select "Tonsillectomy" → Review content, including images and media files, focus on "Workup" and "Preoperative Details"]

■ On your mobile device, you can access the same information: [Pathway: Medscape → Enter "Tonsillectomy" into the search field → Select "Tonsillectomy" → Review content, including images and media files, focus on "Workup" and "Preoperative Details"]

e **eResource 9-4:** To support your preoperative teaching, you utilize several resources:

■ DrawMD (www.drawmd.com) on your mobile device to show the parents an image with annotations to visually present anatomy:

■ [Pathway: DrawMD Pediatrics → Select "New Drawings" → Select "Mouth and Thoat Pediatrics" → Select appropriate "stamp" and add text or additional drawing → Select "Save"]

■ [Pathway: DrawMD Pediatrics → Select "New Drawings" → Select "Tonsils and Adenoids Pediatrics" → Select appropriate "stamp" and add text or additional drawing → Select "Save"]

Exercise 9-5: *Fill-in*

A _____ _____ is required to differentiate between a viral and bacterial throat infection.

Exercise 9-6: *Multiple-choice question*

Which type of bacterial infection is the main culprit for causing tonsillitis and pharyngitis?

    A. *Escherichia coli*

    B. *Moraxella catarrhalis*

    C. Group A beta-hemolytic streptococci

    D. Methicillin-resistant *Staphylococcus aureus*

Exercise 9-7: *Select all that apply*

Which signs and symptoms observed in a sleeping child would indicate a possible hemorrhage after being postoperative from a T&A?

    ❏ Excessive drooling

    ❏ Frequent swallowing

    ❏ Nausea or vomiting

    ❏ Elevated temperature

    ❏ Severe headache

Exercise 9-8: *True or false*

Children with respiratory infections or influenza (viral) should not receive aspirin due to the link with Reye syndrome.

_____ True

_____ False

Answers to this chapter begin on page 141.

eResource 9-5: To reinforce your understanding of postoperative care and patient teaching, continue your review of Medscape:
■ Online: [Pathway: www.medscape.org → Under the tab "Reference," select "References & Tools" → Enter "Tonsillectomy" into the search field → Select "Tonsillectomy" → Review content, focus on "Postoperative Details," "Follow-up," "Complications," and "Outcome and Prognosis"]
■ On your mobile device, you can access the same information: [Pathway: Medscape → Enter "Tonsillectomy" into the search field → Select "Tonsillectomy" → Review content, focus on "Postoperative Details," "Follow-up," "Complications," and "Outcome and Prognosis"]

Unfolding Case Study #9-2 ■ Brock

Sixteen-month-old Brock has been experiencing repeated conjunctivitis bilaterally and chronic otitis media (OM) in his left ear. He has been on numerous antibiotic therapies with no signs of improvement. At the ENT appointment, a decision is made to do a myringotomy and tympanoplasty (ear tube insertion).

 eResource 9-6: To prepare for your preoperative teaching, review the following in Medscape:
■ Online: [Pathway: www.medscape.org → Under the tab "Reference," select "References & Tools" → Enter "myringotomy" into the search field → Select "myringotomy" → Review content, including images and media files, focus on "Overview," "Preprocedural Care, and "Technique"; repeat with "ear tube insertion"]
■ On your mobile device, you can access the same information: [Pathway: Medscape → Enter "myringotomy" into the search field → Select "myringotomy" → Review content, including images and media files, focus on "Overview," "Preprocedural Care," and "Technique"; repeat with "ear tube insertion"]

Brock was given a prescription of antibiotic eye drops to put in each eye to eliminate the conjunctivitis and these same drops are ordered for the left ear. He is to return to the hospital outpatient surgical unit in 2 days for the surgery. The parents have a lot of questions so you prepare materials for preoperative teaching.

 eResource 9-7: To support your preoperative teaching, you utilize several resources on your mobile device:
■ DrawMD (www.drawmd.com) on your mobile device to show the parents an image with annotations to visually present anatomy and the planned procedures: [Pathway: DrawMD ENT → Select "New Drawings" → Select "Ear, Pediatric ENT" → Select appropriate "stamp" and add text or additional drawing to reflect current infection → Select "Save"; repeat for ear tube insertion]

Answers to this chapter begin on page 141.

■ Medscape: [Pathway: Medscape → Enter "ear anatomy" into the search field → Select "ear anatomy" → Review content, including images and media files; select appropriate media file to support your teaching]

Exercise 9-9: *Matching*

Match the terminology involving OM in Column A to the definition in Column B.

Column A	**Column B**
A. OM	_____ Middle ear inflammation with fluid
B. Acute OM	_____ Rapid onset of symptoms lasting 3 weeks
C. OM with effusion	_____ Middle ear effusion lasting beyond 3 months
D. Chronic OM with effusion	_____ Middle ear inflammation without pathogens
E. Otitis interna	_____ External auditory canal inflammation
F. Otitis externa	_____ Labyrinth of the ear inflammation

Exercise 9-10: *Select all that apply*

The interventions important in the nursing care of the child experiencing chronic OM include.

❏ Frequent audiologist evaluations

❏ Penicillin antibiotic therapy

❏ Antihistamines as needed

❏ Analgesics if pain presentation

❏ Instructions to keep ears dry

❏ Antipyretics if elevated temperature

Exercise 9-11: *Fill-in*

List four signs and symptoms expected to be exhibited in children experiencing OM.

1. _____
2. _____
3. _____
4. _____

Exercise 9-12: *True or false*

When you assess the child with OM, the assessment that is of little or no concern includes obtaining a history, day care attendance, smoke exposure, and bottle propping.

_____ True

_____ False

Answers to this chapter begin on page 141.

Exercise 9-13: *Multiple-choice question*

Which situation would cause concern for you to consider possible hearing loss with a child?

    A. A young child with a vocabulary of 900 or more words.

    B. An infant that does not startle to loud sounds.

    C. The older child that answers questions appropriately.

    D. Any age child speaking loudly during conversation.

Exercise 9-14: *Fill-in*

Levels of hearing loss are determined by the decibels (dB) of sound and normal sound is heard in _____ dB.

 eResource 9-8: You want to provide additional educational material to the parents regarding hearing loss and early detection.
- Online: [Pathway: www.healthychildren.org → Select "Tips and Tools" from tool bar → Select "Symptom Checker" → Select "A–Z" tab → Select "H" → Scroll down to select "hearing loss" → Tab to view or listen to content]
- Mobile App (downloaded for Android [goo.gl/FTPQLH] or iOS [goo.gl/7b1Fwm]): [Pathway: HealthyChildren → On the Home Page, scroll down to select "Conditions" under the "Health Issues" section → Select "H" → Scroll down to select "hearing loss" → Tab to view or listen to content]

Unfolding Case Study #9-3 Kylie

Kylie is a 1-week-old infant born prematurely at 32 weeks gestation. She remains in the neonatal intensive care unit (NICU) related to low birth weight (LBW) and other visual impairments. She is being followed by an ophthalmologist and was diagnosed with retinopathy of prematurity (ROP). The parents understand the complications of ROP include myopia, glaucoma, and blindness and that medical follow-up is essential to prevent these complications in the future.

 eResource 9-9: To reinforce your understanding and ability to provide additional teaching to the parents, refer to Medscape:
- Online: [Pathway: www.medscape.org → Under the tab "Reference," select "References & Tools" → Enter "retinopathy of prematurity" into the search field → Select "retinopathy of prematurity" → Review content, focusing on "treatment & management" and "follow-up"]
- On your mobile device, you can access the same information: [Pathway: Medscape → Enter "retinopathy of prematurity" into the search field → Select "retinopathy of prematurity" → Review content, focusing on "treatment & management" and "follow-up"]

Once Kylie is stable, she may have to have eye correction with laser surgery. Her parents are very attentive to her needs in the NICU and visit daily to assist the nurses and provide adequate bonding.

Exercise 9-15: *Matching*

Match the terminology of visual impairments in Column A to the definition in Column B.

Column A	**Column B**
A. Nystagmus	_____ Misalignment of the eyes
B. ROP	_____ Irregular bouncing of the eyes
C. Strabismus	_____ Poor visual development in a normal eye
D. Amblyopia	_____ Opacity of lens of the eye present at birth
E. Congenital cataracts	_____ Incomplete retinal vascularization in prematurity
F. Astigmatism	
G. Infantile glaucoma	_____ Uneven curvature of the cornea(s)
	_____ Genetic obstruction of aqueous humor flow

eResource 9-10: To reinforce your understanding of these visual impairments, refer to Skyscape's Outline in Clinical Medication on your mobile device: [Pathway: Outline in Clinical Medication → Enter "Strabismus" → Review content; repeat with "Retinopathy of prematurity," "Amblyopia," and "Astigmatism"]

Exercise 9-16: *True or false*

The risk factors associated with ROP include low birth weight, prematurity, sepsis, high light intensity, and hypothermia.

_____ True

_____ False

Exercise 9-17: *Multiple-choice question*

Strabismus may occur in cases of resolved ROP. Which explanation best describes the rationale for prescribing daily eye patching?

    A. Eye patching of the stronger eye will strengthen the weaker eye.

    B. Eye patching of the weaker eye will strengthen the eye muscles.

    C. Eye patching allows the affected eye time to revascularize.

    D. Eye patching allows the unaffected eye time to revascularize.

Exercise 9-18: *Select all that apply*

The common causes of ROP in infants include:

    ❏ Low oxygen levels of arterial blood

    ❏ High oxygen levels of arterial blood

    ❏ Prematurity prior to 32 weeks gestation

Answers to this chapter begin on page 141.

❏ Exposure to extreme phototherapy

❏ Maternal infections or toxic exposure

❏ Exposure to colder temperatures

Exercise 9-19: *Fill-in*

The term "legal blindness" refers to vision of less than _____ or peripheral vision less than _____ degrees.

Exercise 9-20: *Fill-in*

Healthy People 2020 has established objectives for the improvement of visual impairment in children and adolescents.

▪ Healthy People 2020: www.healthypeople.gov

▪ Click on 2020 Topics and Objectives—Objectives A-Z—Healthy People 2020.

▪ In Search box, type in reduce blindness and visual impairment in children and adolescents.

▪ Click on the right side of chart on Tech Specs.

▪ The target percentage method is _____ % of visual improvement for children and adolescents.

Answers to this chapter begin on page 141.

Answers

Exercise 9-1: *True or false*

Antibiotics have been proven to be effective in treating viral infections such as the common cold.

_____ True

___X___ **False**

Exercise 9-2: *Fill-in*

The common cold is also known as **nasopharyngitis** and is responsible for making children sick with an estimated six to ten colds per year.

Exercise 9-3: *Select all that apply*

Clinical manifestations associated with the common cold include:

☒ **Irritability**

☒ **Nasal discharge**

☒ **Headache**

☒ **Fever**

☒ **Rhinitis**

☒ **Muscle aches**

❑ Afebrile seizures

Exercise 9-4: *Multiple-choice question*

Which intervention is a priority in preventing the spread of nasopharyngitis?

A. **It is contagious and requires strict handwashing—YES, handwashing is the most important aspect of care.**

B. It is not contagious and is not a concern for others—NO, it is contagious.

C. It does not produce fever so others are not at risk of infection—NO, it is an infection that causes a fever and is contagious.

D. It does cause fever but others are not at risk of infection—NO, it is an infection that causes a fever and is contagious.

Exercise 9-5: *Fill-in*

A **throat culture** is required to differentiate between a viral and bacterial throat infection.

Exercise 9-6: *Multiple-choice question*
Which type of bacterial infection is the main culprit for causing tonsillitis and pharyngitis?
A. *Escherichia coli*—NO, this is not the most common cause.
B. *Moraxella catarrhalis*—NO, this is not the most common cause.
C. Group A beta-hemolytic streptococci—YES, this bacteria is the most common cause of tonsillitis.
D. Methicillin-resistant *Staphylococcus aureus*—NO, this is not the most common cause.

Exercise 9-7: *Select all that apply*
Which signs and symptoms observed in a sleeping child would indicate a possible hemorrhage after being postoperative from a T&A?
☒ **Excessive drooling**
☒ **Frequent swallowing**
❑ Nausea or vomiting
❑ Elevated temperature
❑ Severe headache

Exercise 9-8: *True or false*
Children with respiratory infections or influenza (viral) should not receive aspirin due to the link with Reye syndrome.
___**X**___ True
_____ False

Exercise 9-9: *Matching*
Match the terminology involving OM in Column A to the definition in Column B.

Column A	Column B
A. OM	__C__ Middle ear inflammation with fluid
B. Acute OM	__B__ Rapid onset of symptoms lasting 3 weeks
C. OM with effusion	
D. Chronic OM with effusion	__D__ Middle ear effusion lasting beyond 3 months
E. Otitis interna	
F. Otitis externa	__A__ Middle ear inflammation without pathogens
	__F__ External auditory canal inflammation
	__E__ Labyrinth of the ear inflammation

Exercise 9-10: *Select all that apply*

The interventions important in the nursing care of the child experiencing chronic OM include.

☒ **Frequent audiologist evaluations**

☒ **Penicillin antibiotic therapy**

❑ Antihistamines as needed

☒ **Analgesics if pain presentation**

☒ **Instructions to keep ears dry**

☒ **Antipyretics if elevated temperature**

Exercise 9-11: *Fill-in*

List four signs and symptoms expected to be exhibited in children experiencing OM.

1. **Pulling or tugging at the ears**
2. **Inattentiveness to noises**
3. **Unexplained fever**
4. **Crying and irritability**

Exercise 9-12: *True or false*

When you assess the child with OM, the assessment that is of little or no concern includes history obtainment, day care attendance, smoke exposure, and bottle propping.

_____True

__**X**__ False

Exercise 9-13: *Multiple-choice question*

Which situation would cause concern for you to consider possible hearing loss with a child?

A. A young child with a vocabulary of 900 or more words—NO, this is an adequate vocabulary.

B. **An infant that does not startle to loud sounds—YES, this is abnormal.**

C. The older child that answers questions appropriately—NO, this is a normal finding.

D. Any age child speaking loudly during conversation—NO, this is may be a normal finding.

Exercise 9-14: *Fill-in*

Levels of hearing loss are determined by the decibels (dB) of sound and normal sound is heard in **0 to 20** dB.

Exercise 9-15: *Matching*

Match the terminology of visual impairments in Column A to the definition in Column B.

Column A	Column B
A. Nystagmus	__C__ Misalignment of the eyes
B. ROP	__A__ Irregular bouncing of the eyes
C. Strabismus	__D__ Poor visual development in a normal eye
D. Amblyopia	__E__ Opacity of lens of the eye present at birth
E. Congenital cataracts	__B__ Incomplete retinal vascularization in prematurity
F. Astigmatism	__G__ Uneven curvature of the cornea(s)
G. Infantile glaucoma	__F__ Genetic obstruction of aqueous humor flow

Exercise 9-16: *True or false*

The risk factors associated with ROP include low birth weight, prematurity, sepsis, high light intensity, and hypothermia.

__X__ True

_____ False

Exercise 9-17: *Multiple-choice question*

Strabismus may occur in cases of resolved ROP. Which explanation best describes the rationale for prescribing daily eye patching?

A. Eye patching of the stronger eye will strengthen the weaker eye—YES, patching the stronger eye will strengthen the weaker one.

B. Eye patching of the weaker eye will strengthen the eye muscles—NO, it will not affect the weak eye.

C. Eye patching allows the affected eye time to revascularize—NO, this does not occur.

D. Eye patching allows the unaffected eye to revasculrize—NO, this does not occur.

Exercise 9-18: *Select all that apply*

The common cause(s) of ROP in infants include:

☐ Low oxygen levels of arterial blood

☒ **High oxygen levels of arterial blood**

☒ **Prematurity prior to 32 weeks gestation**

☒ **Exposure to extreme phototherapy**

☒ **Maternal infections or toxic exposure**

☒ **Exposure to colder temperatures**

Exercise 9-19: *Fill-in*

The term "legal blindness" refers vision of less than **20/200** or peripheral vision less than **20** degrees.

Exercise 9-20: *Fill-in*

Healthy People 2020 has established objectives for the improvement of visual impairment in children and adolescents.

- Healthy People 2020: www.healthypeople.gov
- Click on 2020 Topics and Objectives—Objectives A-Z—Healthy People 2020.
- In Search box, type in reduce blindness and visual impairment in children and adolescents.
- Click on the right side of chart on Tech Specs.
- The target percentage method is <u>**10**</u>% visual improvement for children and adolescents.

10

Children With Respiratory Health Care Needs

Vicki A. Martin

Unfolding Case Study #10-1 ▬ Judy

Judy is a 6-month-old who is being admitted to the pediatric unit from the emergency department with a diagnosis of laryngotracheobronchitis (LTB), commonly known as croup, and suspicion of respiratory syncytial virus (RSV). She has been running a fever for the last 24 hours of 102° F with a seal-like barking cough at night until she gags. She was admitted since the health care provider was not sure if the croup was viral or bacterial. The infant looked pale, was irritable and lethargic. Both parents were concerned that the infant was not acting like her normal self. She was admitted for intravenous fluids, diagnostic and laboratory testing, and 24-hour observation to rule out epiglottitis or other respiratory distress disorders.

Exercise 10-1: *Fill-in*
The majority of the cases of croup are caused by _____ and epiglottitis is caused by

_____.

Exercise 10-2: *True or false*
Croup symptoms most often occur at night and have sudden presentation.
_____ True
_____ False

e   **eResource 10-1:** To learn more about the clinical manifestations of croup, you review:
- ▇ MerckMedicus Online on your mobile device: [Pathway: www .merckmedicus.com → Select "Merck Manual" → Select "Merck Manual for Healthcare Professionals" → Enter "Croup" into the search field → Select "Croup" → Select and review the following content: "Signs & Symptoms" and "Diagnosis"]
- ▇ Video, *Baby With Croup Stridor Barking Cough*: goo.gl/1sbKPv

Answers to this chapter begin on page 160.

Exercise 10-3: *Multiple-choice question*

Which technique is essential in ruling out epiglottitis in children?

    A. Throat culture

    B. Sputum culture

    C. Lateral neck radiograph

    D. Chest radiograph

 eResource 10-2: To reinforce your understanding of epiglottitis, visit Medscape:
- Online [Pathway: www.medscape.org → Under the tab "Reference," select "References & Tools" → Enter "epiglottitis" into the search field → Under the "Overview" tab, review "Pathophysiology" and "Etiology"]
- On your mobile device, you can access the same information: [Pathway: Medscape → Enter "epiglottitis" into the search field → Under the "Overview" tab, review "Pathophysiology" and "Etiology"]

Exercise 10-4: *Select all that apply*

Medical interventions for the treatment of croup or LTB include:

❑ Corticosteroids

❑ Racemic epinephrine

❑ Humidified air

❑ Increased fluid intake

❑ Upright positioning

❑ Calm environment

❑ Ice collar to neck

Exercise 10-5: *Fill-in*

List the most common symptoms associated with croup or LTB.

1. _____

2. _____

3. _____

4. _____

5. _____

Exercise 10-6: *True or false*

The age group most affected with croup or LTB are the 1- to 8-year-olds.

_____ True

_____ False

eResource 10-3: To learn more about laryngotracheobronchitis (croup), refer to Epocrates Online: [Pathway: online.epocrates.com → Under the "Diseases" tab, enter "LTB" in the search field → Select "laryngotracheobronchitis" → Review "Highlights," "Diagnosis," and "Treatment"]

Answers to this chapter begin on page 160.

Judy was diagnosed with RSV via nasal-pharyngeal washings or enzyme-linked immunosorbent assay (ELISA). The laboratory specimens validated a viral infection. She was experiencing difficulty breathing, so she was placed on oxygen via nasal cannula at 1 liter along with continuous pulse oximetry monitoring. An IV was started with D5 ¼ normal saline to prevent dehydration from being febrile. The health care provider wrote orders for nasopharyngeal suctioning as needed and prednisolone IV for a one-time dose.

 eResource 10-4: Refer to the medication resources you have on your mobile device to review precautions when administering prednisone:

- Skyscape's RxDrugs [Pathway: RxDrugs → Enter "prednisone" into the search field → Select "prednisone" → Select "Warnings/Precautions" and review content]
- Epocrates [Pathway: Epocrates → Enter "prednisone" into the search field → Select "prednisone" → Scroll down to review "Contraindications/Cautions" and "Adverse Reactions" and review content]

Exercise 10-7: *Fill-in*

RSV is also known as _____.

Exercise 10-8: *True or false*

RSV is a highly contagious virus in infants and toddlers and may be contracted through direct contact with respiratory secretions or from particles on inanimate objects contaminated with the virus.

_____ True

_____ False

Exercise 10-9: *Select all that apply*

The peak incidence of RSV or bronchiolitis occurs in the following seasons:

- ❑ Spring
- ❑ Summer
- ❑ Winter
- ❑ Fall

 eResource 10-5: To review your understanding about respiratory syncytial virus infection, refer to Medscape:

- Online: [Pathway: www.medscape.org → Under the tab "Reference," select "References & Tools" → Enter "Respiratory Syncytial Virus" into the search field → Under the "Overview" tab, review "Practice Essentials," "Pathophysiology," and "Etiology"]
- On your mobile device, you can access the same information: [Pathway: Medscape → Enter "Respiratory Syncytial Virus" into the search field → Under the "Overview" tab, review "Practice Essentials," "Pathophysiology," and "Etiology"]

Answers to this chapter begin on page 160.

Exercise 10-10: *Multiple-choice question*

The only monoclonal antibody approved that can prevent severe RSV disease in susceptible infants and toddlers is which medication?

    A. Remicade

    B. Synagis

    C. Methotrexate

    D. Humira

 eResource 10-6: To review your understanding about medication utilized in the treatment of RSV, again refer to Medscape:

    ▪ Online: [Pathway: www.medscape.org → Under the tab "Reference," select "References & Tools" → Enter "Respiratory Syncytial Virus" into the search field → Under the "Medication" tab, review all the content]

    ▪ On your mobile device, you can access the same information: [Pathway: Medscape → Enter "Respiratory Syncytial Virus" into the search field → Under the "Medication" tab, review all the content]

Exercise 10-11: *Fill-in*

List the priority nursing interventions required in the management of RSV or broncholitis.

    1. _____

    2. _____

    3. _____

    4. _____

    5. _____

    6. _____

    7. _____

 eResource 10-7: To reinforce teaching, the nurse shows the parents a video, *Broncholitis*: goo.gl/z5oRU7

Unfolding Case Study #10-2 ▨ Derrick

Derrick is a 7-year-old living at home with his parents and three other siblings. Two siblings are older and one sibling is younger. Derrick developed asthma when he was a baby. Both of his parents are smokers but they do not smoke in the house. He has one cat and one dog that live in the house with them. He has to use his albuterol metered-dose inhaler (MDI) on a daily to every-other-day basis. In certain seasons, he appears to have asthmatic episodes more frequently. His mother administers diphenhydramine (Benadryl) for his runny nose in spring and winter months. He only visits the health care provider (HCP) every 6 months and as needed. He has not been to the emergency department since 1 year ago when he had the pulmonary function tests (PFTs) completed. They were within desirable limits at that time.

Exercise 10-12: *Fill-in*

Based on this information, what patient education is essential to provide to the parents in managing the asthma?

1. _____
2. _____
3. _____
4. _____
5. _____

 eResource 10-8: To reinforce patient teaching, you play the Centers for Disease Control and Prevention (CDC) podcast, *Asthma—What You Need to Know*: goo.gl/KCpa8

Exercise 10-13: *True or false*

Asthma is a chronic airway disorder characterized by hyperresponsiveness, airway edema, and mucus production, which accounts for 13 million lost school days per year.

_____ True

_____ False

 eResource 10-9: To learn more about asthma and its triggers, visit Medscape:
■ Online: [Pathway: www.medscape.org → Under the tab "Reference," select "References & Tools" → Enter "asthma" into the search field → Under the "Overview" tab, review "Pathophysiology" and "Etiology"]
■ On your mobile device, you can access the same information: [Pathway: Medscape → Enter "asthma" into the search field → Under the "Overview" tab, review "Pathophysiology" and "Etiology"]

Exercise 10-14: *Multiple-choice question*

The only inhalant rescue drug for managing an asthmatic episode that is available as an MDI or nebulizer is which medication?

A. Ipratropium

B. Prednisolone

C. Fluticasone

D. Albuterol

 eResource 10-10: To review your understanding of rescue medication, view the following video, *Asthma: Type of Asthma Medications*; goo.gl/oSze0k

Exercise 10-15: *Matching*

Match the respiratory terms in Column A to the correct description in Column B.

Column A	**Column B**
A. Cyanosis	_____ Wet crackling sounds in the lungs
B. Wheezing	_____ A collapsed or airless portion of the lung
C. Tachypnea	_____ Enlargement of terminal phalanx of finger(s)
D. Hypoxia	_____ High-pitched inspiration due to obstruction
E. Rales	_____ Increased respiratory rate
F. Rhonchi	_____ Oxygen deficiency
G. Stridor	_____ High-pitched musical sound on expiration
H. Atelectasis	_____ Blue-tinged skin or mucous membranes
I. Clubbing	_____ Low-pitched snoring sound in lungs
J. Retractions	_____ Inward pulling of soft tissue with respiration

eResource 10-11: To reinforce your assessment skills, listen to
- Practical Clinical Skills Heart and Lung Sounds: [Pathway: goo.gl/KjzYuC → Select "Lung Sounds" → Select "Basic Lung Sounds" → Listen to lung sounds]
- To learn more about respiratory wheezing, listen to The Merck Manual of Patient Symptoms Podcast, *Wheezing*: goo.gl/BA2cb
- To hear other samples of wheezing lung sounds go to:
  - Wheeze: goo.gl/692Fm
  - Wheezes—Expiratory: goo.gl/azJjo
  - Wheezes—Monophonic: goo.gl/P64fE
  - Wheezes—Polyphonic: goo.gl/G3PDI

Exercise 10-16: *Fill-in*

There are numerous patient education programs for educating others about asthma. Look at the CDC to search for this information to promote a nation of breathing easier.
- In Search box, type in www.cdc.gov/asthma
- Click on the basic information section
- Click on the facts area under basic information
- How many people die every day from asthma? _____
- In 2010, how many children suffered from asthma? _____

Exercise 10-17: *Select all that apply*

The severity of asthma ranges from vigorous exercise to daily symptoms that interfere with quality of life. The National Asthma Education and Prevention Program (2007) developed an asthma severity classification system for children not taking long-term control medication. The severity ranges include:
- ❑ Intermittent
- ❑ Partial intermittent
- ❑ Severe intermittent

Answers to this chapter begin on page 160.

❑ Mild persistent

❑ Moderate persistent

❑ Severe persistent

Exercise 10-18: *Fill-in*

The American Academy of Allergy, Asthma and Immunology (AAAAI) formulated an asthma action plan for emergency management of asthma.

■ In Search box, type in www.aaaai.org

■ Click on the first listing for the AAAAI

■ Search asthma action plan

■ What are the three color-coded sections of the asthma action plan?

_____, _____, and _____.

■ The red section of the asthma action plan requires which action? _____

e   **eResource 10-12:** You want to provide Derrick and his family with an action plan and other resources to take home with them, so you provide the following:

■ American Lung Associations *Asthma Action Plan*: goo.gl/r44xne

■ CDC's brochures:

  ■ *Helping Your Child Gain Control Over Asthma*: goo.gl/Q6bz0L

  ■ *You Can Control Asthma: A Guide to Understanding Asthma and Its Triggers:* goo.gl/zTlW8s

■ CDC's podcasts:

  ■ *Don't Let Asthma Keep You Out of the Game:* goo.gl/wZ9EiS

  ■ *Creating an Asthma-Friendly School*: goo.gl/WAumrQ

Exercise 10-19: *True or false*

When administering MDIs to children, best practices do not require the use of an aerochamber to increase the bioavailability of medication in the lungs.

_____ True

_____ False

e   **eResource 10-13:** Prior to finalizing your patient teaching, you review the proper techniques for using a MDI. You plan to show Derrick the technique prescribed by his physician:

■ *Using a metered dose inhaler with a spacer:* goo.gl/HD4edy

■ *Using a metered dose inhaler one to two inches from mouth:* goo.gl/Dmg1vQ

■ *Using a metered dose inhaler (inhaler in mouth):* goo.gl/mLWwpw

Unfolding Case Study #10-3 ■ Ella

Ella was born prematurely at 28 weeks gestation. She was intubated and admitted to the neonatal intensive care unit (NICU) immediately after birth. She has remained there for the past 30 days. She has been receiving oxygen via nasal

Answers to this chapter begin on page 160.

cannula, intravenous fluids (IVFs), special high-calorie formula with feedings, and a multitude of respiratory treatments. She is being monitored closely in the NICU and the nurses along with her family are working toward a discharge home. Her parents are aware she will have special needs and they are prepared to provide her care. Her mother has given up her job as a secretary to be a stay-at-home mother to provide the demanding care Ella will need. Ella was diagnosed with chronic lung disease or bronchopulmonary dysplasia (BPD) over the past month due to pulmonary immaturity and acute lung injury.

Exercise 10-20: *Fill-in*

Which factors pose an increased risk for infants and children for the development of chronic lung disease?

1. _____

2. _____

3. _____

eResource 10-14: To reinforce your understanding of bronchopulmonary dysplasia, including the prognosis and complications, refer to Medscape:

- Online: [Pathway: www.medscape.org → Under the tab "Reference," select "References & Tools" → Enter "bronchopulmonary dysplasia" into the search field → Review content under the "Follow-up" tab]
- On your mobile device, you can access the same information: [Pathway: Medscape → Enter "bronchopulmonary dysplasia" into the search field → Review content under the "Follow-up" tab]
- View a mini-lecture about *Newborn Lung Diseases*: goo.gl/uN2Ja4

Exercise 10-21: *True or false*

Tachypnea and increased effort of breathing are characteristic of chronic lung disease and since these symptoms can continue after discharge with exertion during oral feedings, infants are discharged with an apnea monitor.

_____ True

_____ False

Exercise 10-22: *Select all that apply*

The most common complications associated with chronic lung disease include:

❏ Pulmonary artery hypertension

❏ Delayed milestones

❏ Postprandial hypotension

❏ Cor pulmonale

❏ Atrial septal defect

❏ Congestive heart failure

❏ Bacterial/viral pneumonia

❏ Failure to thrive

Answers to this chapter begin on page 160.

Exercise 10-23: *Multiple-choice question*

An infant has moderate respiratory distress, increased effort of breathing, a respiratory rate (RR) of 42, and is mildly cyanotic. What is a priority nursing intervention?

A. Airway maintenance and oxygen by mask

B. Airway maintenance and reassessment

C. 100% oxygen and oxygen saturation monitoring

D. 100% oxygen and provide comfort measures

Exercise 10-24: *True or false*

The number of normal alveoli is reduced by one half to two thirds in infants with chronic lung disease.

_____ True

_____ False

Exercise 10-25: *Fill-in*

Infants with chronic lung disease are prone to _____ _____ _____ syndrome and require constant apnea monitoring for respiratory and cardiac status.

 eResource 10-15: Ella's parents have many questions and are particularly concerned about the prognosis for their daughter. You provide the following:
- *Brighter Prospects for Premature Babies*: goo.gl/DgrbLB

Unfolding Case Study #10-4 ▨ Emma Grace

Emma Grace is a 6-year-old female diagnosed with cystic fibrosis at birth. She lives with her parents. Her father is in the military and they move frequently. Her mother is a stay-at-home mom so she can be attentive to Emma Grace's special needs. She requires pancreatic enzymes prior to all large snacks and meals, wearing a chest physiotherapy vest several times daily, daily monitoring of temperature, and lung auscultations daily.

 eResource 10-16: To learn more about pancreatic enzyme replacement, consult Medscape: [Pathway: Medscape → Enter "pancreatic enzyme replacement" into the search field → Select "Pancreatic Enzyme Replacement Therapy" and review content]

Emma Grace has just started first grade and has an order from the health care provider to be home schooled during the cold and flu season. The mother is to report any unusual respiratory signs and symptoms to the health care provider. She has only been in schools for 2 weeks and she appears to be pale and tired. Her mother is monitoring the situation closely.

Answers to this chapter begin on page 160.

Exercise 10-26: *Fill-in*

Cystic fibrosis results in thickened, tenacious secretions in organs and glands, which include:

1. _____
2. _____
3. _____
4. _____
5. _____

e **eResource 10-17:** To hear what a cough of a child with CF sounds like, listen to this recording: goo.gl/Lhc9kZ

Exercise 10-27: *True or false*

In cystic fibrosis, the sweat glands produce a larger amount of chloride, leading to a salty taste to the skin and fluid and electrolyte issues with dehydration.

_____ True

_____ False

Exercise 10-28: *Select all that apply*

The clinical manifestations common to the cystic fibrosis child include:

❑ Meconium ileus at birth
❑ Delayed growth
❑ Bulky, greasy stools
❑ Voracious appetite
❑ Increased weight
❑ Chronic cough
❑ Barrel-shaped chest

Exercise 10-29: *Multiple-choice question*

You are caring for a cystic fibrosis child who receives pancreatic enzymes with large snacks and meals. Which statement by the mother demonstrates a good understanding of proper administration of the supplemental enzymes?

    A. "I will stop the enzymes if my child is given any antibiotics."
    B. "I will decrease the dose by half if my child is having greasy stools."
    C. "I will give the enzymes between meals to provide the best absorption."
    D. "I will give the enzymes at the beginning of every meal and large snack."

Exercise 10-30: *Select all that apply*

The nursing management of cystic fibrosis should include:

❑ Minimizing pulmonary complications
❑ Promoting growth and development
❑ Facilitating coping of child and family
❑ Promoting child's self esteem

Answers to this chapter begin on page 160.

eResource 10-18: To reinforce your understanding of cystic fibrosis, refer to the resources on your mobile device:

- Skyscape's Outline in Clinical Medication on your mobile device: [Pathway: Outline in Clinical Medication → Enter "cystic fibrosis" → Review content]
- Medscape: [Pathway: Medscape → Enter "cystic fibrosis" into the search field → Review "Practice Essentials" under "Overview" and "Long-Term Monitoring" under "Treatment"]

Unfolding Case Study #10-5 ▓ Nick

Nick is a 14-year-old adolescent who is just getting over influenza and mononucleosis. He was home bound from school for extreme lethargy, high fevers, and severe sore throat.

 eResource 10-19: To learn more about mononucleosis, its incidence, pathophysiology, and treatment:

- Medscape on your mobile device: [Pathway: Medscape → Enter "Mononucleosis" into the search field → Under the "Overview" tab, review "Pathophysiology" and "Etiology"]
- Skyscape's Outline in Clinical Medication on your mobile device: [Pathway: Outline in Clinical Medication → Enter "Mononucleosis" → Review content]
- View the videos:
  - *Mononucleosis—Treatment and More*: goo.gl/6Lb0tQ
  - *Mononucleosis*: goo.gl/mtPdqs

After being home bound for 1 month, Nick is finally cleared by the health care provider to return to school. His first week back to school appeared to go well. The second week, Nick started relapsing and experienced the same type of symptoms he previously had. His mother took him to the health care provider. Nick was admitted to the pediatric unit for possible pneumonia. As soon as he arrived onto the pediatric floor, a portable chest radiograph was performed at the bedside. An IV was initiated and intravenous fluids (IVFs) were begun. The chest x-ray did reveal infiltrates and pneumonia, so IV antibiotics were started to treat the respiratory infection.

Exercise 10-31: *Multiple-choice question*
Which factors contribute to infants and children being at increased risk for upper respiratory obstruction as compared to adults?

    A. Small tonsils and narrow nasal passages

    B. Small trachea and narrow nasal passages

    C. Underdeveloped trachea and small tongue

    D. Underdeveloped sinuses and cylinder-shaped pharynx

Answers to this chapter begin on page 160.

Exercise 10-32: *True or false*

Pneumonia is caused by a virus, bacteria, fungus, or *Mycoplasma* and is usually a self-limited disease.

_____ True

_____ False

Exercise 10-33: *Select all that apply*

The clinical manifestations associated with pneumonia include:

❏ Decreased respiratory rate

❏ Cough

❏ Headaches

❏ Chills

❏ Lethargy

❏ Chest/abdomen pain

❏ Fever

❏ Previous upper respiratory infection

e **eResource 10-20:** To learn more about risk for pneumonia, consult the *Pneumonia Severity Index Calculator*: goo.gl/CgxSN

Exercise 10-34: *Fill-in*

Infectious mononucleosis is also known as the "kissing disease" or _____ _____.

Exercise 10-35: *Multiple-choice question*

Which methods are important in diagnosing pneumonia?

 A. Chest radiograph and complete blood count

 B. Sputum culture and blood culture

 C. Incentive spirometry and pulmonary function test

 D. Health assessment and sputum culture

e **eResource 10-21:** To learn more about respiratory wheezing, listen to The Merck Manual of Patient Symptoms Podcast, *Wheezing*: goo.gl/BA2cb

e **eResource 10-22:** To hear other samples of wheezing lung sounds go to:
 ▪ *Wheeze*: goo.gl/692Fm
 ▪ *Wheezes—Expiratory*: goo.gl/azJjo
 ▪ *Wheezes—Monophonic*: goo.gl/P64fE
 ▪ *Wheezes—Polyphonic*: goo.gl/G3PDI

Exercise 10-36: *True or false*

The nursing management of mononucleosis is primarily symptomatic and the pneumococcal vaccine is available to reduce contracting the disease.

_____ True

_____ False

Answers to this chapter begin on page 160.

eResource 10-23: To learn more about the pneumococcal vaccine, check out Children's Hospital of Philadelphia's (CHOP) *Vaccines on the Go* (download Android (goo.gl/gW0xnI) or iOS (goo.gl/gW0xnI) or iOS (goo.gl/VHzkLQ): [Pathway: CHOP Vaccines → Select "Vaccines" → Enter "pneumonococcus" into the search field → Select "pneumonococcus" → Read about the vaccine. Be sure to tap the "disease" tab to read about the disease]

Exercise 10-37: *Select all that apply*
Bacterial infections of the respiratory system commonly occur as complications of influenza infections and include:
❑ Pneumonia
❑ Otitis media
❑ Upper respiratory infections
❑ Acute myositis
❑ Reye syndrome
❑ Meningitis
❑ Encephalitis

Exercise 10-38: *Fill-in*
Reye syndrome is a rare, acute encephalopathy associated with _____ use in the influenza-infected child and results in fatality.

 eResource 10-24: You provide instructional materials regarding Reye syndrome to Nick and his parents, reinforcing that it is rare but important to be aware of. You share a comprehensive resource from HealthyChildren.org and direct them specifically to the "conditions" resource and the information regarding "Reye syndrome":

■ Online: [Pathway: www.healthychildren.org → Select "Health Issues" from tool bar → Select "Conditions" → Select "A–Z" tab → Select "R" → Scroll down to select "Reye syndrome" → Tab to view or listen to content]
■ Mobile App (downloaded for Android [goo.gl/FTPQLH] or iOS [goo.gl/FTPQLH] or iOS [goo.gl/7b1Fwm]): [Pathway: HealthyChildren → On the Home Page, scroll down to select "Conditions" under the "Health Issues" section → Select "R" → Scroll down to select "Reye syndrome" → Tab to view or listen to content]

Answers to this chapter begin on page 160.

Answers

Exercise 10-1: *Fill-in*

The majority of the cases of croup are caused by **parainfluenza virus** and epiglottitis is caused by *Haemophilus influenzae* **type B**.

Exercise 10-2: *True or false*

Croup symptoms most often occur at night and have sudden presentation.

___**X**__ True

_____ False

Exercise 10-3: *Multiple-choice question*

Which technique is essential in ruling out epiglottitis in children?

A. Throat culture—NO, this is for bacterial infections.

B. Sputum culture—NO, this is for bacterial infections.

C. Lateral neck radiograph—YES, x-rays reveal any edema of the epiglottis.

D. Chest radiograph—NO, this is for lung issues, lower in the respiratory tract.

Exercise 10-4: *Select all that apply*

Medical interventions for the treatment of croup or LTB include:

☒ **Corticosteroids**

☒ **Racemic epinephrine**

☒ **Humidified air**

☒ **Increased fluid intake**

☒ **Upright positioning**

☒ **Calm environment**

❏ Ice collar to neck

Exercise 10-5: *Fill-in*

List the most common symptoms associated with croup or LTB.

1. **Mucus production**

2. **Increased temperature**

3. **Hoarseness**

4. **Barking cough**

5. **Inspiratory stridor**

Exercise 10-6: *True or false*
The age group most affected with croup or LTB are the 1- to 8-year-olds.

_____ True

___X___ **False—Most affected are the 3-month to 3-year-olds.**

Exercise 10-7: *Fill-in*
RSV is also known as **bronchiolitis.**

Exercise 10-8: *True or false*
RSV is a highly contagious virus in infants and toddlers and may be contracted through direct contact with respiratory secretions or from particles on inanimate objects contaminated with the virus.

___X___ **True**

_____ False

Exercise 10-9: *Select all that apply*
The peak incidence of RSV or bronchiolitis occurs in the following seasons:

☒ **Spring**

❑ Summer

☒ **Winter**

❑ Fall

Exercise 10-10: *Multiple-choice question*
The only monoclonal antibody approved that can prevent severe RSV disease in susceptible infants and toddlers is which medication?

A. Remicade

B. Synagis

C. Methotrexate

D. Humira

Exercise 10-11: *Fill-in*
List the nursing interventions required in the management of RSV or broncholitis.

1. **Administer oxygen**

2. **Maintain hydration**

3. **Administer antipyretics**

4. **Suction secretions**

5. **Monitor oxygen saturation**

6. **Monitor blood gases and pulmonary function tests**

7. **Administer inhalation medications**

Exercise 10-12: *Fill-in*

Based on this information, what patient education is essential to provide to the parents in managing the asthma?

1. <u>**Animal dander is a common trigger of asthma**</u>
2. <u>**Report any asthma issues to the health care provider or go to the emergency department**</u>
3. <u>**Do not allow the MDI to expire or become empty**</u>
4. <u>**Offer smoking cessation information to the parents**</u>
5. <u>**Medical follow-up is essential for managing asthma**</u>

Exercise 10-13: *True or false*

Asthma is a chronic airway disorder characterized by hyperresponsiveness, airway edema, and mucus production, which accounts for 13 million lost school days per year.

___**X**___ True

_____ False

Exercise 10-14: *Multiple-choice question*

The only inhalant rescue drug for managing an asthmatic episode that is available with an MDI or nebulizer is which medication?

A. Ipratropium—NO, it is a bronchodilator for maintenance of asthma.

B. Prednisolone—NO, it is a steroid for maintenance of asthma/inflammation.

C. Fluticasone—NO, it is a corticosteroid inhalant for maintenance of asthma.

D. Albuterol—YES, it is the drug of choice for rescuing asthmatic episodes.

Exercise 10-15: *Matching*

Match the respiratory terms in Column A to the correct description in Column B.

Column A		Column B
A. Cyanosis	__E__	Wet crackling sounds in the lungs
B. Wheezing	__H__	A collapsed or airless portion of the lung
C. Tachypnea	__I__	Enlargement of terminal phalanx of finger(s)
D. Hypoxia	__G__	High-pitched inspiration due to obstruction
E. Rales	__C__	Increased respiratory rate
F. Rhonchi	__D__	Oxygen deficiency
G. Stridor	__B__	High-pitched musical sound on expiration
H. Atelectasis	__A__	Blue-tinged skin or mucous membranes
I. Clubbing	__J__	Inward pulling of chest with respiration
J. Retractions	__F__	Low-pitched snoring sound in lungs

Exercise 10-16: *Fill-in*

There are numerous patient education programs for educating others about asthma. Look at the CDC to search for this information to promote a nation of breathing easier.

- In Search box, type in www.cdc.gov/asthma
- Click on the basic information section
- Click on the facts area under basic information
- How many people die every day from asthma? __9__
- In 2010, how many children suffered from asthma?
  7 million = 1 of 11 children

Exercise 10-17: *Select all that apply*

The severity of asthma ranges from vigorous exercise to daily symptoms that interfere with quality of life. The National Asthma Education and Prevention Program (2007) developed an asthma severity classifications system for children not taking long-term control medication. The severity ranges include:

☒ **Intermittent**

❑ Partial intermittent

❑ Severe intermittent

☒ **Mild persistent**

☒ **Moderate persistent**

☒ **Severe persistent**

Exercise 10-18: *Fill-in*

The American Academy of Allergy, Asthma and Immunology (AAAAI) formulated an asthma action plan for emergency management of asthma.

- In Search box, type in www.aaaai.org
- Click on the first listing for the AAAAI
- Search asthma action plan
- What are the three color-coded sections of the asthma plan? **green, yellow,** and **red** .
- The red section of the asthma action plan requires which action?
  Seek medical assistance immediately

Exercise 10-19: *True or false*

When administering MDIs to children, best practices do not require the use of an aerochamber to increase the bioavailability of medication in the lungs.

_____ True

___X___ **False**

Exercise 10-20: *Fill-in*

Which factors pose an increased risk for infants and children for the development of chronic lung disease?

  1. Lower birth weights

  2. Male gender

  3. White race

Exercise 10-21: *True or false*

Tachypnea and increased effort of breathing are characteristic of chronic lung disease and since these symptoms can continue after discharge with exertion during oral feedings, infants are discharged with an apnea monitor.

  ___**X**___ True

  _____ False

Exercise 10-22: *Select all that apply*

The most common complications associated with chronic lung disease include:

☒ **Pulmonary artery hypertension**

☒ **Delayed milestones**

❑ Postprandial hypotension

☒ **Cor pulmonale**

❑ Atrial septal defect

☒ **Congestive heart failure**

☒ **Bacterial/viral pneumonia**

☒ **Failure to thrive**

Exercise 10-23: *Multiple-choice question*

An infant has moderate respiratory distress, increased effort of breathing, a respiratory rate (RR) of 42, and is mildly cyanotic. What is a priority nursing intervention?

  A. Airway maintenance and oxygen via mask—NO, there is no airway problem at this time.

  B. Airway maintenance and reassessment—NO, there is no airway problem at this time.

  C. **100% oxygen and oxygen saturation monitoring—YES, the O$_2$ saturation needs immediate attention as shown by the cyanosis.**

  D. 100% oxygen and provide comfort measures—NO, the poor saturation needs to be addressed.

Exercise 10-24: *True or false*

The number of normal alveoli is reduced by one half to two thirds in infants with chronic lung disease.

  _____ True

  ___**X**___ **False—Alveoli are reduced by one third to one half.**

Exercise 10-25: *Fill-in*
Infants with chronic lung disease are prone to **sudden infant death syndrome (SIDS)** and require constant apnea monitoring for respiratory and cardiac status.

Exercise 10-26: *Fill-in*
Cystic fibrosis results in thickened, tenacious secretions in organs and glands, which include:

1. **Exocrine glands**
2. **Pancreas**
3. **Sweat glands**
4. **Respiratory tract**
5. **Gastrointestinal tract**

Exercise 10-27: *True or false*
In cystic fibrosis, the sweat glands produce a larger amount of chloride, leading to a salty taste to the skin and fluid and electrolyte issues with dehydration.

___**X**___ True

_____ False

Exercise 10-28: *Select all that apply*
The clinical manifestations common to the cystic fibrosis child include:

☒ **Meconium ileus at birth**
☒ **Delayed growth**
☒ **Bulky, greasy stools**
☒ **Voracious appetite**
❑ Increased weight
☒ **Chronic cough**
☒ **Barrel-shaped chest**

Exercise 10-29: *Multiple-choice question*
You are caring for a cystic fibrosis child who receives pancreatic enzymes. Which statement by the mother demonstrates a good understanding of proper administration of the supplemental enzymes?

A. "I will stop the enzymes if my child is given any antibiotics."—NO, the enzymes must be continued.
B. "I will decrease the dose by half if my child is having greasy stools."—NO, the full dose of enzymes must be continued.

C. "I will give the enzymes between meals to provide the best absorption."—NO, they need to be given with meals.

D. "I will give the enzymes at the beginning of every meal and large snack." —YES, this is the proper administration.

Exercise 10-30: *Select all that apply*

The nursing management of cystic fibrosis should include:

☒ **Minimizing pulmonary complications**

☒ **Promoting growth and development**

☒ **Facilitating coping of child and family**

☒ **Promoting child's self esteem**

Exercise 10-31: *Multiple-choice question*

Which factors contribute to infants and children being at increased risk for upper respiratory obstruction as compared to adults?

A. Small tonsils and narrow nasal passages—NO, tonsils are large.

B. Small trachea and narrow nasal passages—YES, this is the anatomical difference.

C. Underdeveloped trachea and small tongue—NO, the tongue is large.

D. Underdeveloped sinuses and cylinder-shaped pharynx—NO, it is narrowing of the passages.

Exercise 10-32: *True or false*

Pneumonia is caused by a virus, bacteria, fungus, or *Mycoplasma* and is usually a self-limited disease.

___**X**___ True

_____ False

Exercise 10-33: *Select all that apply*

The clinical manifestations associated with pneumonia include:

❑ Decreased respiratory rate

☒ **Cough**

☒ **Headaches**

☒ **Chills**

☒ **Lethargy**

☒ **Chest/abdomen pain**

☒ **Fever**

☒ **Previous upper respiratory infection**

Exercise 10-34: *Fill-in*

Infectious mononucleosis is also known as the "kissing disease" or **Epstein-Barr virus (EBV)**.

Exercise 10-35: *Multiple-choice question*

Which methods are important in diagnosing pneumonia?

A. **Chest radiograph and complete blood count—YES, this is the best way since it looks at the lungs through x-ray and assesses the white blood cell count for infection.**

B. Sputum culture and blood culture—NO, this doesn't visualize the extent of the pneumonia in the lungs.

C. Incentive spirometry and pulmonary function test—NO, this doesn't visualize the extent of the pneumonia in the lungs.

D. Health assessment and sputum culture—NO, this doesn't visualize the extent of the pneumonia in the lungs.

Exercise 10-36: *True or false*

The nursing management of mononucleosis is primarily symptomatic and the pneumococcal vaccine is available to reduce contracting the disease.

___**X**___ True

_____ False

Exercise 10-37: *Select all that apply*

Bacterial infections of the respiratory system commonly occur as complications of influenza infections and include:

☒ **Pneumonia**

☒ **Otitis media**

☒ **Upper respiratory infections**

☒ **Acute myositis**

☒ **Reye syndrome**

❑ Meningitis

❑ Encephalitis

Exercise 10-38: *Fill-in*

Reye syndrome is a rare, acute encephalopathy associated with **aspirin** use in the influenza-infected child and results in fatality.

11

Children With Cardiovascular Health Care Needs

Susan Parnell Scholtz

Unfolding Case Study #11-1 ▓ Louis

The pediatric intensive care unit (PICU) that you are assigned to is in a tertiary inpatient organization and is the regional center for pediatric cardiology. You like working with infants and children with cardiac defects because it is very interesting. Understanding cardiac anomalies is a challenge but you review your notes from school often and read cardiac nursing journals to keep up to date.

 eResource 11-1: In addition to reading journals, you also reviewed material provided by The Merck Manual Online: [Pathway: www .merckmedicus.com → Select "Merck Manual" → Select "Merck Manual for Healthcare Professionals" → Enter "cardiac anomalies" into the search field → Select "Overview of Congenital Cardiovascular Anomalies" to access and review content]

Exercise 11-1: *Matching*
Select the disorder in Column A and match it with the correct description in Column B.

Column A	Column B
A. Transposition of the great arteries (TGA)	_____ This disorder is common in neonates and is due to persistent fetal circulation. It is characterized by a left to right shunt.
B. Tetralogy of Fallot	_____ Left to right shunting occurs because of an opening between the two atria.
C. Patent ductus arteriosus (PDA)	_____ Because of an opening between the ventricles, there is an increase in pulmonary blood flow.
D. Atrial septal defect (ASD)	_____ This common cardiac defect is characterized by four distinct defects causing the heart to shunt from right to left.
E. Ventricular septal defect (VSD)	_____ This cyanotic heart defect occurs when the aorta serves as the outflow tract for the heart.

You take report on three patients for your 12-hour shift.

Exercise 11-2: *True or false*

Identify if the following statements about the cardiac system in the child are true or false.

_____ The right ventricle of a newborn is considerably larger than the left ventricle at birth.

_____ Recent advances in neonatal medicine have enabled the neonate with a VSD to lead a long life.

_____ Cardiac disease affects many systems but does not affect physical growth.

_____ The femoral artery is an ideal site to assess a young child's central pulses.

_____ Since young children are restless, it is acceptable to auscultate the pulse for 15 seconds.

_____ A functional murmur in a child requires further evaluation.

The first patient you receive report about is Louis, a neonate who is being readmitted for a cardiac anomaly. A thorough interview of the parent is critical during a cardiac assessment. You want to ensure that the health history interview time is used effectively, and prepare a list of questions to ask the parents that would provide important information about the child's cardiac status.

Exercise 11-3: *Select all that apply*

Which of the following questions would be a priority to ask during the interview of a parent whose infant may have a cardiac disorder?

❑ Does your baby have any color changes around his mouth during his feedings?

❑ How old were you when you became pregnant with Louis?

❑ Do you feel that Louis tires easily and naps more than would be expected?

❑ Do you feel Louis has met his developmental milestones?

❑ Has Louis been growing steadily in both height and weight?

 eResource 11-2: To supplement your understanding of perinatal assessment of congenital anomalies, visit NursesLearning.com: goo.gl/0RrB9r

Louis' mother answers all your questions but you can tell she is very apprehensive and worried. You try to stay calm and focused during your interview and choose words carefully so you don't further upset her. Louis' history is typical but his condition was not an emergency so he was sent home from the newborn nursery and his parents are now bringing him back for a "complete workup."

 eResource 11-3: To be better able to provide support to Louis' mother, you want to review additional materials. You remember you went to a continuing education program recently. You pull out those materials to review:

■ Notes from a presentation, *Pediatric Cardiovascular Assessment*, by Janet M. Prozzillo, BSN, RN, CPN, on: goo.gl/DXWycI

Answers to this chapter begin on page 178.

■ A video: *Assessment of the Newborn: Cardiopulmonary Assessment and Cardiac Anomalies*: goo.gl/fPCim7

His mother stays with him the entire hospitalization and accompanies him to every test. She has many questions. You provide patient teaching materials from the American Heart Association (AHA).

 eResource 11-4: Since Louis' mother has a smartphone, you provide the link to the AHA's *Web Booklet: If Your Child Has a Congenital Heart Defect*: goo.gl/8G3B0U

As Louis' mother has opportunity to review materials and get her questions answered, she appears more comfortable. She wants to get additional materials to share with Louis' grandparents.

 eResource 11-5: You provide her with a link to order more materials for free from the AHA: educationpackets.heart.org

Exercise 11-4: *Multiple-choice question*

Which of the following symptoms is typically the first indication of a congenital heart disorder in an infant?

    A. Cyanosis

    B. Decreased pulse

    C. Congestive heart failure

    D. Heart murmur

Unfolding Case Study #11-2 Abe

Another patient assigned to your care is Abe, an infant scheduled for surgery in the morning to correct a large cardiac defect, an ASD. He was discharged from the nursery until the scheduled surgery.

 eResource 11-6: To learn more about ASD, refer to:
■ MerckMedicus Online on your mobile device: [Pathway: www
.merckmedicus.com → Select "Merck Manual" → Select "Merck Manual
for Healthcare Professionals" → Enter "atrial septal defect" into the
search field → Select "atrial septal defect—pediatric" to access and
review content]
■ Medscape:
    ■ Online: [Pathway: www.medscape.org → Under the tab "Reference,"
    select "References & Tools" → Enter "atrial septal defect" into
    the search field → Under the "Overview" tab, review "Problem,"
    "Pathophysiology," and "Etiology"]
    ■ On your mobile device, you can access the same information:
    [Pathway: Medscape → Enter "atrial septal defect" into the
    search field → Under the "Overview" tab, review "Problem,"
    "Pathophysiology," and "Etiology"]

Answers to this chapter begin on page 178.

Exercise 11-5: *Select all that apply*

Which of the following statements, if made by the mother, indicates that she understands preoperative care of her infant?

- ❑ "I may need to stop breastfeeding if he tires too easily."
- ❑ "I may need to learn how to give my son nasogastric feedings during the night."
- ❑ "Abe's immunizations will be delayed until the surgery has been done."
- ❑ "I need to keep Abe away from crowds because of the chance of infection."
- ❑ "It is important that I cuddle and rock him so he knows he is loved."

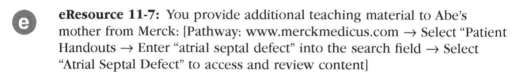 **eResource 11-7:** You provide additional teaching material to Abe's mother from Merck: [Pathway: www.merckmedicus.com → Select "Patient Handouts → Enter "atrial septal defect" into the search field → Select "Atrial Septal Defect" to access and review content]

While assessing Abe, you notice a vital sign that is not within normal limits.

Exercise 11-6: *Multiple-choice question*

Which of the following findings should be reported to the primary care provider?

- A. Blood pressure 80/55
- B. Pulse rate 100/bpm
- C. Respirations 34
- D. Temperature 100.6

After Abe's assessment is complete, you move onto your third patient in the PICU.

Unfolding Case Study #11-3 ▦ Ellen

Ellen is an infant diagnosed with congestive heart failure; the etiology has been determined to be pulmonary venous congestion.

Exercise 11-7: *Multiple-choice question*

Which of the following findings is <u>not</u> typically found in a child with pulmonary venous congestion?

- A. Resting bradycardia
- B. Impaired weight gain
- C. Circumoral cyanosis associated with feeding
- D. Adventitious breath sounds

Exercise 11-8: *Multiple-choice question*

Which of the following is the primary initial goal of managing congestive heart failure?

- A. Calm the child to relieve respiratory distress
- B. Administer diuretics to promote excretion of excessive fluid
- C. Improve tissue perfusion
- D. Correct arrhythmias

Answers to this chapter begin on page 178.

Ellen will undergo a process known as digitalization to lessen the workload of her heart. Her mother asks, "What is that?"

 eResource 11-8: Using the online medical dictionary provided by WebMD, you look up the term to make sure you give her the proper explanation: goo.gl/ZxMPC: [Pathway: WebMD Dictionary → Enter "digitalization" into the search field → View results]

Exercise 11-9: *Multiple-choice question*
Which of the following medications will be given to digitalize Ellen?
A. Lanoxin
B. Propanolol
C. Carvedilol
D. Captopril

Ellen is receiving a maintenance dose of digoxin and furosemide (Lasix) to manage her congestive heart failure.

 eResource 11-9: To learn more about these drugs and precautions, consult:
- Skyscape's RxDrugs on your mobile device: [Pathway: Skyscape → Select "RxDrugs" → Enter "Lasix" into the search field → Scroll down to view "Warnings/precautions"; repeat with "digoxin"]
- Epocrates on your mobile device: [Pathway: Epocrates → Enter "Lasix" into the search field → Scroll down to view "Warnings," "Contraindications/ Cautions," and "Adverse Reactions"; repeat with "digoxin"]

Exercise 11-10: *Matching*
Identify common side effects of digoxin and Lasix in Column A and match them with the drug related to each in Column B.

Column A	Column B
_____ K levels less than 3.5 mEq/L	A. Digoxin
_____ Sinus bradycardia	B. Lasix
_____ Excessive diuresis	
_____ Hypomagnesemia	
_____ Arrhythmias	

Exercise 11-11: *Fill-in*
Digoxin should be withheld and the primary care provider notified when the infant's heart rate is less than _____.

Exercise 11-12: *Ordering*
Beginning with the highest priority (1), rank the nursing interventions that Ellen should receive to manage her congestive heart failure from 1 to 6.
_____ Weigh all of Ellen's diapers and measure urine specific gravity
_____ Monitor oxygen saturation via pulse oximetry

Answers to this chapter begin on page 178.

———— Monitor Ellen's cardiac output

———— Elevate the head of Ellen's bed while sleeping

———— Maintain a calorie count to ensure nutrition is maintained

———— Involve the parents in Ellen's care

Once you have all three of your patients assessed and their interventions completed, you ask your colleague, Tom, if he needs assistance with his nursing care. Tom tells you he too has three patients assigned to him, none of whom are acute. He asks you if you have time to take a pulse oximetry reading on Marta in room 302.

 eResource 11-10: To learn more about pulse oximetry prior to performing the procedure, consult Medscape on your mobile device: [Pathway: Medscape → Enter "pulse oximetry" into the search field → Select "pulse oximetry" and review content]

Unfolding Case Study #11-4 ▨ Marta

Marta is a 5-year-old who presented to the clinic today. Her mother noted that ever since she had a sore throat 3 weeks ago, "She hasn't been her normal self." Upon auscultation of her heart, the nurse noted the presence of a murmur that was never documented before. An exam of the integumentary system reveals a pink skin rash located primarily on her abdomen. Marta was admitted to the PICU.

Exercise 11-13: *Select all that apply*

Based upon this initial examination, the clinic nurse should determine:

❑ If the child has complained of pain in her large joints

❑ If there is the presence of a group A *Streptococcus* infection

❑ If there is an elevation in C-reactive protein

❑ If there is a decrease in hemoglobin

❑ If there is an increase in the erythrocyte sedimentation rate

A diagnosis of acute rheumatic fever has been made and it has been explained to her mother who is tearful.

 eResource 11-11: To learn more about acute rheumatic fever, consult:
■ MerckMedicus Online on your mobile device: [Pathway: www .merckmedicus.com → Select "Merck Manual" → Select "Merck Manual for Healthcare Professionals" → Enter "Acute Rheumatic Fever" into the search field → Select "Rheumatic Fever" to access and review content]
■ Medscape:
  ■ Online: [Pathway: www.medscape.org → Under the tab "Reference," select "References & Tools" → Enter "Rheumatic Fever" into the search field → Review content]
  ■ On your mobile device, you can access the same information: [Pathway: Medscape → Enter "Rheumatic Fever" into the search field → Review content]

Answers to this chapter begin on page 178.

Exercise 11-14: *Multiple-choice question*

Which of the following interventions should be anticipated in the care of Marta?

    A. Place Marta on bedrest until carditis is ruled out.

    B. Medicate the child with Tylenol to manage pain.

    C. Perform active range of motion on the child during the acute phase.

    D. Assure the parents that the child is now immune from further recurrences.

You check Marta's pulse oximeter and it is 97% so you report it to Tom and ask him if there is anything else you can do for him. He says no but thank you; he is off to assess Isabella.

Unfolding Case Study #11-5 Isabella

Isabella, age 5, is a preschooler who was diagnosed with Kawasaki disease. Since there is no specific blood test to diagnose the disorder, four out of five diagnostic criteria must be evident to diagnose it.

Exercise 11-15: *Multiple-choice question*

Which of the following findings is not a diagnostic criterion for Kawasaki disease?

    A. Pyrexia more than 5 days

    B. Peeling of the palms of the hands and soles of the feet 2 weeks after onset

    C. Positive group A *Streptococcus* test

    D. Bilateral inflammation of conjunctiva

    E. Strawberry tongue

eResource 11-12: Refer to Medscape on your mobile device to learn more about Kawasaki disease diagnostic criteria: [Pathway: Medscape → Enter "Kawasaki" into the search field → Select "Kawasaki Disease Diagnostic Criteria" and review content]

Exercise 11-16: *Fill-in*

_____ is the medication that will be administered to Marta to decrease the risk for a coronary artery aneurysm in the child with Kawasaki disease.

Your charge nurse asks you to assist Paula with getting Trinh, a preprocedure patient, ready and you agree since you just made nursing care rounds and all three of your infants' parents are in the room and your patients are all comfortable.

Unfolding Case Study #11-6 Trinh

Trinh, age 9 years, is scheduled for a cardiac catheterization to evaluate the status of her cardiac disorder. A sedative had been administered 30 minutes ago.

Answers to this chapter begin on page 178.

eResource 11-13: To review the preoperative education to provide to Trinh and her parents, you review:

Video, *Heart Health Cardiac Catheterization Surgery PreOp® Patient Education:* goo.gl/pvInPs

Exercise 11-17: *Ordering*
Prioritize the nursing interventions in terms of their importance beginning with the highest priority from 1 to 5.

_____ Ask the child to void and document the results.

_____ Support the family members who are anxious about the procedure.

_____ Monitor for respiratory depression.

_____ Assess the child's baseline cardiac status.

_____ Answer any questions the child may have before the catheterization.

 eResource 11-14: To learn more about the procedure, refer to Medscape:

- Online: [Pathway: www.medscape.org → Under the tab "Reference," enter "Cardiac Catheterization" into the search field → Select "Cardiac Catheterization of the Left Heart" and review content under the "Overview" tab; be sure to look at the multimedia files and also review content under "Periprocedural care" and "Technique"]
- On your mobile device, you can access the same information: [Pathway: Medscape → Enter "Cardiac Catheterization" into the search field → Select "Cardiac Catheterization of the Left Heart" and review content under the "Overview" tab; be sure to look at the multimedia files and also review content under "Periprocedural care" and "Technique"]
- Look at several images depicting the procedure:
  American Heart Association's Cardiac Catheterization: goo.gl/D66Vs8
  Medline Plus images of Cardiac Catheterization:
  goo.gl/CR5R0I
  goo.gl/crxv2Q

After the cardiac catheterization procedure, Trinh is brought back to the PICU and you assist getting her into bed.

Exercise 11-18: *Select all that apply*
Identify nursing interventions that should be implemented immediately following the cardiac catheterization procedure.

❏ Direct pressure should be placed on the site of insertion of the catheter and guide wires.

❏ Assess the area proximal to the incision.

❏ Apply a pressure dressing over the catheter site for several hours.

❏ Elevate the head of the bed until comfort has been achieved.

❏ Place the child on bed rest for approximately 6 hours following the procedure.

❏ Encourage fluid intake.

Answers to this chapter begin on page 178.

You and your colleagues know that you must watch Trinh closely for bleeding from the catheterization site.

Exercise 11-19: *Multiple-choice question*
Which of the following findings is a late manifestation of hypovolemic shock?

    A. Tachycardia

    B. Greater than 3-second capillary refill

    C. Pallor

    D. Hypotension

(e) eResource 11-15: To learn more about the signs, symptoms, and management of hypovolemic shock, refer to Skyscape's Outline in Clinical Medicine on your mobile device: [Pathway: Outline in Clinical Medicine → Enter "hypovolemia" → Select "shock" → Review content]

(e) eResource 11-16: To review postprocedure care for Trinh, consult Medscape again:

■ Online: [Pathway: www.medscape.org → Under the tab "Reference," enter "cardiac catheterization" into the search field → Select "Cardiac Catheterization of the Left Heart" and review content under the "Overview" tab; be sure to look at the multimedia files; also review content under "periprocedural care" and "technique"]

■ On your mobile device, you can access the same information: [Pathway: Medscape → Enter "cardiac catheterization" into the search field → Select "Cardiac Catheterization of the Left Heart" and review content under the "Overview" tab; be sure to look at the multimedia files and also review content under "periprocedural care" and "technique"]

Exercise 11-20: *Multiple-choice question*
Which of the following statements should be made by Trinh's nurse to her parents regarding discharge?

    A. "A fever is normal within the first 24 hours following a cardiac catheterization."

    B. "The foot on the side of the catheterization may temporarily feel numb for a few days following the procedure."

    C. "There may be decreased circulation in the foot on the side of the catheterization."

    D. "Report any increase in the bruise at the catheter site."

Trinh does fine after the catheterization and is scheduled to go home the following morning since it is already late. You ask your colleagues before the end of the shift if they need anything but they are fine and also finishing up their work. You check your infants one more time before you write out your S-B-A-R (Situation, Background, Assessment, Recommendations) reports for the nurse on the next shift.

(e) eResource 11-17: For a comprehensive review of SBAR and Huddles and to see additional examples of charting, read *A Guide For Collaborative Structured Communication*: goo.gl/zEX7ut

Answers to this chapter begin on page 178.

Answers

Exercise 11-1: *Matching*

Select the disorder in Column A and match it with the correct description in Column B.

Column A	Column B
A. Transposition of the great arteries (TGA)	__C__ This disorder is common in neonates and is due to persistent fetal circulation. It is characterized by a left to right shunt.
B. Tetralogy of Fallot	__D__ Left to right shunting occurs because of an opening between the two atria.
C. Patent ductus arteriosus (PDA)	__E__ Because of an opening between the ventricles, there is an increase in pulmonary blood flow.
D. Atrial septal defect (ASD)	__B__ This common cardiac defect is characterized by four distinct defects causing the heart to shunt from right to left.
E. Ventricular septal defect (VSD)	__A__ This cyanotic heart defect occurs when the aorta serves as the outflow tract for the heart.

Exercise 11-2: *True or false*

Identify if the following statements about the cardiac system in the child are true or false.

__True__ **The right ventricle of a newborn is considerably larger than the left ventricle at birth—YES, this dynamic occurs secondary to high levels of pulmonary resistance during fetal life.**

__True__ **Recent advances in neonatal medicine have enabled the neonate with a VSD to lead a long life—YES, this structural defect results in an opening between the ventricles and at one time was incompatible with life.**

__False__ Cardiac disease affects many systems but does not affect physical growth— NO, children with cardiac disease tend to be smaller in stature and have lower than normal body weight.

__True__ The femoral artery is an ideal site to assess a young child's central pulses— YES, palpation of the femoral artery is the recommended pulse point in a young child.

__False__ Since young children are often restless, it is acceptable to auscultate the pulse for 15 seconds—NO, pulses should be palpated as opposed to auscultated in the young child for 1 full minute.

__False__ A functional murmur in a child requires further evaluation—NO, a functional murmur is benign and a common finding in the child and does not require further evaluation.

Exercise 11-3: *Select all that apply*

Which of the following questions would be a priority to ask during the interview of a parent whose infant may have a cardiac disorder?

☒ **Does your baby have any color changes around his mouth during his feedings?—YES, the infant with a cardiac disorder may experience circumoral cyanosis (bluish color around the mouth) during feeding, which may indicate his oxygen saturations are decreasing because of the amount of energy and exertion that is made during feeding.**

☒ **How old were you when you became pregnant with Louis?—YES, maternal age at this point has been related to VSD.**

☒ **Do you feel that Louis tires easily and naps more than would be expected?— YES, the infant may tire easily due to decreased oxygen levels.**

❑ Do you feel Louis has met his developmental milestones?—NO, the infant most likely will meet his social, language, fine, and gross motor milestones regardless of the anomaly; however, growth in terms of height and weight may be compromised.

☒ **Has Louis been growing steadily in both height and weight?—YES, growth in terms of height and weight may be delayed in a child with a cardiac disorder.**

Exercise 11-4: *Multiple-choice question*

Which of the following symptoms is typically the first indication of a congenital heart disorder in an infant?

A. Cyanosis—NO, although cyanosis is typically found in many cardiac defects, it is not typically the first sign.

B. Decreased pulse—NO, although an abnormal pulse is typically found in many cardiac defects, it is not typically the first sign.

C. Congestive heart failure—NO, this occurs with increased shunting.

D. Heart murmur—YES, auscultation of a heart murmur is often the first sign of a congenital heart defect.

Exercise 11-5: *Select all that apply*

Which of the following statements, if made by the mother, indicates that she understands preoperative care of her infant?

☐ "I may need to stop breastfeeding if he tires too easily."—NO, feedings should not last longer than 30 minutes and may need to be supplemented.

☒ **"I may need to learn how to give my son nasogastric feedings during the night."—YES, this is done for infants who have problems gaining or maintaining their weight.**

☐ "Abe's immunizations will be delayed until the surgery has been done."—NO, A regular immunization schedule will be maintained in order to prevent the child from infections.

☒ **"I need to keep Abe away from crowds because of the chance of infection."—YES, children with congenital heart defects have difficulty with hypoxia associated with respiratory infections.**

☒ **"It is important that I cuddle and rock him so he knows he is loved."—YES, attachment can be affected in children with a chronic illness; therefore, mediators of attachment are critical.**

Exercise 11-6: *Multiple-choice question*

Which of the following findings should be reported to the primary care provider?

A. Blood pressure 80/55—NO, this is a normal finding for an infant.

B. Pulse rate 100/bpm —NO, this is a normal finding for an infant.

C. Respirations 34—NO, this is a normal finding for an infant.

D. **Temperature 100.6—YES, this could be indicative of an infection and children with cardiac disease are at risk for respiratory infections.**

Exercise 11-7: *Multiple-choice question*

Which of the following findings is <u>not</u> typically found in a child with pulmonary venous congestion?

A. **Resting bradycardia—YES, children with congestive heart failure secondary to pulmonary venous congestion typically experience tachycardia.**

B. Impaired weight gain—NO, children with congestive heart failure with pulmonary venous congestion tire easily during feedings and therefore have trouble gaining weight.

C. Circumoral cyanosis associated with feeding—NO, children with congestive heart failure with pulmonary venous congestion have dyspnea and cyanosis associated with feeding.

D. Adventitious breath sounds—NO, children with congestive heart failure with pulmonary venous congestion experience sounds such as crackles, wheezing, cough.

Exercise 11-8: *Multiple-choice question*

Which of the following is the primary initial goal of managing congestive heart failure?

A. Calm the child to relieve respiratory distress—NO, while it is important to comfort the child, the pathological changes associated with congestive heart failure must be managed first.

B. Administer diuretics to promote excretion of excessive fluid—NO, while it is important to relieve the body of excessive fluids, arrhythmias must be corrected first because they can be life-threatening.

C. Improve tissue perfusion—NO, while it is important to facilitate tissue perfusion, arrhythmias must be corrected first because they can be life-threatening.

D. Correct arrhythmias—**YES, arrhythmias can be life-threatening and are often the cause of the congestive heart failure.**

Exercise 11-9: *Multiple-choice question*

Which of the following medications will be given to digitalize Ellen?

A. Lanoxin—YES, lanoxin is the drug that most efficiently improves cardiac output.

B. Propanolol—NO, there are few data to support efficacy of this drug in clinical improvement of congestive heart failure.

C. Carvedilol—NO, there are few data to support efficacy of this drug in clinical improvement of congestive heart failure.

D. Captopril—NO, this medication is used to treat congestive heart failure but is not used in digitalization.

Exercise 11-10: *Matching*

Identify common side effects of digoxin and Lasix in Column A and match them with the drug related to each in Column B.

Column A	Column B
B K levels less than 3.5 mEq/L	A. Digoxin
A Sinus bradycardia	B. Lasix
B Excessive diuresis	
B Hypomagnesemia	
A Arrhythmias	

Exercise 11-11: *Fill-in*

Digoxin should be withheld and the primary care provider notified when the infant's heart rate is less than **100 bpm**.

Exercise 11-12: *Ordering*

Beginning with the highest priority (1), rank the nursing interventions that Ellen should receive to manage her congestive heart failure from 1 to 6.

___4___ Weigh all of Ellen's diapers and measure urine specific gravity. **Diuresis is promoted by use of diuretics and strict intake and output should be maintained.**

___1___ Monitor oxygen saturation via pulse oximetry. **Airway is the priority in nursing care of the child with congestive heart failure.**

___3___ Monitor the cardiac output. **Once there is an effective breathing pattern established, circulation assumes the next priority.**

___2___ Elevate the head of Ellen's bed while sleeping. **Elevating the child's head will improve the infant's breathing. Semi-Fowler's position is recommended for the older child.**

___5___ Maintain a calorie count to ensure nutrition is maintained. **Infants and children with congestive heart failure often have difficulty gaining or maintaining weight.**

___6___ Involve parents in Ellen's care. **Once Ellen's physiological needs are met, the psychosocial needs of both the infant and parents should be met.**

Exercise 11-13: *Select all that apply*

Based upon this initial examination, the clinic nurse should determine:

☒ **If the child has complained of pain in her large joints—YES, pain in the large joints is one of the classic symptoms of rheumatic fever.**

☒ **If there is the presence of a group A *Streptococcus* infection—YES, an untreated or residual *Streptococcus* infection predisposes the child to acute rheumatic fever.**

☒ **If there is an elevation in C-reactive protein—YES, this test measures inflammation and is commonly elevated in acute rheumatic fever.**

❑ If there is a decrease in hemoglobin—NO, hemoglobin levels should not be affected in acute rheumatic fever.

☒ **If there is an increase in the erythrocyte sedimentation rate—YES, this test measures inflammation and is commonly elevated in acute rheumatic fever.**

Exercise 11-14: *Multiple-choice question*

Which of the following interventions should be anticipated in the care of Marta?

A. Place Marta on bedrest until carditis is ruled out—YES, there is an increased risk for the development of carditis within the first month after diagnosis of acute rheumatic fever.

B. Medicate the child with Tylenol to manage pain—NO, the medication of choice to manage joint pain in children with acute rheumatic fever is aspirin.

C. Perform active range of motion on the child during the acute phase—NO, during the acute phase, the child's painful joints should be gently moved.

D. Assure the parents that the child is now immune from further recurrences—NO, there is a risk for recurrences throughout the life span.

Exercise 11-15: *Multiple-choice question*

Which of the following findings is not a diagnostic criterion for Kawasaki disease?

A. Pyrexia more than 5 days—NO, this is a diagnostic criterion.

B. Peeling of the palms of the hands and soles of the feet 2 weeks after onset—NO, this is a diagnostic criterion.

C. **Positive group A** *Streptococcus* **test—YES, this is not related to Kawasaki disease.**

D. Bilateral inflammation of conjunctiva—NO, this is a diagnostic criterion.

E. Strawberry tongue—NO, this is a diagnostic criterion.

Exercise 11-16: *Fill-in*

Intravenous immune globulin (IVIG) is the medication that will be administered to Marta to decrease the risk for a coronary artery aneurysm in the child with Kawasaki disease.

Exercise 11-17: *Ordering*

Prioritize the nursing interventions in terms of their importance beginning with the highest priority from 1 to 5.

___**3**___ Ask the child to void and document the results. **Once airway and circulation needs are addressed, the child should void prior to transport to the catheterization lab.**

___**5**___ Support the family members who are anxious about the procedure. **Once the child's physiological and psychosocial needs are met, the parents' needs should be addressed.**

___**1**___ Monitor for respiratory depression. **This assessment is particularly important since the child has received a sedative, which could cause respiratory depression.**

___**2**___ Assess the child's baseline cardiac status. **This measure would be done second to assess circulation. Airway and breathing assessment are the two priorities.**

___**4**___ Answer any questions the child may have before the catheterization. **Once the child's physiological needs are met, the psychosocial needs of the child and family must be addressed.**

Exercise 11-18: *Select all that apply*

Identify nursing interventions that should be implemented immediately following the cardiac catheterization procedure.

☒ **Direct pressure should be placed on the site of insertion of the catheter and guide wires—YES, this measure is done to prevent bleeding from the catheterization site.**

❑ Assess the area proximal to the incision—NO, the area distal to the site would be assessed, which would be the lower extremity.

☒ **Apply a pressure dressing over the catheter site for several hours—YES, this measure is done to prevent bleeding from the catheterization site.**

❑ Elevate the head of the bed until comfort has been achieved—NO, the child must lie flat to prevent hip flexion, which could predispose the child to bleeding.

☒ **Place the child on bed rest for approximately 6 hours following the procedure—YES, this is to prevent disruption of the clot, which could predispose the child to a hemorrhage.**

☒ **Encourage fluid intake—YES, fluids will help to flush the contrast out of the system.**

Exercise 11-19: *Multiple-choice question*

Which of the following findings is a late manifestation of hypovolemic shock?
A. Tachycardia—NO, this is an early sign in hypovolemia and indicates compensatory efforts.
B. Greater than 3-second capillary refill—NO, this is an early sign in hypovolemia and indicates compensatory efforts.
C. Pallor—NO, this is an early sign in hypovolemia and indicates compensatory efforts.
D. **Hypotension—YES, this is a late sign of hypovolemia.**

Exercise 11-20: *Multiple-choice question*

Which of the following statements should be made by Trinh's nurse to her parents regarding discharge?
A. "A fever is normal within the first 24 hours following a cardiac catheterization."—NO, this finding should be reported to the physician.
B. "The foot on the side of the catheterization may temporarily feel numb for a few days following the procedure."—NO, paresthesia is an abnormal finding and should be reported to the physician.
C. "There may be decreased circulation in the foot on the side of the catheterization."—NO, this is an abnormal finding and must be reported to the physician.
D. **"Report any increase in the bruise at the catheter site."—YES, this finding could indicate bleeding and must be reported to the physician for further evaluation.**

12

Children With Hematological Health Care Needs

Vicki A. Martin

Unfolding Case Study #12-1 ▨ Michael

Michael is a 9-month-old infant. He lives with his single mother and one older sibling of school age in government housing. Michael and his mother both are on Women, Infants, and Children (WIC) services for healthy nutrition. In previous months, he and his mother were anemic and both are being followed in the local health department for WIC services. The program monitors their dietary intake and blood levels to ensure adequate nutrition. Their services are modified as needed depending on the health assessment.

Exercise 12-1: *Fill-in*
WIC services are available to those meeting the requirements in South Carolina to ensure healthy nutrition.
- ▨ In the Search box, type in "WIC programs in SC"
- ▨ Click on the first listing labeled "Apply for WIC online "with www .benefitsapplication.com/under the listing
- ▨ What is the goal of the WIC program?

  _____
  _____.

Exercise 12-2: *Fill-in*
List four eligibility requirements in order to receive WIC services:

1. _____
2. _____
3. _____
4. _____

Exercise 12-3: *True or false*
Anemia is the most common blood disorder in infants and children.

_____ True

_____ False

Exercise 12-4: *Multiple-choice question*
Which group of children is most at risk of developing iron-deficiency anemia?
  A. School-age children participating in after-school programs
  B. Breastfed infants younger than 6 months of age
  C. Two- to 4-year-olds attending day care every day
  D. Infants and children from 6 months to 2 years of age

Exercise 12-5: *Select all that apply*
Anemia ranges from mild to severe. Clinical manifestations associated with anemia include:

  ❑ Dizziness
  ❑ Fainting
  ❑ Cardiac murmurs
  ❑ Shortness of breath
  ❑ Tachycardia
  ❑ Pale skin
  ❑ High fever
  ❑ Abdominal pain

e **eResource 12-1:** Refer to Medscape to reinforce your understanding of anemia: [Pathway: Medscape → Enter "anemia" into the search field → Select "anemia" → Review content in "overview"; be sure to review content under "etiology"]

Exercise 12-6: *Matching*
Match the hematological terms in Column A to the correct description in Column B.

Column A	Column B
A. Hematopoiesis	_____ Decreased hemoglobin and hematocrit
B. Erythropoiesis	
C. Polycythemia	_____ Cell defenders against microorganisms
D. Anemia	
E. Red blood cells	_____ Supply oxygenation to body tissue
F. White blood cells	
G. Platelets	_____ Facilitate blood coagulation
	_____ Above-average increase in red blood cells
	_____ Process forming cellular blood elements
	_____ Production of blood cells

Answers to this chapter begin on page 193.

Exercise 12-7: *Multiple-choice question*

Which foods are good dietary sources of iron and are useful in treating anemia?

    A. Cow's milk and applesauce

    B. Meat and sweet potatoes

    C. White rice and fish sticks

    D. Sweet peas and carrots

 eResource 12-2: To review normal serum blood levels, refer to:
- Epocrates Online: [Pathway: online.epocrates.com → Select "Tables" tab → Scroll down and select "Lab Reference" and review content]
- Global RPh: goo.gl/BrHnj

Unfolding Case Study #12-2 Alex

Alex is an 8-year-old boy with a history of hemophilia. He was diagnosed when he was just over 1 year old. He lives with his mother, father, and two sisters. One sister is older and the other is younger. He attends elementary school but requires factor replacement at the children's hematological outpatient clinic routinely. The family has adjusted well to his medical diagnosis but they are concerned about his health. He cannot play any type of contact sports so he has learned to be a computer savvy child.

 eResourse 12-3: To refresh your memory about hemophilia, refer to Medscape:
- Online: [Pathway: www.medscape.org → Under the tab "Reference" → Enter "Hemophilia" into the search field → Select "Hemophilia A" and review content]
- On your mobile device, you can access the same information: [Pathway: Medscape → Select "Reference" → Enter "Hemophilia" into the search field → Select "Hemophilia A" and review content]

Alex has had several hospitalizations for hemarthrosis since he was 4 years old. He requires close monitoring with all activities at home and school.

One day while at school, Alex falls down while walking back to class after recess. He sustains an abrasion and a small contusion on his left knee. The school nurse contacts his parents since the wound will not stop bleeding and the contusion increases in size. Alex is taken to the local emergency department.

Exercise 12-8: *Multiple-choice question*

When a child experiences hemarthrosis, which nursing intervention is a priority in preventing permanent joint dysfunction?

    A. Initiating active and passive range-of-motion exercises

    B. Administering aspirin to relieve pain and inflammation

    C. Applying moist, hot packs to the affected joint

    D. Elevating and immobilizing the affected joint

Answers to this chapter begin on page 193.

eResource 12-4: To learn more about hemarthrosis, again refer to
Medscape:
- Online: [Pathway: www.medscape.org → Under the tab "Reference" →
Enter "Hemarthrosis" into the search field → Select "Pediatric Factor
VII Deficiency" and review content]
- On your mobile device, you can access the same information: [Pathway:
Medscape → Select "Reference" → Enter "Hemarthrosis" into the search
field → Select "Pediatric Factor VII Deficiency" and review content]

Exercise 12-9: *Fill-in*

The most common type of hemophilia is hemophilia _____ and it is referred to as
classic hemophilia.

Exercise 12-10: *True or false*

Classic hemophilia is treated with an infusion of factor IX replacement.

_____ True

_____ False

 eResource 12-5: To learn more about this procedure, again refer to
Medscape:
- Online: [Pathway: www.medscape.org → Under the tab "Reference" →
Enter "Factor IX" into the search field → Select "Factor IX (Rx)" and
review content]
- On your mobile device, you can access the same information:
[Pathway: Medscape → Select "Reference" → Enter "Factor IX" into the
search field → Select "Factor IX (Rx)" and review content]

Exercise 12-11: *Matching*

Match the type of hemophilia in Column A to the correct description in Column B.

Column A	Column B
A. Classic or hemophilia A	_____ Factor XI deficiency
B. Christmas or hemophilia B	_____ Factor VIII deficiency
C. Hemophilia C	_____ Factor IX deficiency

Exercise 12-12: *Select all that apply*

Hemophilia ranges from mild to severe. Clinical manifestations associated with hemophilia include:

- ❑ Epistaxis
- ❑ Hematuria
- ❑ Hemarthrosis
- ❑ Bruise easily
- ❑ Prone to hemorrhaging
- ❑ Swollen, painful joints

Answers to this chapter begin on page 193.

Exercise 12-13: *Fill-in*

List information that is essential in educating the family of the hemophiliac child.

1. _____

2. _____

3. _____

4. _____

5. _____

 eResource 12-6: To reinforce your patient teaching, you show the parents a video, *Hemophilia Presentation* goo.gl/1yRh5L

Exercise 12-14: *True or false*

Hemophilia A and hemophilia B are X-linked recessive disorders more commonly expressed in males.

_____ True

_____ False

Unfolding Case Study #12-3 Valerie

Valerie is a 13-year-old African American female with sickle cell anemia (SCA). She is an only child. She resides with her mother and grandmother in a two-bedroom apartment. She has been experiencing frequent sickle cell crises since becoming an adolescent. She is off for the summer and is enjoying shopping with her friends while playing basketball. Her mother brings her to the outpatient hematology clinic for complaints of severe generalized pain after a basketball game. She is admitted to the pediatric intensive care unit (PICU) for sickle cell crisis. Her vital signs are as follows:

Temperature: 100° F

Pulse: 115 beats/minute

Respirations: 32 breaths/minute

Blood pressure: 100/70

White blood cell (WBC) count: 12,000 cells/mm³

Platelet count: 140,000 cells/mm³

Oxygen saturation: 88%

 eResource 12-7: To reinforce your understanding of sickle cell anemia, you refer to the following resources:
■ Skyscape's Outline in Clinical Medication on your mobile device: [Pathway: Outline in Clinical Medication → Enter "sickle cell anemia" → Review content]
■ Epocrates Online: [Pathway: online.epocrates.com → Under the "Diseases" tab, enter "sickle cell anemia" in the search field → Select "sickle cell" and review content]

Answers to this chapter begin on page 193.

Exercise 12-15: *Multiple-choice question*

What should you anticipate as a priority medical intervention for the child being admitted in a vaso-occlusive crisis?

     A. Intravenous (IV) antibiotics and oxygen

     B. Complete blood count (CBC) and IV fluids

     C. IV pain medications and IV fluids

     D. Transfusion of platelets

 eResource 12-8: To read more about vaso-occlusive crisis management, refer to Medscape:

    ■ Online: [Pathway: www.medscape.org → Select "Reference" → Enter "sickle cell" into the search field → Select "sickle cell anemia" → Under the "Treatment and Management" tab, review "Vaso-Occlusive Crisis Management"]

    ■ On your mobile device, you can access the same information: [Pathway: Medscape → Select "Reference" → Enter "sickle cell" into the search field → Select "sickle cell anemia" → Under the "Treatment and Management" tab, review "Vaso-Occlusive Crisis Management"]

Exercise 12-16: *True or false*

The most common cause of sickle cell crisis is related to dehydration factors.

_____ True

_____ False

Exercise 12-17: *Matching*

Match the type of sickle cell crisis in Column A to the correct description in Column B.

Column A	Column B
A. Vaso-occlusive crisis	_____ Excessive blood pooling in liver and spleen
B. Sequestration crisis	
C. Aplastic crisis	_____ Aggregation of sickled cells within a vessel
	_____ A decrease in erythropoiesis

Exercise 12-18: *Select all that apply*

Clinical manifestations associated with sickle cell anemia include:

    ❏ Delayed growth and puberty

    ❏ Painful episodes

    ❏ Dehydration

    ❏ Hand–foot syndrome

    ❏ Able to weight bear

    ❏ Cerebral vascular accident

Answers to this chapter begin on page 193.

❑ Abdominal pain

❑ Enuresis

❑ Severe anemia

e **eResource 12-9:** To review information regarding clinical manifestations of sickle cell anemia, consult Medscape:

- Online: [Pathway: www.medscape.org → Select "Reference" → Enter "sickle cell" into the search field → Select "sickle cell anemia" → Under the "Clinical Presentation" tab and review content]
- On your mobile device, you can access the same information: [Pathway: Medscape → Select "Reference" → Enter "sickle cell" into the search field → Select "sickle cell anemia" → Under the "Clinical Presentation" tab and review content]

Exercise 12-19: *Fill-in*

When one parent has sickle cell disease and the other is a carrier for the disease, there is a _____% chance each child conceived will carry the disease and a _____% chance each child conceived will have the disease.

Exercise 12-20: *Fill-in*

Education is available to the general public on sickle cell anemia and sickle cell disease to promote healthier living since it is not curable.

- In the Search box, type in www.sicklecelldiease.org
- Click on the listing labeled lifescript.com under the listing
- What are some of the life style changes to manage sickle cell disease?

_____, _____, _____,

_____, and _____.

Unfolding Case Study #12-4 ▧ Spencer

Spencer is an 8-month-old diagnosed with beta-thalassemia major (Cooley's anemia). He is of Mediterranean descent and lives with both parents. He was diagnosed at 6 months of age due to failure-to-thrive symptoms and laboratory testing with low hemoglobin (Hgb), low hematocrit (Hct), elevated bilirubin, and elevated iron level. He has been managed well with the chelation agent Desferal. He has to have periodic packed red blood cell (PRBC) transfusions to provide adequate hemoglobin for proper oxygenation of tissue.

Exercise 12-21: *Fill-in*

The two types of thalassemias are _____ thalassemia and _____ thalassemia.

Exercise 12-22: *Matching*

Match the hematological terms in Column A to the correct description in Column B.

Column A	Column B
A. Hemosiderosis	_____ Iron-containing pigment of red blood cells
B. Anisocytosis	_____ Variation in the shape of red blood cells
C. Poikilocytosis	_____ Volume of erythrocytes packed by centrifugation
D. Hemoglobin	_____ Excessive supply of iron
E. Hematocrit	_____ Variation in the size of erythrocytes

Exercise 12-23: *Select all that apply*

Clinical manifestations exhibited in the child with beta-thalassemia major include:

❏ Jaundice
❏ Bronze skin
❏ Protruding forehead
❏ Maxillary prominence
❏ Malocclusion
❏ Pointed nose
❏ Close-set eyes
❏ Pathologic fractures

e **eResource 12-10:** To learn more about beta-thalassemia major, refer to The Merck Manual/MerckMedicus Online on your mobile device: [Pathway: www.merckmedicus.com → Select "Merck Manual" → Select "Merck Manual for Healthcare Professionals" → Enter "beta-thalassemia major" into the search field (Note: If you include "major" into the search, the keywords associated with this particular diagnosis will be highlighted) → Select "beta-thalassemia major" to access and review content]

Exercise 12-24: *True or false*

Beta-thalassemia major presents itself during the first 6 months of life after Hb F is replaced by Hb A.

_____ True
_____ False

Exercise 12-25: *Multiple-choice question*

What are the potential side effects of Desferal?

A. Hypertension with rapid IV infusion.
B. Cardiac complications with rapid IV infusion.
C. Tea-colored urine and cyanosis.
D. Blotchy erythema and skin flushing.

Answers to this chapter begin on page 193.

Answers

Exercise 12-1: *Fill-in*

WIC services are available to those meeting the requirements in South Carolina to ensure healthy nutrition.

- In Search box, type in "WIC programs in SC"

- Click on the first listing labeled "Apply for WIC online" with www.benefitsapplication .com/ under the listing

- What is the goal of the WIC program? **To provide healthy, iron-fortified nutrition to women, infants, and children meeting eligibility requirements in the state of South Carolina related to income levels.**

Exercise 12-2: *Fill-in*

List four eligibility requirements in order to receive WIC services:

1. **Infants up to 1 year of age**

2. **Children up to 5 years of age**

3. **Pregnant and postpartum women**

4. **Breastfeeding mothers**

Exercise 12-3: *True or false*

Anemia is the most common blood disorder in infants and children.

   X   True

_____ False

Exercise 12-4: *Multiple-choice question*

Which group of children is most at risk of developing iron-deficiency anemia?

A. School-age children participating in after school-programs—NO, after school programs many times provide nutrition.

B. Breastfed infants younger than 6 months of age—NO, breastfed babies are usually not anemic due to the mother's dietary intake.

C. Two- to 4-year-olds attending day care every day—NO, day care centers many times provide nutritious food.

D. **Infants and children from 6 months to 2 years of age—YES, children this age have picky eating habits and are very active.**

Exercise 12-5: *Select all that apply*

Anemia ranges from mild to severe. Clinical manifestations associated with anemia include:

☒ **Dizziness**

☒ **Fainting**

☒ **Cardiac murmurs**

☒ **Shortness of breath**

☒ **Tachycardia**

☒ **Pale skin**

❏ High fever

☒ **Abdominal pain**

Exercise 12-6: *Matching*

Match the hematological terms in Column A to the correct description in Column B.

Column A	Column B	
A. Hematopoiesis	__D__	Decreased hemoglobin and hematocrit
B. Erythropoiesis		
C. Polycythemia	__F__	Cell defenders against microorganisms
D. Anemia		
E. Red blood cells	__E__	Supply oxygenation to body tissues
F. White blood cells		
G. Platelets	__G__	Facilitate blood coagulation for clotting
	__C__	Above-average increase in red blood cells
	__B__	Process forming cellular blood elements
	__A__	Production of blood cells

Exercise 12-7: *Multiple-choice question*

Which foods are good dietary sources of iron and are useful in treating anemia?

A. Cow's milk and applesauce—NO, these provide vitamins D and C.

B. Meat and sweet potatoes—YES, meat is the best source of iron.

C. White rice and fish sticks—NO, fish is good but not as high in iron as red meat.

D. Sweet peas and carrots—NO, vegetables are high in vitamins but not as high in iron as meat.

Exercise 12-8: *Multiple-choice question*

When a child experiences hemarthrosis, which nursing intervention is a priority in preventing permanent joint dysfunction?

A. Initiating active and passive range-of-motion exercises—NO, range of motion may increase the bleeding.

B. Administering aspirin to relieve pain and inflammation—NO, aspirin will decrease clotting.

C. Applying moist, hot packs to the affected joint—NO, warm packs will increase circulation and bleeding to the area.

D. Elevating and immobilizing the affected joint—YES, this along with ice will give the joint time to decrease the bleeding.

Exercise 12-9: *Fill-in*

The most common type of hemophilia is hemophilia _____**type A**_____ and it is referred to as classic hemophilia.

Exercise 12-10: *True or false*

Classic hemophilia is treated with an intravenous infusion of factor IX replacement.

_____ True

___**X**___ **False**

Exercise 12-11: *Matching*

Match the type of hemophilia in Column A to the correct description in Column B.

Column A	Column B
A. Classic or hemophilia A	__C__ Factor XI deficiency
B. Christmas or hemophilia B	__A__ Factor VIII deficiency
C. Hemophilia C	__B__ Factor IX deficiency

Exercise 12-12: *Select all that apply*

Hemophilia ranges from mild to severe. Clinical manifestations associated with hemophilia include:

☒ **Epistaxis**

☒ **Hematuria**

☒ **Hemarthrosis**

☒ **Bruise easily**

☒ **Prone to hemorrhaging**

❑ Swollen, painful joints

Exercise 12-13: *Fill-in*

List information that is essential in educating the family of the hemophiliac child.

1. <u>**Use soft-bristled toothbrushes**</u>

2. <u>**Avoid contact sports**</u>

3. <u>**Apply pressure to any bleed for 10 to 15 minutes**</u>

4. <u>**Maintain a healthy weight**</u>

5. <u>**Wear a medic alert bracelet**</u>

Exercise 12-14: *True or false*

Hemophilia A and hemophilia B are X-linked recessive disorders more commonly expressed in males.

__**X**__ True

_____ False

Exercise 12-15: *Multiple-choice question*

What should you anticipate as a priority medical intervention for the child being admitted in a vaso-occlusive crisis?

A. Intravenous (IV) antibiotics and oxygen—NO, there is no infection.

B. Complete blood count (CBC) and IV fluids—NO, a CBC is not necessary.

C. IV pain medications and IV fluids—YES, it is painful and fluids increase circulation and decrease blood viscosity.

D. Transfusion of platelets—NO, they are already clotting abnormally.

Exercise 12-16: *True or false*

The most common cause of sickle cell crisis is related to dehydration factors.

__**X**__ True

_____ False

Exercise 12-17: *Matching*

Match the type of sickle-cell crisis in Column A to the correct description in Column B.

Column A	Column B	
A. Vaso-occlusive crisis	__**B**__	Excessive blood pooling in liver and spleen
B. Sequestration crisis	__**A**__	Aggregation of sickled cells within a vessel
C. Aplastic crisis	__**C**__	A decrease in erythropoiesis

Exercise 12-18: *Select all that apply*

Clinical manifestations associated with sickle cell anemia include:

☒ **Delayed growth and puberty**

☒ **Painful episodes**

☒ **Dehydration**

☒ **Hand–foot syndrome**

❏ Able to weight bear

☒ **Cerebral vascular accident**

☒ **Abdominal pain**

☒ **Enuresis**

☒ **Severe anemia**

Exercise 12-19: *Fill-in*

When one parent has sickle cell disease and the other is a carrier for the disease, there is a __**50**__ % chance each child conceived will carry the disease and a __**50**__ % chance each child conceived will have the disease.

Exercise 12-20: *Fill-in*

Education is available to the general public on sickle cell anemia and sickle cell disease to promote healthier living since it is not curable.

▧ In the Search box, type in www.sicklecelldiease.org

▧ Click on the listing labeled lifescript.com under the listing

▧ What are some of the life style changes to manage sickle cell disease? **Eat a well-balanced diet, take a folic acid supplement, drink plenty of water, get sufficient rest, and avoid physical and emotional stress**.

Exercise 12-21: *Fill-in*

The two types of thalassemias are **alpha** thalassemia and **beta** thalassemia.

Exercise 12-22: *Matching*

Match the hematological terms in Column A to the correct description in Column B

Column A	Column B	
A. Hemosiderosis	__D__	Iron-containing pigment of red blood cells
B. Anisocytosis	__C__	Variation in the shape of red blood cells
C. Poikilocytosis	__E__	Volume of erythrocytes packed by centrifugation
D. Hemoglobin	__A__	Excessive supply of iron
E. Hematocrit	__B__	Variation in the size of erythrocytes

Exercise 12-23: *Select all that apply*
Clinical manifestations exhibited in the child with beta-thalassemia major include:

☒ **Jaundice**

☒ **Bronze skin**

☒ **Protruding forehead**

☒ **Maxillary prominence**

☒ **Malocclusion**

❑ Pointed nose

❑ Close-set eyes

☒ **Pathologic fractures**

Exercise 12-24: *True or false*
Beta-thalassemia major presents itself during the first 6 months of life after Hb F is replaced by Hb A.

_____ True

___**X**___ **False—It is replaced in the second 6 months of life.**

Exercise 12-25: *Multiple-choice question*
What are the potential side effects of Desferal?

A. Hypertension with rapid IV infusion—NO, this would be hypotension.

B. Cardiac complications with rapid IV infusion—NO, this is not a side effect.

C. Tea-colored urine and cyanosis—NO, cyanosis should not happen.

D. Blotchy erythema and skin flushing—YES, these are potential side effects.

13

Nursing Care of Children With Musculoskeletal Health Care Needs

Susan Parnell Scholtz

Unfolding Case Study #13-1 ▬ Raiza and Alyssa

The newborn nursery is a great place to work and you never mind being "pulled" there from the orthopedic unit when they are in need of another nurse. Because the charge nurse knows your varied nursing background, she assigns you to two newborns that have orthopedic concerns. This is a great opportunity for you to assess younger patients than you normally do on the orthopedic unit and you get to interact with their parents.

 eResource 13-1: To review your skills, view the following videos:
- *Physical Exam—Newborn Normal* goo.gl/OqENLQ
- *Head to Toe Examination of the Neonate* goo.gl/UFwQlY
- *Newborn Assessment and Exam Just After Birth by Nurse* goo.gl/cEA3Bo

The first newborn you assess is Raiza. Raiza is a newborn who was diagnosed with talipes equinovarus immediately after birth. In order to correct this structural defect, treatment must begin immediately.

Exercise 13-1: *Multiple-choice question*

You prepare Raiza's parents for the typical treatment of talipes equinovarus and gather patient education to teach the parents about:

- A. Serial casting
- B. Surgical correction of the disorder
- C. Simple exercises
- D. Application of a brace

eResource 13-2: To reinforce your understanding of this diagnosis and the treatment, refer to Epocrates Online: [Pathway: online.epocrates.com → Under the "Diseases" tab, enter "talipes equinovarus" in the search field → Select "talipes equinovarus" and review content]

Exercise 13-2: *Select all that apply*

Raiza has plaster casts applied to both legs. Which of the following instructions should be given to the parent for cast care in the first 24 to 48 hours postprocedure?

❑ Use only the palms to reposition the cast until dry.

❑ Assess the circulation of the toes every 4 hours during the first 24 hours.

❑ Petal the edges of the cast if they are ragged or rough.

❑ Notify the physician if there is a fever.

❑ Normal color should return in 3 seconds when the nail bed is blanched.

 eResource 13-3: To supplement your patient teaching, you show Raiza's parents the following video, *Orthopedic Clubfoot Care at Phoenix Children's Hospital*: goo.gl/C9uO2W

Exercise 13-3: *Multiple-choice question*

Which of the following nursing diagnoses would not be appropriate for the infant who has been casted for a clubfoot deformity?

A. Mobility: Physically impaired related to restricted movement secondary to casted legs.

B. Skin integrity: Risk for impairment due to pressure points or rough edges from the leg casts.

C. Parenting: Risk for alteration in parenting related to the birth of a child with a structural defect.

D. Pain: Acute pain related to casting of both lower extremities.

The second newborn you assess is Alyssa. She has a positive Ortolani sign as well as a positive Barlow sign. Based on her initial assessment, the nurse practitioner believes Alyssa has congenital hip dislocation.

 eResource 13-4: To learn more about Alyssa's condition, refer to Medscape:

■ Online: [Pathway: www.medscape.org → Select "Reference" → Enter "congenital hip dislocation" into the search field → Select "Developmental Dysplasia of the Hip" → Review content]

■ On your mobile device, you can access the same information: [Pathway: Medscape → Select "Reference" → Enter "congenital hip dislocation" into the search field → Select "Developmental Dysplasia of the Hip" → Review content]

Exercise 13-4: *Multiple-choice question*

In addition to the positive Ortolani and Barlow signs, congenital hip dislocation in the infant may be recognized during physical assessment as:

A. Shortening of the limb on the unaffected side

B. Limited adduction of the affected hip

C. Restricted abduction of the affected hip

D. Equalized skin folds of the thighs on abduction of the hips

Alyssa's diagnosis of congenital hip dislocation has been confirmed by an x-ray.

Exercise 13-5: *Multiple-choice question*

Based on an understanding of the pathology of congenital hip dislocation, the nurse is aware that treatment for a newborn may consist of which of the following?

A. Pavlik harness

B. Bryant's traction

C. Hip spica cast

D. Closed reduction

Exercise 13-6: *Multiple-choice question*

Alyssa is placed in Bryant's traction to correct congenital hip dislocation. Which of the following measures should be done for this child?

A. Cleanse the pins every shift to prevent infection.

B. Keep the child's buttocks slightly elevated off the bed.

C. Place the weights on the bed to prevent interference.

D. Remove the weights frequently to allow for ambulation.

 eResource 13-5: To prepare to care for Alyssa and to provide teaching to Alyssa's parents, refer to MerckMedicus Online using your mobile device: [Pathway: www.merckmedicus.com → Select "Merck Manual" → Select "Merck Manual for Healthcare Professionals" → Enter "Bryant Traction" into the search field → Select "Modified Bryant's traction after exstrophy repair" → Review content]

In order to place Alyssa into the correct traction, you accompany her and her parents to the orthopedic unit. The transfer is complete and you answer questions for the parents. One of the questions they have is how common is this in newborns and you explain that it is fairly common as well as other orthopedic conditions. The discussion is a good review for you!

Exercise 13-7: *Fill-in*

Identify the orthopedic disorder commonly diagnosed in children.

_____ is in-toeing and internal rotation, which originates from the femoral head.

_____ is in-toeing that occurs from internal rotation that occurs at the tibia.

_____ causes pain below the knee and is due to thickening of the tibia tuberosity.

_____ is an infection of the long ends of the bone.

_____ is a painful infection of the hip characterized by pyrexia and pain.

Alyssa's parents are both college educated and ask how the congenital hip dislocation was detected. You explain to them about various orthopedic examination techniques that are used to determine if a person has an orthopedic problem.

Exercise 13-8: *Matching*

Select the term in Column A that matches the definition of a movement that is used during physical assessment of the musculoskeletal system in Column B.

Column A	Column B
A. Galeazzi test	_____ While an infant is supine, flex the infant's knees so the ankles touch the buttocks. Determine if knees are level in this position.
B. Ortolani's test	
C. Internal rotation	_____ Act of straightening an extremity at a joint.
D. Flexion	_____ Movement of the extremity away from the midline of the body.
E. Adduction	
F. Supinate	_____ Turn or rotate the arm so that the palm of the hand faces upward.
G. Abduction	
H. Extension	_____ Movement of the extremity toward the midline of the body.
I. Barlow's sign	_____ Turn or rotate the arm so that the palm of the hand points downward.
J. Pronate	
	_____ Act of bending an extremity at a joint.
	_____ While lying on back, arms behind head, flex the knee and bring the leg inward toward other leg.
	_____ Place anterior pressure on infant's greater trochanter while the hips and knees are flexed, and gently rotate.
	_____ Adduct the infant's hip while placing gentle pressure on the knees to determine instability of the hip.

Unfolding Case Study #13-2 ▨ Skylar

Thirteen-year-old Skylar was referred to the orthopedic unit for treatment of scoliosis. The diagnosis was made following routine screening by her school nurse.

Exercise 13-9: *Multiple-choice question*

Skylar's mother asks the nurse, "What is the cause of idiopathic scoliosis? Is it something we could have detected earlier?" Which of the following statements is most accurate?

    A. "This disorder is typically detected prenatally by means of an ultrasound."

    B. "This order is genetic and cannot be prevented."

Answers to this chapter begin on page 207.

C. "The cause is unknown but symptoms do not typically present until pre-pubescence."

D. "This disorder is a result of hormonal changes in the adolescent girl."

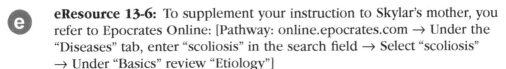 **eResource 13-6:** To supplement your instruction to Skylar's mother, you refer to Epocrates Online: [Pathway: online.epocrates.com → Under the "Diseases" tab, enter "scoliosis" in the search field → Select "scoliosis" → Under "Basics" review "Etiology"]

You begin your focused assessment of Skylar and look specifically for signs of scoliosis.

Exercise 13-10: *Select all that apply*
Which of the following are signs of idiopathic scoliosis?
- ❑ Skylar's hem on her skirt seems uneven
- ❑ Asymmetry when performing the Adam's forward bend test
- ❑ Pain when asked to bend at the waist
- ❑ In-toeing that originates from the acetabulum
- ❑ One scapula appears to be higher than the others

Skylar's curve was measured at 40 degrees. The primary care provider decides to begin her treatment with application of a Boston brace.

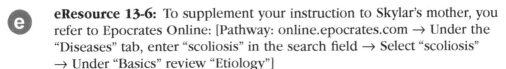 **eResource 13-7:** You show Skylar and her mother the following video, *Scoliosis—Curvature of the Spine*, to reinforce your patient teaching: goo.gl/4FLbLc

Exercise 13-11: *Multiple-choice question*
Which of the following statements made by Skylar indicates that further instruction is needed?
A. "I can remove my brace for 1 hour a day to bathe."
B. "The goal of my brace is to prevent an increase in spinal curvature."
C. "Since my curve is 40 degrees, there is a good chance I will need surgery."
D. "I may not be able to run track this spring because of my brace."

Skylar's curvature does not respond to the bracing and it appears that the curve has increased. She undergoes surgery and has just returned to the orthopedic unit.

Exercise 13-12: *Ordering*
Prioritize Skylar's postoperative care from 1 to 5 beginning with the highest priority.
_____ Administer pain medication around the clock especially during the first 48 hours postoperatively.
_____ Apply pulse oximeter
_____ Monitor the child's circulation and neurovascular status
_____ Encourage the child to relax using nonpharmacologic pain management techniques
_____ Logroll Skylar every 2 hours

Answers to this chapter begin on page 207.

Exercise 13-13: *Multiple-choice question*

Skylar is receiving morphine sulfate to control her postoperative pain. Which of the following findings is a side effect of morphine?

    A. Pruritis

    B. Respiratory depression

    C. Severe hypotension

    D. Bradycardia

 eResource 13-8: To review your understanding of this medication, consult the following resources on your mobile device:

    ■ Skyscape's RxDrugs: [Pathway: Skyscape → Select "RxDrugs" → Enter "Morphine" into the search field → Select "Morphine (Injectable)" and review content, focusing on warnings and side effects]

    ■ Epocrates: [Pathway: Epocrates → Enter "Morphine" into the search field → select "Morphine Sulfate" and review content, focusing on warnings and side effects]

Skylar does well postoperatively and her recovery is uneventful. You discuss discharge instructions with Skylar and her mother.

Exercise 13-14: *Multiple-choice question*

Which of the following activities are permitted upon discharge?

    A. Gym class

    B. Walking

    C. Lifting 15 pounds

    D. Twisting at the waist

Unfolding Case Study #13-3   Liam

Liam is a 5-year-old boy who presented in the emergency department with a chief complaint of pain and swelling of his patella. His mother reports that he has been experiencing low-grade fevers in the morning and seems to be "stiff" when he arises in the morning. His kindergarten teacher reports that Liam sits on the bench at the playground and no longer plays at recess. The tentative diagnosis for Liam is juvenile rheumatoid arthritis and he is being admitted to have definitive tests done.

 eResource 13-9: To review your understanding of juvenile rheumatoid arthritis, refer to Medscape:

    ■ Online: [Pathway: www.medscape.org → Select "Reference" → Enter "juvenile arthritis" into the search field → Select "juvenile rheumatoid arthritis" → Under the "Treatment and Management" tab, review content]

    ■ On your mobile device, you can access the same information: [Pathway: Medscape → Select "Reference" → Enter "juvenile arthritis" into the search field → Select "juvenile rheumatoid arthritis" → Under the "Treatment and Management" tab, review content]

Answers to this chapter begin on page 207.

Exercise 13-15: *Select all that apply*
Liam's nurse is reviewing his diagnostic findings from his blood work. Which of the following findings would be expected in a child with juvenile rheumatoid arthritis?

❑ Elevated sedimentation rate
❑ Positive antinuclear antibody test (ANA)
❑ C-reactive protein greater than 10 mg/L
❑ Positive rheumatoid factor test
❑ Low vitamin D levels
❑ Low hemoglobin levels

 eResource 13-10: To reinforce your understanding of the diagnostic results, refer to Epocrates Online: [Pathway: online.epocrates.com → Under the "Diseases" tab, enter "Juvenile Rheumatoid Arthritis" in the search field → Select "Juvenile Rheumatoid Arthritis" → Under "Diagnosis" select "Tests" and review content]

Exercise 13-16: *Multiple-choice question*
Which of the following medications is a tumor necrosis factor blocker that is used to treat rheumatoid arthritis?

A. Orencia
B. Trexall
C. Humira
D. Prednisolone

Liam is started on treatment. His parents and teacher are asked to keep a log of how he participates and if and when he complains of discomfort and in what joint. Juvenile rheumatoid arthritis is a chronic condition that will need close follow-up.

Your nursing supervisor asks you to go down to the emergency department to take care of an orthopedic case since it is so busy in the emergency department and the wait time is approaching 1 hour.

Unfolding Case Study #13-4 ▒ Casey

Fourteen-year-old Casey is admitted to the emergency department with a fractured wrist. You assist with a fiberglass cast application to her wrist done by the physician assistant. Casey will be able to be discharged. You want to make both Casey and her parents aware of the importance of neurovascular assessment. You would like the parents to be aware of abnormal findings related to the casted extremity.

Exercise 13-17: *Multiple-choice question*
Which of the following findings should be reported to the primary care provider immediately?

A. An increase in pain out of proportion to the injury and diminished pulses
B. Itchiness under the cast

Answers to this chapter begin on page 207.

    C. Rapid capillary filling of the nail beds

    D. Irritation around the cast edges

Exercise 13-18: *Multiple-choice question*

When teaching Casey home management of her cast, you should include which of the following instructions?

    A. Cleanse the cast daily with warm soapy water and a soft brush

    B. Gently knock on the cast at the injury site to assess for pain

    C. Use a tongue depressor to scratch under the cast

    D. Notify the physician if she feels any "hot spots" under the cast

 eResource 13-11: To reinforce your patient teaching, you provide the following video instructions, *How to Care for Your Child's Cast*: goo.gl/iAmcvY

Casey and her parents seem to understand when and when not to call the primary care provider. They are also provided with the emergency department's telephone number in case they have any questions. Your 12-hour shift is over and it has been an interesting one that has taken you to three different units. You know that one of the joys of being a nurse is that the variety of situations it places you in leaves no time to become bored!

Answers

Exercise 13-1: *Multiple-choice question*

You prepare Raiza's parents for the typical treatment of talipes equinovarus and gather patient education to teach the parents about:

A. **Serial casting—YES, a series of casts must be applied immediately after birth since ossification occurs and the deformity could become permanent.**
B. Surgical correction of the disorder—NO, surgery is only considered in extreme cases of clubfoot.
C. Simple exercises—NO, exercise alone does not correct talipes equinovarus.
D. Application of a brace—NO, application of the Denis Browne splint, which is attached to reverse laced shoes, is not the treatment used in the newborn.

Exercise 13-2: *Select all that apply*

Riaza has plaster casts applied to both legs. Which of the following instructions should be given to the parent for cast care in the first 24 to 48 hours postprocedure?

☒ **Use only the palms to reposition the cast until dry—YES, there is a chance for indentation of the cast when fingertips are used, which could cause pressure on the skin and disrupt skin integrity.**
☐ Assess the circulation of the toes every 4 hours during the first 24 hours—NO, during the first 2 hours postcast, the circulation should be check every 30 minutes and then every 2 hours for the first 24 hours.
☒ **Petal the edges of the cast if they are ragged or rough—YES, moleskin can be used to petal rough edges of the cast in order to maintain skin integrity.**
☒ **Notify the physician if there is a fever—YES, if the fever is sudden and unrelated to a respiratory infection, or so on, it should be reported.**
☒ **Normal color should return in 3 seconds when the nail bed is blanched—YES, this return to normal color indicates normal capillary refill.**

Exercise 13-3: *Multiple-choice question*

Which of the following nursing diagnoses would not be appropriate for the infant who has been casted for a clubfoot deformity?

A. Mobility: Physically impaired related to restricted movement secondary to casted legs—NO, this is an appropriate nursing diagnosis for the child who has been immobilized by a plaster cast.
B. Skin integrity: Risk for impairment due to pressure points or rough edges from the leg casts—NO, this is an appropriate nursing diagnosis since pressure spots or rough edges could cause a break in the skin integrity.

C. Parenting: Risk for alteration in parenting related to the birth of a child with a structural defect—NO, this is an appropriate nursing diagnosis since the parent must grieve the loss of the fantasized infant and attach to the child with a leg deformity.

D. **Pain: Acute pain related to casting of both lower extremities—YES, this is an inappropriate nursing diagnosis because pain is not a normal finding in the child who has been casted for talipes equinovarus. It is a finding that should be reported to the primary care provider.**

Exercise 13-4: *Multiple-choice question*

In addition to the positive Ortolani and Barlow signs, congenital hip dislocation, in the infant may be recognized during physical assessment as:

A. Shortening of the limb on the unaffected side—NO, the limb on the affected side will appear shorter because it is not within the femoral head.

B. Limited adduction of the affected hip—NO, adduction is unaffected.

C. **Restricted abduction of the affected hip—YES, there is limited abduction of the extremities on the same side as the affected hip.**

D. Equalized skin folds of the thighs on abduction of the hips—NO, there will be asymmetry of the gluteal folds.

Exercise 13-5: *Multiple-choice question*

Based on an understanding of the pathology of congenital hip dislocation, the nurse is aware that treatment for a newborn may consist of which of the following?

A. **Pavlik harness—YES, a Pavlik harness is a flexion abductor used to stabilize the hip.**

B. Bryant's traction—NO, typically Bryant's traction is used after 6 months when the soft tissues have shortened. This treatment may be done prior to surgery.

C. Hip spica cast—NO, a hip spica cast is typically applied after surgery and is not the first choice of treatment for congenital hip dislocation.

D. Closed reduction—NO, this is not the first method of treatment for a newborn diagnosed with congenital hip dislocation. Double diapering or application of a Pavlik harness is the first intervention.

Exercise 13-6: *Multiple-choice question*

Alyssa is placed in Bryant's traction to correct congenital hip dislocation. Which of the following measures should be done for this child?

A. Cleanse the pins every shift to prevent infection—NO, Bryant's traction is a form of skin traction and there are no pins inserted.

B. **Keep the child's buttocks slightly elevated off the bed—YES, this provides counter-traction.**

C. Place the weights on the bed to prevent interference—NO, weights must be free swinging to maintain a constant pull from the weights.

D. Remove the weights frequently to allow for ambulation—NO, removal of the weights are done as ordered but not frequently. It is important not to lose the correction that has been achieved.

Exercise 13-7: *Fill-in*

Identify the orthopedic disorder commonly diagnosed in children.

Femoral anteversion is in-toeing and internal rotation, which originates from the femoral head.

Tibial torsion is in-toeing that occurs from internal rotation that occurs at the tibia.

Oshgood Schlatter causes pain below the knee and is due to thickening of the tibia tuberosity.

Osteomyelitis is an infection of the long ends of the bone.

Septic hip is a painful infection of the hip characterized by pyrexia and pain.

Exercise 13-8: *Matching*

Select the term in Column A that matches the definition of a movement that is used during physical assessment of the musculoskeletal system in Column B.

Column A	**Column B**
A. Galeazzi test	__A__ While an infant is supine, flex the infant's knees so the ankles touch the buttocks. Determine if knees are level in this position.
B. Ortolani's test	
C. Internal rotation	
D. Flexion	
E. Adduction	__H__ Act of straightening an extremity at a joint.
F. Supinate	__E__ Movement of the extremity away from the midline of the body.
G. Abduction	
H. Extension	__F__ Turn or rotate the arm so that the palm of the hand faces upward.
I. Barlow's sign	
J. Pronate	__G__ Movement of the extremity toward the midline of the body.
	__J__ Turn or rotate the arm so that the palm of the hand points downward.
	__D__ Act of bending an extremity at a joint.
	__C__ While lying on back, arms behind head, flex the knee and bring the leg inward toward other leg.
	__B__ Place anterior pressure on infant's greater trochanter while the hips and knees are flexed, and gently rotate.
	__I__ Adduct the infant's hip while placing gentle pressure on the knees to determine instability of the hip.

Exercise 13-9: *Multiple-choice question*

Skylar's mother asks the nurse, "What is the cause of idiopathic scoliosis? Is it something we could have detected earlier?" Which of the following statements is most accurate?

A. "This disorder is typically detected prenatally by means of an ultrasound."—NO, although programmed for this disorder at the time of conception, it typically does not present until the pre-pubertal period.

B. "This order is genetic and cannot be prevented."—NO, the cause is unknown.

C. "The cause is unknown but symptoms do not typically present until pre-pubescence."—YES, there is no known cause for idiopathic scoliosis and changes are not prominent until secondary sex characteristics appear such as widening of the hips.

D. "This disorder is a result of hormonal changes in the adolescent girl."—NO, the cause is unknown and changes do occur during pre-pubescence but is not related to hormones.

Exercise 13-10: *Select all that apply*

Which of the following are signs of idiopathic scoliosis?

☒ **Skylar's hem on her skirt seems uneven—YES, uneven hip height is a sign of scoliosis.**

☒ **Asymmetry when performing the Adam's forward bend test—YES, this is a simple screening test that identifies asymmetry of the trunk.**

❑ Pain when asked to bend at the waist—NO, there is no pain associated with scoliosis.

❑ In-toeing that originates from the acetabulum—NO, this symptom is associated with femoral anteversion.

☒ **One scapula appears to be higher than the others—YES, an uneven scapula is a sign of scoliosis.**

Exercise 13-11: *Multiple-choice question*

Which of the following statements made by Skylar indicates that further instruction is needed?

A. "I can remove my brace for 1 hour a day to bathe."—YES, any corrective device can be removed 1 hour for bathing.

B. "The goal of my brace is to prevent an increase in spinal curvature."—NO, this statement is correct. The goal is to maintain existing curvature and not allow it to progress.

C. "Since my curve is 40 degrees, there is a good chance I will need surgery."—NO, this statement is correct because curves 40 or greater typically need surgery. Since the curse is 40 degrees, they may be giving the brace a trial.

D. "I may not be able to run track this spring because of my brace."—NO, this statement is correct because the brace cannot come off during regular activities.

Exercise 13-12: *Ordering*

Prioritize Skylar's postoperative care from 1 to 5 beginning with the highest priority.

___3___ Administer pain medication around the clock especially during the first 48 hours postoperatively. **Pain management assumes priority once airway, breathing, and circulatory status are satisfactory.**

___1___ Apply pulse oximeter. **Airway is the priority postoperatively. If the oxygen saturation is decreased, oxygen must be applied.**

___2___ Monitor the child's circulation and neurovascular status. **Once airway and breathing are adequate, circulation must be assessed.**

___5___ Encourage the child to relax using nonpharmacologic pain management techniques. **Complementary therapies are important to institute once the physical needs of the child have been met.**

___4___ Logroll the child every 2 hours. **Repositioning the child is important to prevent pooling of respiratory secretions. Ideally, it is done after pain management has been instituted.**

Exercise 13-13: *Multiple-choice question*

Skylar is receiving morphine sulfate to control her postoperative pain. Which of the following findings is a side effect of morphine?

A. Pruritis—YES, this is a common reported side effect of morphine.

B. Respiratory depression—NO, this is an adverse reaction to morphine.

C. Severe hypotension—NO, this is an adverse reaction to morphine.

D. Bradycardia—NO, this is an adverse reaction to morphine.

Exercise 13-14: *Multiple-choice question*

Which of the following activities are permitted upon discharge?

A. Gym class—NO, bending or twisting at the waist and strenuous activities are not permitted.

B. Walking—YES, walking including climbing stairs is permitted.

C. Lifting 15 pounds—NO, lifting cannot exceed 10 pounds.

D. Twisting at the waist—NO, bending or twisting at the waist and strenuous activities are not permitted.

Exercise 13-15: *Select all that apply*

Liam's nurse is reviewing his diagnostic findings from his blood work. Which of the following findings would be expected in a child with juvenile rheumatoid arthritis?

☒ **Elevated sedimentation rate—YES, increased sedimentation indicates there is inflammation in the body but is not specific to juvenile rheumatoid arthritis.**

☒ **Positive antinuclear antibody test (ANA)—YES, this test screens for autoimmune diseases. Juvenile rheumatoid arthritis is believed to be an autoimmune disease.**

☒ **C-reactive protein greater than 10 mg/L—YES, this elevation indicates inflammation.**

☒ **Positive rheumatoid factor test—YES, this test indicates juvenile rheumatoid arthritis.**

☐ Low vitamin D levels—NO, low vitamin D levels can lead to problems with bone density but has no relationship to juvenile rheumatoid arthritis.

☒ **Low hemoglobin levels—YES, low hemoglobin is often found in children with juvenile rheumatoid arthritis.**

Exercise 13-16: *Multiple-choice question*

Which of the following medications is a tumor necrosis factor blocker that is used to treat rheumatoid arthritis?

A. Orencia—NO, Orencia is an immune suppressant used in autoimmune disorders.

B. Trexall—NO, Trexall is a disease-modifying antirheumatic drug.

C. Humira—YES, Humira reduces pain and morning stiffness.

D. Prednisolone—NO, prednisolone is a corticosteroid used to decrease inflammation.

Exercise 13-17: *Multiple-choice question*

Which of the following findings should be reported to the primary care provider immediately?

A. An increase in pain out of proportion to the injury and diminished pulses— YES, these findings in addition to paresthesias could indicate compartment syndrome.

B. Itchiness under the cast—NO, this is a common occurrence due to increased perspiration and warmth. It is bothersome to the child but is not an emergency.

C. Rapid capillary filling of the nail beds—NO, this is a normal finding when circulation is adequate.

D. Irritation around the cast edges—NO, this finding typically occurs with plaster casts and can be prevented by petaling with moleskin but is not an emergency.

Exercise 13-18: *Multiple-choice question*

When teaching Casey home management of her cast, you should include which of the following instructions?

A. Cleanse the cast daily with warm soapy water and a soft brush—NO, the cast should be protected from water and soiling.

B. Gently knock on the cast at the injury site to assess for pain—NO, this is not a good indicator of pain.

C. Use a tongue depressor to scratch under the cast—NO, inserting any object under the cast to scratch will impair skin integrity.

D. Notify the physician if she feels any "hot spots" under the cast—YES, "hot spots" under a cast could signify infection.

14

Nursing Care of Children With Gastrointestinal Health Care Needs

Susan Parnell Scholtz

Unfolding Case Study #14-1 ▪ Charlie

Charlie is a 15-month-old toddler who is admitted to the pediatric unit with a diagnosis of gastroenteritis. According to his mother, he had approximately eight loose stools and has "not been able to tolerate any fluids or solids." Auscultation of the abdomen reveals the presence of bowel sounds in all four quadrants that occur every 5 seconds, as well as the presence of loud stomach growling.

Exercise 14-1: *Multiple-choice question*
Based on this initial assessment, you document the findings as:

    A. Normoactive bowel sounds present

    B. Hypoactive bowel sounds present

    C. Hyperactive bowel sounds with borborygmi

    D. Slight decrease in bowel sounds noted

(e)   **eResource 14-1:** To learn more about clinical presentation of children with gastroenteritis, refer to Epocrates Online: [Pathway: online.epocrates .com → Under the "Diseases" tab, enter "gastroenteritis" in the search field → Select "Viral gastroenteritis in children" → Review "Highlights," "Basics," and "Diagnosis"]

After Charlie is admitted to the pediatric unit, you weigh him and he is 23 pounds; however, his weight prior to the gastroenteritis was 24 pounds, 5 ounces.

Exercise 14-2: *Select all that apply*
To further assess for signs of moderate dehydration, which would you include?

    ❑ Parched mucous membranes

    ❑ No tears

    ❑ Tachycardia

    ❑ Capillary refill in less than 2 seconds

❑ Urine output of 1.0 to 2.0 mL urine/kg/hr

❑ Poor skin recoil/turgor with 2 seconds return after pinching

 eResource 14-2: To check your understanding of the clinical presentation of dehydration, consult Medscape:

■ Online: [Pathway: www.medscape.org → Select "Reference" → Enter "dehydration" into the search field → Select "dehydration" → Review content under "Overview" and "Clinical Presentation"]

■ On your mobile device, you can access the same information: [Pathway: Medscape → Select "Reference" → Enter "dehydration" into the search field → Select "dehydration" → Review content under "Overview" and "Clinical Presentation"]

As the primary nurse for Charlie, you call the primary care provider for orders and receive and order for an IV and isolation. Charlie is admitted to the appropriate single-patient room.

Exercise 14-3: *Multiple-choice question*

Until a causative organism has been identified, you should institute _____ precautions.

    A. Universal

    B. Droplet

    C. Contact

    D. Airborne

After getting Charlie settled in his room, you finish the discharge teaching for a school-age child, Martin, who was admitted yesterday for rotavirus.

Exercise 14-4: *Multiple-choice question*

When planning to complete discharge instructions for the child who is being discharged with a diagnosis of gastroenteritis related to rotavirus and dehydration, which of the following statements, if made by the parent, would indicate that further teaching is needed?

    A. "I will continue to only give my child glucose water until I am sure the diarrhea has stopped."

    B. "I now realize the importance of the rotavirus vaccine, which may have prevented this illness."

    C. "I will notify my pediatrician if his urine output is less than 20 mL per hour."

    D. "I will change his diapers at least every 2 hours to minimize skin irritation."

You reinforce Martin's discharge instructions with his parents and refer him to the pediatrician for a follow-up visit. They understand the appropriate diet as well as the manifestations of a repeat infection. Currently Charlie is resting comfortably as you await the stool cultures that will identify the causative agent.

Answers to this chapter begin on page 221.

Unfolding Case Study #14-2 ▨ Sadie

Sadie was diagnosed at birth with a unilateral, complete cleft lip and palate. Although the family was made aware of the defect following a three-dimensional in-utero ultrasound, the mother is having difficulty comprehending the care of the child with a cleft lip. Sadie has been transferred from the newborn nursery to the pediatric unit so you can assist the parents in understanding the care needed for Sadie until her reparative surgery can be completed.

 eResource 14-3: To reinforce your understanding of clinical management of a child with this diagnosis, refer to Epocrates Online: [Pathway: online.epocrates.com → Under the "Diseases" tab, enter "cleft lip" in the search field → Select "cleft lip and palate" and read content]

Exercise 14-5: *Multiple-choice question*
Which of the following statements, made by the mother immediately after birth, indicates the need for further assessment?
    A. "Although I knew my child would be born with cleft lip, I really didn't know what to expect."
    B. "I think it would be helpful to talk with another mother whose child was born with cleft lip."
    C. "I can't help but wonder if it was something I did during my pregnancy that caused this to happen."
    D. "I am so glad that my sister and her family live nearby."

 eResource 14-4: To supplement your teaching of the parents, you show them a video, *Cleft Lip and Palate*, an animation that depicts the surgical repair and expected outcome: goo.gl/nW5fNM

You discuss with the mother the care that you are providing to Sadie, who is otherwise a healthy newborn. The mother seems to be reluctant to participate.

Exercise 14-6: *Multiple-choice question*
Which of the following interventions should you make to assist the mother with Sadie's feedings?
    A. Encourage the mother to bottle feed since babies born with cleft lip often experience feeding problems.
    B. Hold the infant in a supine position to facilitate swallowing.
    C. Burp the baby after every 15 to 30 mL of formula.
    D. Position the child in a prone position immediately after feeding.

Once Sadie's parents are comfortable caring for her and providing her with safe feedings that reduce the chance of aspiration, she is discharged. Her cleft lip repair surgery is scheduled for 1 month later, and you tell her mother that you will make sure you are on the schedule since her mother and you have built a trusting relationship. When Sadie is readmitted at a month old, you are surprised at how

Answers to this chapter begin on page 221.

big she has become. She is a happy and alert infant. You proceed to complete the preoperative instructions.

Exercise 14-7: *Ordering*

Sadie has her cleft lip repaired and has just returned from the operating room. Prioritize her care immediately postoperatively by placing the numbers 1 to 6 next to the task.

_____ Apply a cool mist for the first 24 hours

_____ Gently suction the oropharynx and nasopharynx avoiding the suture lines

_____ Apply elbow immobilizers that are removed every 2 hours

_____ Medicate for pain with analgesics as ordered

_____ Cleanse the suture line with normal saline

_____ Encourage the parents to hold and soothe the child

 eResource 14-5: To review pre- and postoperative care for Sadie, refer to Medscape:

- Online: [Pathway: www.medscape.org → Select "Procedures" → Enter "cleft palate" into the search field → Select "Reconstructive Surgery for Cleft Palate" and review content, focusing on "Treatment and Management"]
- On your mobile device, you can access the same information: [Pathway: Medscape → Select "Procedures" → Enter "cleft palate" into the search field → Select "Reconstructive Surgery for Cleft Palate" and review content, focusing on "Treatment and Management"]

Sadie recovers well and her mother stays in her room the entire time and assists with her care.

Exercise 14-8: *Multiple-choice question*

Based upon an understanding of common complications associated with cleft lip and palate, you make several referrals for evaluations. Which of the following services is not typically needed in a child with cleft lip and palate?

    A. Speech therapist

    B. Ear, nose, and throat specialist

    C. Dentist

    D. Neurologist

Sadie is discharged home and is scheduled for her cleft palate repair in 2 months. Sadie's mother is distressed at the thought of another surgery but verbalizes to you that she is happy that the lip repair will help her to cope better with Sadie's appearance.

Unfolding Case Study #14-3   Frank

After a 3-day weekend off, you return to work and are given report on a new admission, Frank. Frank, an 11-week-old boy, is admitted to the pediatric unit with a diagnosis of "rule out pyloric stenosis."

Answers to this chapter begin on page 221.

Exercise 14-9: *Multiple-choice question*

As the admitting nurse beginning the interview, which question will you ask?

    A. "Can you describe to me a typical feeding routine, specifically, what occurs after he finishes his bottle?"

    B. "Describe the typical color of his stool and any changes you may have noticed."

    C. "Have you noticed that your child has bouts of constipation?"

    D. "Do you think your child is experiencing abdominal pain?"

e   **eResource 14-6:** To reinforce your understanding of pyloric stenosis, refer to MerckMedicus Online on your mobile device: [Pathway: www .merckmedicus.com → Select "Merck Manual" → Select "Merck Manual for Healthcare Professionals" → Enter "pyloric stenosis" into the search field → Select the results in "Merck Manual Pro" → Select "Hypertrophic Pyloric Stenosis" to access and review content]

A diagnosis of pyloric stenosis is made and Frank is scheduled to have a pyloromyotomy performed.

Exercise 14-10: *Multiple-choice question*

Which of the following orders would be anticipated in the immediate preoperative care of the child with a diagnosis of pyloric stenosis?

    A. Frequent burping with feedings

    B. Give 50 mL of glucose water via nasogastric tube

    C. Elevate the head of the bed during feedings

    D. Keep child nothing by mouth (NPO)

e   **eResource 14-7:** To learn more about this procedure, view this video tutorial, *Laparoscopic Pyloromyotomy*: goo.gl/n0C3nB

Frank has the surgery and is admitted back to the pediatric unit after spending several hours in the postanesthesia recovery unit (PACU). Frank is extremely cranky after the surgery and the first night hardly sleeps at all. The first postoperative day is much better and he is using his pacifier and fluids by mouth are started gradually. By the third postoperative day, Frank is tolerating solid food and is being prepared for discharge the following day.

Exercise 14-11: *Select all that apply*

Which of the following instructions regarding Frank's care is appropriate?

    ❏ Tub baths should be done to keep the incision clean

    ❏ Burp the child after every 30 to 60 mL

    ❏ Discontinue breastfeeding until the pediatrician recommends

    ❏ Notify the physician if the child's temperature is greater than 101.4° F

    ❏ Place child in an upright position for 30 minutes following the feeding

Frank's mother is instructed to use Tylenol if Frank shows signs of discomfort.

Answers to this chapter begin on page 221.

eResource 14-8: In addition to medication instructions, Frank's mother is shown the following video, *Pyloromyotomy (Pyloric Stenosis Repair) Discharge Instructions*: goo.gl/VkCt4X

Exercise 14-12: *Calculation*

The nurse practitioner orders 40 mg of Tylenol by mouth every 4 hours for pain. The Tylenol is dispensed in 160 mg/5 mL. How many mL should Frank receive in one dose?

Frank will follow up with the pediatrician and the parents are instructed to bring him to the emergency department if he should have any projectile vomiting.

Unfolding Case Study #14-4 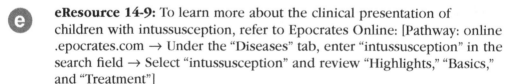 Tanya

Tanya is a 2-year-old toddler who is admitted to the pediatric unit with a diagnosis of intussusception. Her parents have noticed that her stools have been like currant jelly and for the past 24 hours she appears to be uncomfortable and guarding her abdomen.

Exercise 14-13: *Multiple-choice question*

The child with a suspected diagnosis of intussusception is admitted with stool that appears gelatinous in consistency and appears to be blood tinged. Based on an understanding of the pathophysiology of this disease, this stool is due to:

    A. Necrosis of the bowel

    B. Diverticulum in the bowel

    C. Fissures in the rectum

    D. Absence of ganglionic cells in the intestine

 eResource 14-9: To learn more about the clinical presentation of children with intussusception, refer to Epocrates Online: [Pathway: online.epocrates.com → Under the "Diseases" tab, enter "intussusception" in the search field → Select "intussusception" and review "Highlights," "Basics," and "Treatment"]

Tanya presents with other manifestations such as pyrexia, and the currant jelly-like stools continue that is now blood tinged. She is scheduled for diagnostic testing.

Exercise 14-14: *Multiple-choice question*

Tanya is scheduled for radiographic tests to rule out intussusception. Based on this information, you should be prepared to:

    A. Administer a saline enema to prep the bowel for the procedure

    B. Obtain a rectal temp to ensure accuracy of the reading

Answers to this chapter begin on page 221.

C. Make the child NPO (nothing by mouth) for a computed tomography (CT) scan of the abdomen

D. Do not administer anything to the child rectally

Tanya's diagnosis of intussusception is confirmed and she is maintained NPO. A procedure to alleviate the telescoping bowel is done successfully under anesthesia.

Unfolding Case Study #14-5 ▨ McKenzie

McKenzie, a 15-year-old girl, is admitted with nausea and vomiting, a white blood cell count of 12,000 mcL, and pain at McBurney's point. Her temperature is slightly elevated at 99.4° F.

Exercise 14-15: *Multiple-choice question*
Based on an understanding of pathophysiology of common gastrointestinal disorders in children, the nurse anticipates the admitting diagnosis is to rule out:
A. Gastroenteritis
B. Appendicitis
C. Peritonitis
D. Ulcerative colitis

As you are admitting McKenzie, she experiences sudden pain relief although nothing has been administered for pain management. You understand that this is a concern and notify the primary care provider. The primary care provider makes the diagnosis of appendicitis.

 eResource 14-10: To review the clinical presentation of appendicitis, consult Medscape:
■ Online: [Pathway: www.medscape.org → Select "Reference" → Enter "appendicitis" into the search field → Select "appendicitis" → Review "Overview" and "Clinical Presentation"]
■ On your mobile device; you can access the same information: [Pathway: Medscape → Select "Reference" → Enter "appendicitis" into the search field → Select "appendicitis" → Review "Overview" and "Clinical Presentation"]

Exercise 14-16: *Select all that apply*
Which of the following symptoms should you look for in a patient who may be at risk for peritonitis?
❑ Dramatic increase in temperature
❑ Septic shock
❑ Deep, prolonged respirations
❑ Chills and shakiness
❑ Increased blood pressure

Answers to this chapter begin on page 221.

McKenzie is taken to surgery immediately for an appendectomy.

 eResource 14-11: To learn more about the surgical procedure and the postoperative considerations, you again consult Medscape:
- Online: [Pathway: www.medscape.org → Select "Procedures" → Enter "appendectomy" into the search field → Select "appendectomy" → Review "Technique" and "Post-Procedure"]
- On your mobile device; you can access the same information: [Pathway: Medscape → Select "Procedures" → Enter "appendectomy" into the search field → Select "appendectomy" → Review "Technique" and "Post-Procedure"]

Postoperatively she is given broad spectrum antibiotics and maintained on IV fluids for 24 hours. In the same room as McKenzie is a 13-year-old girl, August, who has celiac disease. McKenzie resumes her normal diet slowly and August maintains her dietary needs with some autonomy by choosing her own meals.

Exercise 14-17: *Select all that apply*

Which of the following menu items could be selected for a child who is diagnosed with celiac disease?
- ❑ French fries
- ❑ Crackers
- ❑ Broiled chicken
- ❑ Bagels
- ❑ Pizza
- ❑ Hard boiled eggs

McKenzie recovers well without complications and is discharged, but before she leaves she exchanges Facebook accounts with August so they can keep in touch. August is thrilled to have a friend who is 15 and McKenzie understands that August needs "acceptance" because her condition is chronic as opposed to hers, which was acute and fixable.

Answers to this chapter begin on page 221.

Answers

Exercise 14-1: *Multiple-choice question*

Based on this initial assessment, you document the findings as:

A. Normoactive bowel sounds present—NO, normal bowel sounds, in the toddler, are heard every 10 to 30 seconds.

B. Hypoactive bowel sounds present—NO, this finding exceeds the normal range of 10 to 30 seconds.

C. **Hyperactive bowel sounds with borborygmi—YES, the 5-second interval of bowel sounds indicates an increase in bowel sounds and the stomach growling indicates hunger.**

D. Slight decrease in bowel sounds noted—NO, this finding exceeds the normal range of 10 to 30 seconds.

Exercise 14-2: *Select all that apply*

To further assess for signs of moderate dehydration, which would you include?

❏ Parched mucous membranes—NO, severe dehydration.

❏ No tears—NO, severe dehydration.

☒ **Tachycardia—YES, tachycardia is a sign of decreased blood volume.**

❏ Capillary refill in less than 2 seconds—NO, mild dehydration.

❏ Urine output of 1.0 to 2.0 mL urine/kg/hr—NO, normal urine output.

☒ **Poor skin recoil/turgor with 2 seconds return after pinching—YES, poor skin turgor is a sign of dehydration.**

Exercise 14-3: *Multiple-choice question*

Until a causative organism has been identified, you should institute _____ precautions.

A. Universal—NO, these precautions should be utilized with all patients and are not specific to any one microorganism.

B. Droplet—NO, this isolation is instituted for patients with a suspected microorganism that can be transmitted via large droplets.

C. Contact—**YES, this isolation is employed for patients with a suspected or diagnosed microorganism that can be infectious via contact.**

D. Airborne—NO, this isolation is used with patients with a suspected or diagnosed microorganism that is spread via small particle residue of droplets.

Exercise 14-4: *Multiple-choice question*

When planning to complete discharge instructions for the child who is being discharged with a diagnosis of gastroenteritis related to rotavirus and dehydration. Which of the following statements, if made by the parent, would indicate that further teaching is needed?

A. **"I will continue to only give my child glucose water until I am sure the diarrhea has stopped"—YES, glucose water will not meet the nutritional or electrolyte requirements of a child who has been moderately dehydrated. The parent does not have an adequate understanding of the child's nutritional requirements.**

B. "I now realize the importance of the rotavirus vaccine, which may have prevented this illness."—NO, the rotavirus vaccine is given at 2, 4, and 6 months of life, which indicates the parent's understanding.

C. "I will notify my pediatrician if his urine output is less than 20 mL per hour."—NO, the child should have a urinary output of 1 to 2 mL of urine/kg/hr, which indicates the parent understands the patient education.

D. "I will change his diapers at least every 2 hours to minimize skin irritation."—NO, the parent understands that frequent stools place the child at risk for impaired skin integrity.

Exercise 14-5: *Multiple-choice question*

Which of the following statements, made by the mother immediately after birth, indicates the need for further assessment?

A. "Although I knew my child would be born with cleft lip, I really didn't know what to expect."—NO, this is a normal response. Mothers typically fantasize about the appearance of their child, and need to assimilate the child's looks with their preconceived image. This behavior occurs regardless of a structural defect.

B. "I think it would be helpful to talk with another mother whose child was born with cleft lip."—NO, this is a normal response and may indicate that referral to a support group would be beneficial.

C. **"I can't help but wonder if it was something I did during my pregnancy that caused this to happen."—YES, this statement may indicate that the mother is experiencing feelings of guilt, which may need to be further explored.**

D. "I am so glad that my sister and her family live nearby."—NO, this response indicates that the mother knows she may need the support of her extended family.

Exercise 14-6: *Multiple-choice question*

Which of the following interventions should you make to assist the mother with Sadie's feedings?

A. Encourage the mother to bottle feed since babies born with cleft lip often experience feeding problems.—NO, breastfeeding is the desired method of feeding for a newborn and can be facilitated by the nursery nurses as well as La Leche representatives.

B. Hold the infant in a supine position to facilitate swallowing—NO, in order to facilitate feeding and swallowing, the newborn should be fed in an upright position.

C. **Burp the baby after every 15 to 30 mL of formula—YES, babies with a cleft lip tend to ingest more air since the suction around the nipple is not tight; therefore, additional burping is needed.**

D. Position the child in a prone position immediately after feeding—NO, the child should be positioned upright for at least 30 minutes after the feeding to prevent aspiration.

Exercise 14-7: *Ordering*

Sadie has her cleft lip repaired and has just returned from the operating room. Prioritize her care immediately postoperatively by placing the numbers 1 to 6 next to the task.

_**1**_ Apply a cool mist for the first 24 hours—**Upon return to the pediatric unit place the child in a cool mist in order to decrease the viscosity of the secretion for effective airway breathing**

_**2**_ Gently suction the oropharynx and nasopharynx avoiding the suture lines—**As the cool mist liquefies the secretions, it will be easier and more effective to gently suction the airway.**

_**4**_ Apply elbow immobilizers that are removed every 2 hours—**Once the airway, breathing, circulation, and pain have been managed, efforts must be made to prevent the child from touching the incision.**

_**3**_ Medicate for pain with analgesics as ordered—**Pain management follows airway in terms of prioritization of patient care.**

_**5**_ Cleanse the suture line with normal saline—**Cleansing of the suture line is important to prevent infection and scarring but assumes importance after the airway has been established and pain managed.**

_**6**_ Encourage the parents to hold and soothe the child—**Psychosocial care is critical once physical needs are met.**

Exercise 14-8: *Multiple-choice question*

Based upon an understanding of common complications associated with cleft lip and palate, you make several referrals for evaluations. Which of the following services is not typically needed in a child with cleft lip and palate?

A. Speech therapist—NO, a speech therapist is often needed to detect speech and hearing problems in a child with cleft palate.

B. Ear, nose, and throat specialist—NO, an ear, nose, and throat specialist is needed because of an increased incidence of otitis media in children with cleft palate.

C. Dentist—NO, normal dentition may be disrupted in children with cleft palate.

D. **Neurologist—YES, there is no clear relation between cleft lip/palate and neurological disorders.**

Exercise 14-9: *Multiple-choice question*

As the admitting nurse beginning the interview, which question will you ask?

A. "Can you describe to me a typical feeding routine, specifically, what occurs after he finishes his bottle?"—YES, typically the infant will present with a voracious appetite that is immediately followed by projectile vomiting of undigested formula.

B. "Describe the typical color of his stool and any changes you may have noticed."—NO, this information would not be relevant to a diagnosis of pyloric stenosis, which is a structural defect of the upper gastrointestinal tract. In severe cases, there may be fewer stools of normal color and consistency.

C. "Have you noticed that your child has bouts of constipation?"—NO, this information would not be relevant to a diagnosis of pyloric stenosis, which is a structural defect of the upper gastrointestinal tract. In severe cases, there may be fewer, smaller stools of normal color and consistency.

D. "Do you think your child is experiencing abdominal pain?"—NO, pain does not typically accompany pyloric stenosis. Immediately after vomiting, the child will be hungry.

Exercise 14-10: *Multiple-choice question*

Which of the following orders would be anticipated in the immediate preoperative care of the child with a diagnosis of pyloric stenosis?

A. Frequent burping with feedings—NO, once the child is scheduled for surgery within the next 8 hours, all fluids will be held to prevent aspiration. Also, because of the structural nature of this problem, all fluids will be immediately regurgitated because there is constriction of the pyloric valve.

B. Give 50 mL of glucose water via nasogastric tube—NO, once the child is scheduled for surgery within the next 8 hours, all fluids will be held to prevent aspiration. Also, because of the structural nature of this problem, all fluids will be immediately regurgitated because there is constriction of the pyloric valve.

C. Elevate the head of the bed during feedings—NO, all feedings will be withheld.

D. Keep child nothing by mouth (NPO)—YES, once the child is scheduled for surgery within the next 8 hours, all fluids will be held to prevent aspiration. Adequate hydration may be achieved by administration of intravenous fluids.

Exercise 14-11: *Select all that apply*

Which of the following instructions regarding Frank's care is appropriate?

❑ Tub baths should be done to keep the incision clean—NO, the child should be given a sponge bath and the incision should be protected from water.

☒ **Burp the child after every 30 to 60 mL—YES, this will decrease gas and abdominal distention from ingested air.**

❑ Discontinue breastfeeding until the pediatrician recommends—NO, breastfeeding may resume as soon as possible postoperatively.

❑ Notify the physician if the child's temperature is greater than 101.4° F—NO, the physician should be notified of any temperature greater than 100° F because of the potential for sepsis.

☒ **Place child in an upright position for 30 minutes following the feeding—YES, this will aid in the digestive process and decrease the possibility of aspiration if the child vomits.**

Exercise 14-12: *Calculation*
Frank will be receiving Tylenol for pain upon discharge. The nurse practitioner orders 40 mg of Tylenol by mouth every 4 hours for pain. The Tylenol is dispensed in 160 mg/5 mL. How many mL should Frank receive in one dose?

1.25 mL

Exercise 14-13: *Multiple-choice question*
The child with a suspected diagnosis of intussusception is admitted with stool that appears gelatinous in consistency and appears to be blood tinged. Based on an understanding of the pathophysiology of this disease, this stool is due to:

A. Necrosis of the bowel—**YES, adequate perfusion of blood to the affected portion of the bowel is obstructed, which results in necrosis and sloughing.**

B. Diverticulum in the bowel—NO, Meckel's diverticulum is characterized by black stools.

C. Fissures in the rectum—NO, a fissure or break in the integrity of the skin would be manifested by frank blood.

D. Absence of ganglionic cells in the intestine—NO, this disorder, Hirschsprung's disease, is characterized by ribbon-like stools or the inability to pass a stool.

Exercise 14-14: *Multiple-choice question*
Tanya is scheduled for radiographic tests to rule out intussusception. Based on this information, the nurse should be prepared to:

A. Administer a saline enema to prep the bowel for the procedure—NO, a nurse should not insert anything into the rectum of a child with rectal bleeding. Also, there is no recommended preparation for the type of radiographic study used in intussusception.

B. Obtain a rectal temp to ensure accuracy of the reading—NO, nothing should be inserted into the rectum of a child with rectal bleeding.

C. Make the child NPO (nothing by mouth) for a computed tomography (CT) scan of the abdomen—NO, prep is needed for an air or barium enema, which is performed by the physician.

D. Do not administer anything to the child rectally—**YES, the nurse should not insert anything into the rectum of a child who has active rectal bleeding.**

Exercise 14-15: *Multiple-choice question*

Based on an understanding of pathophysiology of common gastrointestinal disorders in children, the nurse anticipates the admitting diagnosis is rule out:

A. Gastroenteritis—NO, gastroenteritis may be characterized by nausea and vomiting; however, the discomfort associated with gastroenteritis does not shoot from the area around the umbilicus to the right lower quadrant of the abdomen.

B. **Appendicitis—YES, the typical presentation of appendicitis includes pain and guarding at McBurney's point as well as nausea, vomiting, and a slight temperature elevation. White blood cell count will be elevated in infections of the appendix.**

C. Peritonitis—NO, this may be caused by a ruptured appendix and is characterized by a washboard-rigid abdomen, a significantly elevated temperature, and a significant elevation of the white blood cell count.

D. Ulcerative colitis—NO, this is an intermittent inflammatory bowel disease characterized by abdominal cramping.

Exercise 14-16: *Select all that apply*

Which of the following symptoms should you look for in a patient who may be at risk for peritonitis?

☒ **Dramatic increase in temperature—YES, hyperpyrexia is noted in individuals with septic shock due to a ruptured appendix.**

☒ **Septic shock—YES, septic shock is associated with a ruptured appendix and peritonitis.**

❑ Deep, prolonged respirations—NO, children with peritonitis and/or septic shock will experience shallow, short respirations.

☒ **Chills and shakiness—YES, chills and shakiness are symptoms experienced with sepsis and septic shock.**

❑ Increased blood pressure—NO, septic shock is associated with hypotension.

Exercise 14-17: *Select all that apply*

Which of the following menu items could be selected for a child who is diagnosed with celiac disease?

☒ **French fries—YES, potatoes do not contain gluten**

❑ Crackers—NO, crackers are made with products such as flour that contain gluten.

☒ **Broiled chicken—YES, poultry and meat are gluten free.**

❑ Bagels—NO, grains are not gluten free.

❑ Pizza—NO, the crust can be a source of gluten unless made specifically to be gluten free.

☒ **Hard boiled eggs—YES, these are gluten free.**

15

Children With Genitourinary Health Care Needs

Vicki A. Martin

Unfolding Case Study #15-1 ▨ Clarisse

Clarisse is a 10-year-old who lives with her aunt since both of her parents were killed in a car accident when she was 5 years old. She has been voiding frequently along with experiencing burning during urination. Her aunt is a nurse in a local family practice office and decides to take a urine specimen in for analyzing the next day. Clarisse goes to school as usual the next day. At about 9:30 the school nurse calls her aunt to report that Clarisse is not feeling well and is running a low-grade temperature. Clarisse is picked up from school and taken to the health care provider. It was determined that she has a urinary tract infection. She was given a prescription for antibiotics and orders to increase fluid intake and to void every 1 to 2 hours. She is cleared to return to school the next day.

Exercise 15-1: *True or false*
Female infants and children are more prone to having urinary tract infections due to the short urethra as compared to boys.

_____ True

_____ False

Exercise 15-2: *Calculation*
The nurse knows the bladder capacity in ounces can be calculated by using the formula (child's age in years + 2 = number of ounces of bladder capacity). Using this formula, what is the bladder capacity of Clarisse?

_____

Exercise 15-3: *Multiple-choice question*
What is the best indicator to the nurse that an antibiotic is providing effective treatment for a urinary tract infection?

      A. Urinary symptoms have subsided within 24 to 48 hours after treatment began.

      B. The oral antibiotics have been completed as the health care provider ordered.

Answers to this chapter begin on page 238.

C. The parents state the child is finally voiding normally.

D. The urine culture is negative at the 72 hour follow-up.

Exercise 15-4: *Fill-in*

Most urinary tract infections in children are caused by _____ _____, a common gram-negative enteric bacterium.

Exercise 15-5: *Select all that apply*

The clinical manifestations of school-age children that are associated with urinary tract infections include:

❏ Fever and chills

❏ Malodorous urine

❏ Abdominal pain

❏ Flank pain

❏ Skin rashes

❏ Constipation

❏ Hematuria

❏ Frequency

❏ Dysuria

ⓔ **eResource 15-1:** To reinforce your understanding of urinary tract infections in children and its management, go to Epocrates Online: [Pathway: online.epocrates.com → Under the "Diseases" tab, enter "urinary" in the search field → Select "Urinary tract infection in children" → Review "Highlights," "Basics," and "Diagnosis"]

Exercise 15-6: *Fill-in*

List four nursing interventions that should be included in the patient education for the parents of a female child with a urinary tract infection.

1. _____

2. _____

3. _____

4. _____

ⓔ **eResource 15-2:** To learn more about nursing interventions for managing urinary tract infections, review the following:

■ NANDA *Nursing Interventions for Urinary Tract Infection (UTI)*: goo .gl/yRKrW9

■ *Nursing Care Plan: A Client with Cystitis*: goo.gl/JzA9Ea

ⓔ **eResource 15-3:** To review patient teaching resources, go to HealthyChildren.org and enter "UTI" into the search field:

■ Online: [Pathway: www.healthychildren.org → Enter "UTI" into the search field → Scroll down to select "Detecting Urinary Tract Infections" → Review or listen to content]

Answers to this chapter begin on page 238.

■ Mobile App (downloaded for Android [goo.gl/FTPQLH] or iOS [goo .gl/7b1Fwm]): [Pathway: HealthyChildren → Enter "UTI" into the search field → Scroll down to select "Detecting Urinary Tract Infections" → Review or listen to content]

Due to Clarisse experiencing frequent urinary tract infections, she has now developed secondary enuresis and requires medical management of this disorder.

eResource 15-4: To learn more about enuresis, refer to Medscape:
■ Online: [Pathway: www.medscape.org → Select "Reference" → Enter "enuresis" into the search field → Select "enuresis" → Review content]
■ On your mobile device, you can access the same information: [Pathway: Medscape → Enter "enuresis" into the search field → Select "enuresis" → Review content]

The health care provider orders oxybutynin chloride (Ditropan) to treat the enuresis.

eResource 15-5: To learn more about oxybutynin chloride (Ditropan), use your mobile device to consult:
■ Skyscape's RxDrugs on your mobile device (www.skyscape.com): [Pathway: Skyscape → Select "RxDrugs" → Enter "Ditropan" into the search field → Select "Ditropan" to review content]
■ Epocrates: [Pathway: Epocrates → Enter "Ditropan" into the search field → Select "Ditropan" → Review content; focus on pediatric dosing and precautions]

Exercise 15-7: *Multiple-choice question*
Which side effect is common with the medication Ditropan for treating enuresis?
    A. Dry mouth and constipation
    B. Cold intolerance and diarrhea
    C. Personality changes and nausea
    D. Nose bleeds and nasal congestion

Exercise 15-8: *True or false*
Secondary enuresis is diagnosed in a child that has never had a dry night.
_____ True
_____ False

Exercise 15-9: *Fill-in*
List six treatment strategies useful in treating enuresis.
    1. _____
    2. _____
    3. _____
    4. _____
    5. _____
    6. _____

Answers to this chapter begin on page 238.

eResource 15-6: To learn more about treatment and management of enuresis, refer to Medscape:
- Online: [Pathway: www.medscape.org → Select "Reference" → Enter "enuresis" into the search field → Select "enuresis" → Select "Treatment and Management" → Review content: "Approach Considerations," "Initial Management," "Alarm Therapy," Pharmacologic Therapy," and "Diet"]
- On your mobile device, you can access the same information: [Pathway: Medscape → Enter "enuresis" into the search field → Select "enuresis" → Select "Treatment and Management" → Review content: "Approach Considerations," "Initial Management," "Alarm Therapy," Pharmacologic Therapy," and "Diet"]

Exercise 15-10: *Matching*

Match the type of enuresis in Column A to the correct description in Column B.

Column A	Column B
A. Primary enuresis	_____ Bedwetting with stress/infections
B. Secondary enuresis	_____ Bedwetting during night and day
C. Diurnal enuresis	_____ Bedwetting every night
D. Nocturnal enuresis	_____ Bedwetting at night time

Unfolding Case Study #15-2 ▧ Rodney

Rodney is a newborn male just born to a young teenage mother. He is being placed into an adoption program since his mother is too young to support and care for him. His mother's parents were against their daughter continuing with the pregnancy. Rodney was born with hypospadias and crytorchidism. These congenital anomalies will require several surgeries for correction so he will have special needs during this crucial infancy stage to promote proper growth and development.

 eResource 15-7: To learn more about treatment and management of hypospadias and cryptorchidism, refer to Medscape:
- Online: [Pathway: www.medscape.org → Select "Reference" → Enter "hypospadias" into the search field → Select "hypospadias" → Review "Overview" and "Clinical Presentation"; repeat with "cryptorchidism"]
- On your mobile device, you can access the same information: [Pathway: Medscape → Enter "hypospadias" into the search field → Select "hypospadias" → Review "Overview" and "Clinical Presentation"; repeat with "cryptorchidism"]

Otherwise, Rodney has no other medical issues. The adoption agency will place Rodney with his new family. Both new parents are older, have been unable to bear a child, and are financially stable. Rodney's new parents have questions about the surgical procedure to correct his hypospadias.

Answers to this chapter begin on page 238.

eResource 15-8: The pediatric surgeon uses Dr DrawMD (www .drawmd.com) on her iPad to show the parents an image with mark-up annotations to visually present anatomy and the planned procedure: [Pathway: DrawMD Pediatrics → Select "New Drawings" → Select "Pediatric Urology" → Select appropriate "stamp" and add text or additional drawing → Select "Save"]

His new mother is a stay-at-home mom and will provide the special care he requires. Rodney is being discharged home with a urinary stent and the parents are trained on the double-diapering technique to prevent infection and skin break-down while maintaining patent urinary flow.

 eResource 15-9: To learn more about these conditions and the procedures to correct them, view:
■ Hypospadias—Surgical Simulator: goo.gl/w63L1V
■ Hypospadias: goo.gl/13btkY
■ Surgery for Undescended Testicle—Frequently Asked Questions: goo.gl/F9TSk7

Exercise 15-11: *Multiple-choice question*
Proper growth and development involves pediatric theorists. Which pediatric theorist contributed the psychosexual aspect of growth and development?
    A. Erik Erikson
    B. Lawrence Kohlberg
    C. Sigmund Freud
    D. Jean Piaget

Exercise 15-12: *Multiple-choice question*
The pictures below depict hypospadias and epispadias. Properly label which picture depicts which congenital anomaly for the nurse's newborn assessment.

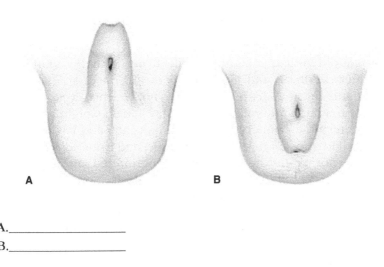

A   B

    A._____
    B._____

Answers to this chapter begin on page 238.

Exercise 15-13: *True or false*

Hypospadias occurs in 1 in 250 live male births in the United States and rates are increasing, most likely due to the increase in premature births and low birth weight.

_____ True

_____ False

Exercise 15-14: *Matching*

Match the type of urinary disorder in Column A to the correct description in Column B.

Column A	Column B
A. Cryptorchidism	_____ Peritoneal fluid in scrotal sac
B. Hypospadias	_____ Meatus on ventral surface of penis
C. Epispadias	_____ Undescended testicles
D. Phimosis	_____ Meatus on dorsal surface of penis
E. Testicular torsion	_____ Penis foreskin cannot be retracted
F. Obstructive uropathy	_____ Emergency with spermatic cord rotation
G. Hydrocele	_____ Structural abnormality of urinary system
H. Bladder exstrophy	_____ Short foreskin causing a curved penis
I. Chordee	_____ Bladder extrudes into abdominal wall

Exercise 15-15: *Fill-in*

List four goals for successful surgical correction in the nursing management of hypospadias or any structural defect of the urinary system.

1. _____

2. _____

3. _____

4. _____

Unfolding Case Study #15-3 ▦ Keith

Keith is a 4-year-old African American male living with his grandparents. His mother died after childbirth and his father is incarcerated. He is brought to the emergency department after his grandmother noticed his eyes, hands, and feet were "puffy." He has had a poor appetite and has gained weight over the past few weeks. He had a respiratory infection 2 to 3 months ago and has not acted playful since then. The child appears to be pale, lethargic, and irritable. Upon assessment, his vital signs are normal but he presents with periorbital and dependent edema with a weight gain of 3 pounds in 1 month. A urinalysis and complete blood work is done. The health care provider determines he has nephrotic syndrome and should be admitted to the pediatric floor at the hospital due to the weight gain and edema issues. He is on daily weights, strict intake and output (I&O), and corticosteroids along with diuretics.

Answers to this chapter begin on page 238.

eResouce 15-10: To learn more about nephrotic syndrome, consult:
- MerckMedicus Online on your mobile device: [Pathway: www .merckmedicus.com → Enter "nephrotic syndrome" into the search field → Select "nephrotic syndrome" to access and review content]
- Medscape:
  - Online: [Pathway: www.medscape.org → Select "Reference" → Enter "nephrotic syndrome" into the search field → Select "nephrotic syndrome" → Review content]
  - On your mobile device, you can access the same information: [Pathway: Medscape → Enter "nephrotic syndrome" into the search field → Select "nephrotic syndrome" → Review content]

Exercise 15-16: *Multiple-choice question*

The typical drug of choice is the corticosteroid prednisolone for the accurate dosing and increased palatability in young children. The usual protocol is to start with a high dose of 2 mg/kg/day up to a maximum of 80 mg/day. What is the expected outcome before discontinuing prednisolone for the treatment of nephrotic syndrome?

A. Administer the drug until the protein increases in the urine.

B. Administer the drug until the child is free of proteinuria for 3 days.

C. The child has an increased appetite and weight loss.

D. The child is able to receive scheduled live virus vaccines.

eResource 15-11: To reinforce your understanding of prednisolone, refer to Epocrates:
- Online: [Pathway: online.epocrates.com → Under the "Drugs" tab, enter "prednisolone" in the search field → Select "prednisolone" → Select "Peds Dosing" and review content]
- On your mobile device: [Pathway: Epocrates → Enter "prednisolone" in the search field → Select "prednisolone" → Scroll down to "Peds Dosing" and review content.]

Exercise 15-17: *True or false*

The common clinical manifestations exhibited in children with nephrotic syndrome include edema, massive proteinuria, and hypoalbuminemia.

_____ True

_____ False

Exercise 15-18: *Matching*

Match the type of renal disorder in Column A to the correct description in Column B.

Column A	Column B
A. Hemolytic uremic syndrome	_____ Progressive, irreversible renal damage
B. Acute renal failure	
C. Chronic renal failure	_____ Increased renal permeability with proteinuria
D. Nephrotic syndrome	
	_____ Main cause of acute renal failure

Answers to this chapter begin on page 238.

Column A   **Column B**

_____ Sudden loss of adequate renal
function

 eResource 15-12: To learn more about these other disorders, refer to:
- MerckMedicus Online: [Pathway: www.merckmedicus.com
  → Enter "Hemolytic uremic syndrome" into the search field → Select
  "Hemolytic uremic syndrome" → Access and review content; repeat
  with "Acute renal failure" and "Chronic renal failure"]
- Medscape:
  - Online: [Pathway: www.medscape.org → Select "Reference"
    → Enter "Hemolytic uremic syndrome" into the search field
    → Select "Hemolytic uremic syndrome" → Access and review
    content; repeat with "Acute renal failure" and "Chronic renal failure"]
  - On your mobile device; you can access the same information: [Pathway:
    Medscape → Enter "Hemolytic uremic syndrome" into the search field
    → Select "Hemolytic uremic syndrome" → Access and review content;
    repeat with "Acute renal failure" and "Chronic renal failure"]

Exercise 15-19: *Fill-in*
Children with kidney disease have restricted diets that are usually low in sodium,
potassium, and phosphorus. List four high-sodium foods the nurse should educate
families to avoid.

1. _____
2. _____
3. _____
4. _____

 eResource 15-13: To supplement your teaching, you refer the parents
to HealthyChildren.org and direct them specifically to the information
regarding "sodium":
- Online and on Mobile device: [Pathway: www.healthychildren
  .org →Enter "sodium" into the search field → Scroll down to select
  "Healthy Children Radio: Sodium (Audio)" and "We Don"t Need to Add
  Salt to Food" → Review and listen to content]
- Mobile App: [Pathway: HealthyChildren → Enter "sodium" into the
  search field → Scroll down to select "Healthy Children Radio: Sodium
  (Audio)" and "We Don"t Need to Add Salt to Food" → Review and
  listen to content]

Exercise 15-20: *Multiple-choice question*
A 3-year-old child with nephrotic syndrome is admitted to the pediatric floor, which
only has semi-private rooms. Which pediatric patient would be the most appropriate
roommate for the nephrotic syndrome child?

    A. A 2-year-old recovering from varicella

    B. A 3-year-old with pneumonia

Answers to this chapter begin on page 238.

C. A 3-year-old with a fractured femur

D. A 6-year-old postoperative tonsillectomy

Exercise 15-21: *Fill-in*

The nurse is preparing to administer an erythropoietin (Epogen) injection to a child with chronic renal failure. The mother asks what the purpose of this drug is. The nurse should respond to the mother that this drug is given to combat _____ .

 eResource 15-14: To reinforce your understanding of this medication, refer to Medscape:
- Online: [Pathway: www.medscape.org → Select "Reference" → Enter "Epogen" into the search field → Select "Epogen" → Access and review content]
- On your mobile device, you can access the same information: [Pathway: Medscape → Enter "Epogen" into the search field → Select "Epogen" → Access and review content]

Exercise 15-22: *Multiple-choice question*

Which type of acid–base imbalance is most often seen in children with renal failure?

A. Respiratory alkalosis

B. Respiratory acidosis

C. Metabolic alkalosis

D. Metabolic acidosis

Exercise 15-23: *True or false*

The vaccines approved for a child with a kidney transplant are DTaP, IPV, MMR, and varicella.

_____ True

_____ False

Exercise 15-24: *Multiple-choice question*

The nurse is caring for a young child with pre-acute renal failure (ARF). Which of the following is the most common cause for this type of ARF?

A. Wilms' tumor

B. Heart failure

C. Vesicoureteral reflux

D. Contrast media diagnostics

Unfolding Case Study #15-4 ▓ Lydia

Lydia is a teenager who recently had a group A beta-hemolytic *Streptococcus* infection. Her parents took her to the doctor and she took half of the antibiotics that were prescribed. She did not tell her parents she had not completed the medications. She thought once she felt better it would be feasible to stop the medication. Medication compliance with teenagers can be problematic. The past few days she has started having headaches, decreased urine output, and blood in the urine. Her mother took her to the clinic. The health care provider did a urinary and blood workup. She was diagnosed with acute glomerulonephritis. All vital signs were normal except her blood pressure was slightly elevated and that was the reason for the headaches. She is to be monitored closely at home. She was ordered to be on bed rest, dietary restrictions such as low-sodium diet, fluid restrictions, and a second dose of antibiotics. The parents were instructed to take her to the emergency department if any renal or respiratory complications occur.

Exercise 15-25: *Select all that apply*

The clinical manifestations of children that are associated with acute glomerulonephritis include:

❑ Nervousness

❑ Dependent edema

❑ Periorbital edema

❑ Decreased urine output

❑ Hematuria

❑ Hypertension

❑ Low sodium

❑ Low potassium

 eResource 15-15: To learn more about acute glomerulonephritis and the clinical presentation, refer to Medscape:

◼ Online: [Pathway: www.medscape.org → Select "Reference" → Enter "acute glomerulonephritis" into the search field → Select "acute glomerulonephritis" → Review content under "Clinical Presentation"]

◼ On your mobile device, you can access the same information: [Pathway: Medscape → Enter "acute glomerulonephritis" into the search field → Select "acute glomerulonephritis" → Review content under "Clinical Presentation"]

Exercise 15-26: *Multiple-choice question*

Which test would the nurse anticipate the health care provider to order for effectively diagnosing acute glomerulonephritis?

A. Antistreptolysin O titer

B. Collection for 24-hour urine

C. Blood cultures

D. Stool cultures

Answers to this chapter begin on page 238.

Exercise 15-27: *True or false*

Nonsteroidal anti-inflammatory drugs (NSAIDs) should not be administered to children with renal function problems as the prostaglandin action can further decrease the glomerular filtration rate.

_____ True

_____ False

Exercise 15-28: *Fill-in*

List four laboratory/diagnostic tests useful in diagnosing acute glomerulonephritis.

1. _____

2. _____

3. _____

4. _____

 eResource 15-16: To learn more about laboratory workup for acute glomerulonephritis, refer to Medscape:

■ Online: [Pathway: www.medscape.org → Select "Reference" → Enter "acute glomerulonephritis" into the search field → Select "acute glomerulonephritis" → Review content under "Workup"]

■ On your mobile device, you can access the same information: [Pathway: Medscape → Enter "acute glomerulonephritis" into the search field → Select "acute glomerulonephritis" → Review content under "Workup"]

Exercise 15-29: *Multiple-choice question*

Which treatment is not used for acute glomerulonephritis but for the treatment of the original strep infection that was responsible for causing the acute glomerulonephritis?

    A. NSAIDs

    B. Antihypertensives

    C. Diuretics

    D. Antibiotics

Exercise 15-30: *Multiple-choice question*

A child with acute glomerulonephritis is in the playroom of the hospital and experiences blurred vision with a headache. Which action should be taken by the nurse?

    A. Check the urine to see if hematuria has increased.

    B. Obtain a blood pressure reading on the child and notify the physician.

    C. Reassure the child and encourage bed rest until the headache improves.

    D. Follow up on serum electrolytes with the medical laboratory.

 eResource 15-17: To reinforce your understanding of the complications associated with acute glomerulonephritis, refer to Epocrates Online: [Pathway: online.epocrates.com → Under the "Diseases" tab, enter "acute glomerulonephritis" in the search field → Select "acute glomerulonephritis" → Under "Follow-up" select "Complications" and review content]

Answers to this chapter begin on page 238.

Answers

Exercise 15-1: *True or false*

Female infants and children are more prone to having urinary tract infections due to the short urethra as compared to boys.

___X___ True

_____ False

Exercise 15-2: *Calculation*

The nurse knows the bladder capacity in ounces can be calculated by using the formula (child's age in years + 2 = number of ounces of bladder capacity). Using this formula, what is the bladder capacity of Clarisse in ounces and mL?

12 oz or 350 mL

10 years old + 2 = 12 ounces of bladder capacity or 350 mL

Exercise 15-3: *Multiple-choice question*

What is the best indicator to the nurse that an antibiotic is providing effective treatment for a urinary tract infection?

A. Urinary symptoms have subsided within 24 to 48 hours after treatment began—NO, a culture has to be done.

B. The oral antibiotics have been completed as the health care provider ordered—NO, a culture has to be done.

C. The parents state the child is finally voiding normally—NO, a culture has to be done.

D. The urine culture is negative at the 72 hour follow-up—YES

Exercise 15-4: *Fill-in*

Most UTIs in children are caused by ***Escherichia coli***, a common gram-negative enteric bacterium.

Exercise 15-5: *Select all that apply*

The clinical manifestations of school-age children that are associated with urinary tract infections include:

☒ **Fever and chills**

☒ **Malodorous urine**

☒ **Abdominal pain**

☒ **Flank pain**

❑ Skin rashes

❑ Constipation

☒ **Hematuria**

☒ **Frequency**

☒ **Dysuria**

Exercise 15-6: *Fill-in*

List four nursing interventions that should be included in patient education for the parents of a young female child with a urinary tract infection.

1. **Wear cotton underpants that are not tight fitting**

2. **Avoid bubble baths and scented soaps**

3. **Wipe front to back after using the bathroom**

4. **Drink plenty of fluids and void often**

Exercise 15-7: *Multiple-choice question*

Which side effect is common with the medication Ditropan for treating enuresis?

A. **Dry mouth and constipation—YES, these are common side effects.**

B. Cold intolerance and diarrhea—NO, the medication is drying.

C. Personality changes and nausea—NO, it should not cause personality changes.

D. Nose bleeds and nasal congestion—NO, this is also not a side effect.

Exercise 15-8: *True or false*

Secondary enuresis is diagnosed in a child that has never had a dry night.

_____ True

___**X**___ **False—Secondary enuresis is when a child starts bedwetting with stress and infections. Primary enuresis is when a child never has a dry night.**

Exercise 15-9: *Fill-in*

List six treatment strategies useful in treating enuresis.

1. **Fluid restriction**

2. **Timed voiding**

3. **Enuresis alarms**

4. **Medications**

5. **Bladder exercises**

6. **Reward system**

Exercise 15-10: *Matching*

Match the type of enuresis in Column A to the correct description in Column B.

Column A		Column B
A. Primary enuresis	**B**	Bedwetting with stress/infections
B. Secondary enuresis	**C**	Bedwetting during night and day
C. Diurnal enuresis	**A**	Bedwetting every night
D. Nocturnal enuresis	**D**	Bedwetting at night time

Exercise 15-11: *Multiple-choice question*

Proper growth and development involves pediatric theorists. Which pediatric theorist contributed the psychosexual aspect of human development?

A. Erik Erikson—NO, Erikson's theory was about psychosocial development.

B. Lawrence Kohlberg—NO, Kohlberg's theory was about moral development.

C. Sigmund Freud—YES

D. Jean Piaget—NO, Piaget's theory was about cognitive development.

Exercise 15-12: *Multiple-choice question*

The pictures below depict hypospadias and epispadias. Properly label which picture depicts which congenital anomaly for the nurse's newborn assessment.

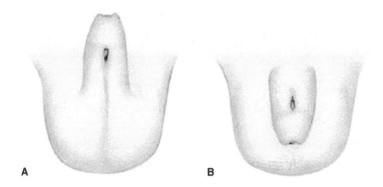

A   B

A. <u>Hypospadias on the ventral surface of the penis</u>

B. <u>Epispadias on the dorsal surface of the penis</u>

Exercise 15-13: *True or false*

Hypospadias occurs in 1 in 250 live male births in the United States and rates are increasing, most likely due to the increase in premature births and low birth weight.

  X   True

_____ False

Exercise 15-14: *Matching*

Match the type of urinary disorder in Column A to the correct description in Column B.

Column A		Column B
A. Cryptorchidism	__G__	Peritoneal fluid in scrotal sac
B. Hypospadias	__B__	Meatus on ventral surface of penis
C. Epispadias	__A__	Undescended testicles
D. Phimosis	__C__	Meatus on dorsal surface of penis
E. Testicular torsion	__D__	Penis foreskin cannot be retracted
F. Obstructive uropathy	__E__	Emergency with spermatic cord rotation
G. Hydrocele	__F__	Structural abnormality of urinary system
H. Bladder exstrophy	__I__	Short foreskin causing a curved penis
I. Chordee	__H__	Bladder extrudes into abdominal wall

Exercise 15-15: *Fill-in*

List four goals for successful surgical correction in the nursing management of hypospadias or any structural defect of the urinary system.

1. **The child will have minimal pain.**
2. **The child will remain free of infection.**
3. **Caregivers will demonstrate an understanding of postoperative care.**
4. **Future sexuality and reproduction will be promoted.**

Exercise 15-16: *Multiple-choice question*

The typical drug of choice is the corticosteroid prednisolone for the accurate dosing and increased palatability in young children. The usual protocol is to start with a high dose of 2 mg/kg/day up to a maximum of 80 mg/day. What is the expected outcome before discontinuing prednisolone for the treatment of nephrotic syndrome?

A. Administer the drug until the protein increases in the urine—NO, the goal is for protein to decrease.

B. **Administer the drug until the child is free of proteinuria for 3 days—YES, the drug must be continued until the child's urine is protein free for 3 days.**

C. The child has an increased appetite and weight loss—NO, the goal is to increase weight.

D. The child is able to receive scheduled live virus vaccines—NO, this will not affect it.

Exercise 15-17: *True or false*

The common clinical manifestations being exhibited in children with nephrotic syndrome include edema, massive proteinuria, and hypoalbuminemia.

__X__ **True**

_____ False

Exercise 15-18: *Matching*

Match the type of renal disorder in Column A to the correct description in Column B.

Column A	Column B
A. Hemolytic uremic syndrome	_____ Progressive, irreversible renal damage
B. Acute renal failure	_____ Increased renal permeability with proteinuria
C. Chronic renal failure	_____ Main cause of acute renal failure
D. Nephrotic syndrome	_____ Sudden loss of adequate renal function

Exercise 15-19: *Fill-in*

Children with kidney disease have restricted diets that are usually low in sodium, potassium, and phosphorus. List four high-sodium foods the nurse should educate families to avoid.

1. **Processed lunchmeats and smoked meats**

2. **Pickles and pickled foods**

3. **Spaghetti and tomato sauce**

4. **Seasonings and potato chips**

Exercise 15-20: *Multiple-choice question*

A 3-year-old child with nephrotic syndrome is admitted to the pediatric floor, which only has semi-private rooms. Which pediatric patient would be the most appropriate roommate for the nephrotic syndrome child?

A. A 2-year-old recovering from varicella—NO, this is an infection control issue.

B. A 3-year-old with pneumonia—NO, this is an infection control issue.

C. A 3-year-old with a fractured femur—YES, noninfectious and same age.

D. A 6-year-old postoperative tonsillectomy—NO, this child is too old.

Exercise 15-21: *Fill-in*

The nurse is preparing to administer an erythropoietin (Epogen) injection to a child with chronic renal failure. The mother asks what the purpose of this drug is. The nurse should respond to the mother that this drug is given to combat **anemia**.

Exercise 15-22: *Multiple-choice question*

Which type of acid–base imbalance is most often seen in children with renal failure?

A. Respiratory alkalosis—NO

B. Respiratory acidosis—NO

C. Metabolic acidosis—YES, metabolic acidosis is seen because they cannot clear waste products efficiently.

D. Metabolic alkalosis—NO

Exercise 15-23: *True or false*
The vaccines approved for a child with a kidney transplant are DTaP, IPV, MMR, and varicella.
_____ True
___**X**___ **False—IPV is the only killed vaccine that is approved.**

Exercise 15-24: *Multiple-choice question*
The nurse is caring for a young child with pre-acute renal failure (ARF). Which explanation is the most common cause for this type of ARF?
A. Wilms' tumor—NO, this is cancer.
B. Heart failure—YES, heart failure produces ineffective pumping to major organs such as the kidneys.
C. Vesicoureteral reflux—NO, this should not affect the kidneys.
D. Contrast media diagnostics—NO, this should not affect the kidneys to the extent of failure.

Exercise 15-25: *Select all that apply*
The clinical manifestations of children that are associated with acute glomerulonephritis include:
☐ Nervousness
☒ **Dependent edema**
☒ **Periorbital edema**
☒ **Decreased urine output**
☒ **Hematuria**
☒ **Hypertension**
☐ Low sodium
☐ Low potassium

Exercise 15-26: *Multiple-choice question*
Which test would the nurse anticipate the health care provider to order for effectively diagnosing acute glomerulonephritis?
A. Antistreptolysin O titer—YES, this would show if the child has an infection.
B. Collection for 24-hour urine—NO, this is not diagnostic for this condition.
C. Blood cultures—NO, this is not diagnostic for this condition.
D. Stool cultures—NO, this is not diagnostic for this condition.

Exercise 15-27: *True or false*
Nonsteroidal anti-inflammatory drugs (NSAIDs) should not be administered to children with renal function problems as the prostaglandin action can further decrease the glomerular filtration rate.
___**X**___ **True**
_____ False

Exercise 15-28: *Fill-in*

List four laboratory/diagnostic tests useful in diagnosing acute glomerulonephritis.

1. **Serum creatinine and BUN**

2. **Erythrocyte sedimentation rate**

3. **Urine dipstick test**

4. **White blood count with differential**

Exercise 15-29: *Multiple-choice question*

Which treatment is not used for acute glomerulonephritis but for the treatment of the original strep infection that was responsible for causing the acute glomerulonephritis?

A. NSAIDs—NO, this is a pain relief and anti-inflammatory medication.

B. Antihypertensives—NO, this should not be needed.

C. Diuretics—NO, this will not help the causative factor.

D. Antibiotics —YES, to fight the infection.

Exercise 15-30: *Multiple-choice question*

A child with acute glomerulonephritis is in the playroom of the hospital and experiences blurred vision with a headache. Which action should be taken by the nurse?

A. Check the urine to see if hematuria has increased—NO, this will not casue cerebral manifestations.

B. Obtain a blood pressure reading on the child and notify the physician—YES, hypertension can affect the vision.

C. Reassure the child and encourage bed rest until the headache improves—NO, an assessment is warranted.

D. Follow up on serum electrolytes with the medical laboratory—NO, an assessment should be done immediately.

16

Children With Endocrine Health Care Needs

Vicki A. Martin

Unfolding Case Study #16-1 Jasper

Jasper is a 14-year-old boy with diabetes mellitus (DM). He was diagnosed with juvenile onset DM at 12 years old, which is also referred to as type 1 DM. He has an insulin pump and manages his care well with the support of his family and endocrinologist. He drinks 1 to 2 liters of water per day to stay well hydrated and to prevent any further DM complications. He does participate in athletics at school. He regulates his blood sugar and insulin needs according to the insulin pump readings. He had baseball practice today and did get somewhat overheated. He drank water and Gatorade to compensate for the dehydration. However, after practice he felt weak and tired.

Exercise 16-1: *Fill-in*
Type 1 DM is the _____ most common chronic disease of childhood in the United States and Europe.

Exercise 16-2: *True or false*
The increase in incidence of type 2 DM among children and adolescents is attributed to the increase in childhood obesity and decrease in physical activity.
_____ True
_____ False

eResource 16-1: To learn more about the epidemiology of type 1 DM, refer to Medscape:
■ Online: [Pathway: www.medscape.org → Select "Reference" → Enter "sickle cell" into the search field → Select "sickle cell anemia" → Under the "Treatment and Management" tab, review "Vaso-Occlusive Crisis Management"]
■ On your mobile device, you can access the same information: [Pathway: Medscape → Select "Reference" → Enter "sickle cell" into the search field → Select "sickle cell anemia" → Under the "Treatment and Management" tab, review "Vaso-Occlusive Crisis Management"]

Answers to this chapter begin on page 255.

Exercise 16-3: *Multiple-choice question*

When planning patient education for the parents of a young child with type 1 DM, which instructions should the nurse include in the teaching?

    A. Limit the physical activity of the child.

    B. Rotate the insulin injection sites.

    C. Do not allow the child to do blood sugar testing.

    D. Recommend a high-calorie, high-fat diet.

 eResource 16-2: To learn more about DM to support your teaching, view the following:

    ▪ *Pathophysiology of Diabetes Mellitus*: goo.gl/okZGk2

    ▪ *What Is a Good Diet for Type 1 Diabetes—Pediatrics Information*: goo.gl/oulH4b

    ▪ *Diabetes Mellitus—Type I vs Type II*: goo.gl/wRm0WG

Exercise 16-4: *Matching*

Match the endocrine terms in Column A to the correct description in Column B.

Column A	Column B
A. Acanthosis	_____ Life-threatening medical emergency
B. Polyphagia	_____ Conversion of glycogen to glucose
C. Polydipsia	_____ Excessive hunger
D. Polyuria	_____ Excessive urine output
E. Glyconeogenesis	_____ Glycogen fixation from noncarbohydrates
F. Diabetic ketoacidosis	_____ Localized fat under skin from insulin
G. Proteolysis	_____ Fat breakdown
H. Lipolysis	_____ Low blood glucose (insulin reaction)
I. Hyperglycemia	_____ High blood glucose (low insulin)
J. Hypoglycemia	_____ Excessive thirst
K. Lipodystrophy	_____ Thickening and darkening of skin
L. Glycogenolysis	_____ Protein breakdown

Exercise 16-5: *Select all that apply*

The clinical manifestations associated with hypoglycemia include:

    ❑ Tachycardia

    ❑ Fatigue

    ❑ Blurred vision

    ❑ Headaches

    ❑ Dizziness

    ❑ Dry skin

Answers to this chapter begin on page 255.

eResource 16-3: To learn more about the clinical presentation of hypoglycemia, refer to:

- MerckMedicus: [Pathway: www.merckmedicus.com → Enter "hypoglycemia" into the search field → Select "hypoglycemia" → Select "Symptoms and Signs" to access and review related content]
- Medscape:
    - Online: [Pathway: www.medscape.org → Select "Reference" → Enter "hypoglycemia" into the search field → Select "hypoglycemia" → Under the "Clinical Presentation" tab, review "History" and "Physical Examination"]
    - On your mobile device, you can access the same information: [Pathway: Medscape → Enter "hypoglycemia" into the search field → Select "hypoglycemia" → Under the "Clinical Presentation" tab, review "History" and "Physical Examination"]
- View the following video, *Hypoglycemia*: goo.gl/hvCqyi

Exercise 16-6: *Select all that apply*

The clinical manifestations associated with hyperglycemia include:

- ❑ Polyuria
- ❑ Polydispsia
- ❑ Fruity breath
- ❑ Shakiness
- ❑ Weak, slow pulse
- ❑ Dry skin

 eResource 16-4: To learn more about the clinical presentation of hyperglycemia, refer to:

- MerckMedicus: [Pathway: www.merckmedicus.com → Enter "hyperglycemia" into the search field → Select "hyperglycemia" → Select "Symptoms and Signs" to access and review related content]
- Medscape:
    - Online: [Pathway: www.medscape.org → Select "Reference" → Enter "hyperglycemia" into the search field → Select "hyperglycemia" → Ender the "Clinical Presentation" tab, review "History" and "Physical Examination"]
    - On your mobile device, you can access the same information: [Pathway: Medscape → Enter "hyperglycemia" into the search field → Select "hyperglycemia" → Under the "Clinical Presentation" tab, review "History" and "Physical Examination"]
- View the following video, *Hyperglycemia*: goo.gl/OHrW2T

DM is the most common disorder of the pancreas in which the islets of Langerhans fail to produce adequate insulin.

Answers to this chapter begin on page 255.

eResource 16-5: To learn more about the standard treatments for type 1 DM and type 2 DM, refer to the American Diabetes Association website: [Pathway: www.diabetes.org → Select "Diabetes Basics" information tab → Select "Type 1 DM" tab → Select "Treatment/Care" tab for Type 1 and review content; repeat for "Type 2 DM"]

Exercise 16-7: *Fill-in*

According to the American Diabetes Association, what is the treatment for type 1 DM? _____ and _____.

According to the American Diabetes Association, what is the treatment for type 2 DM? _____, _____, _____, and _____.

Exercise 16-8: *Multiple-choice question*

Which diabetic testing has the capacity to check compliance with blood sugars over a 2- to 3-month period?

    A. Urine ketone testing

    B. C-peptide testing

    C. Blood glucose monitoring

    D. Hemoglobin A1C monitoring

 eResource 16-6: To develop a nursing care plan for Jasper, refer to the following resource:

    ■ *Diabetes Mellitus:* goo.gl/ZB2OK4

    ■ *Nursing Care Plan Index:* goo.gl/NKEJMM

    ■ *Nursing Outcomes Index:* goo.gl/IxdH2o

Unfolding Case Study #16-2 ■ Liza

Liza is a 7-year-old African American female. She was diagnosed with precocious puberty when she was 6 since she had early breast development, mood swings, and was larger than the average child her age. She is being monitored closely by the pediatrician to ensure proper growth and development and was started on gonadotropin-releasing hormone analog injections every 3 to 4 weeks. Her excessive sexual maturation has been slowly stabilizing and she will continue the injections until the pubertal age of 10 to 12 years old. The neurologist ruled out a brain tumor and her family was relieved.

 eResource 16-7: To learn more about the treatment of precocious puberty, refer to the following resources on your mobile device:

    ■ Epocrates Online: [Pathway: online.epocrates.com → Under the "Diseases" tab, enter "precocious puberty" in the search field → Select "precocious puberty" → Review content, focusing on "Highlights" and "Treatment"]

Answers to this chapter begin on page 255.

- Medscape:
  - Online: [Pathway: www.medscape.org → Select "Reference" → Enter "precocious puberty" into the search field → Select "precocious puberty" → Review content under "Overview" and "Treatment and Management"]
  - On your mobile device, you can access the same information: [Pathway: Medscape → Enter "precocious puberty" into the search field → Select "precocious puberty" → Review content under "Overview" and "Treatment and Management"]

Exercise 16-9: *True or false*

In precocious puberty, the child develops sexual characteristics before the age of puberty, which include girls and boys at the ages of 10 to 12 years.

_____ True

_____ False

Exercise 16-10: *Select all that apply*

The clinical manifestations associated with precocious puberty include:

- ❏ Facial acne
- ❏ Headaches
- ❏ Mood swings
- ❏ Accelerated growth
- ❏ Advanced bone age
- ❏ Early breast development
- ❏ Pigmented skin
- ❏ Adult body odor

e **eResource 16-8:** To learn more about the clinical manifestations of precocious puberty, refer to Medscape:
- Online: [Pathway: www.medscape.org → Select "Reference" → Enter "precocious puberty" into the search field → Select "precocious puberty" → Review content under "Clinical Presentation"]
- On your mobile device, you can access the same information: [Pathway: Medscape → Enter "precocious puberty" into the search field → Select "precocious puberty" → Review content under "Clinical Presentation"]

Exercise 16-11: *Multiple-choice question*

The newest treatment for precocious puberty is an implant for continuous release of which medication?

- A. Histrelin
- B. Baclofen
- C. Morphine
- D. Insulin

Answers to this chapter begin on page 255.

Exercise 16-12: *Fill-in*

Often, children with precocious puberty develop _____ _____ _____ and _____ related to the body image disturbances and impaired social interactions.

 eResource 16-9: To learn more about the psychosocial considerations of precocious puberty, refer to:
- Epocrates Online: [Pathway: online.epocrates.com → Under the "Diseases" tab, enter "precocious puberty" in the search field → Select "precocious puberty" → Select "Follow-up" and review content under "Complications"]
- *Precocious Puberty* video, which explores these important issues: goo.gl/dHGejK

Unfolding Case Study #16-3 ▨ Harold

Harold is a 16-year-old who received a head injury this year as a quarterback on the high school football team. He was recently diagnosed with diabetes insipidus or nephrogenic diabetes insipidus after waking up at night with complaints of excretion of large amounts of urine (polyuria) and excessive thirst (polydipsia). He is being treated by a neurologist for this condition with intranasal desmopressin acetate (DDAVP). He reports feeling much better while being on this medication.

 eResource 16-10: To reinforce your understanding of DDAVP, consult the following resources on your mobile device:
- Skyscape's RxDrugs on your mobile device (www.skyscape.com): [Pathway: Skyscape → Select "RxDrugs" → Enter "Desmopressin Acetate" into the search field → Select "Desmospray" to review content related to "desmopressin (nasal)]
- Epocrates: [Pathway: Epocrates → Enter "Desmopressin Acetate" into the search field → Select "Desmopressin nasal" and review content]

He has not been cleared to play football at this time. He is anxious to start playing football again and is compliant with all orders.

Exercise 16-13: *Fill-in*

Diabetes insipidus or nephrogenic diabetes insipidus is caused by a hormone deficiency with _____.

Exercise 16-14: *Multiple-choice question*

Which diagnostic test is essential in diagnosing diabetes insipidus?
- A. Blood toxicology
- B. Urine toxicology
- C. Water deprivation test
- D. Water intoxication test

Answers to this chapter begin on page 255.

eResource 16-11: To learn more about the causes of diabetes insipidus (or nephrogenic diabetes insipidus) and diagnostic workup, refer to Medscape:
- Online: [Pathway: www.medscape.org → Select "Reference" → Enter "Diabetes insipidus" into the search field → Select "Diabetes insipidus" → Review content under "Overview"]
- On your mobile device, you can access the same information: [Pathway: Medscape → Enter "Diabetes insipidus" into the search field → Select "Diabetes insipidus" → Review content under "Overview"]

Exercise 16-15: *Select all that apply*

The clinical manifestations associated with diabetes insipidus or nephrogenic diabetes insipidus include:

- ❏ Decreased urine osmolality
- ❏ Increased urine osmolality
- ❏ Decreased urine specific gravity
- ❏ Increased urine specific gravity
- ❏ Hypernatremia
- ❏ Hyponatremia
- ❏ Extreme dehydration

 eResource 16-12: To learn more about the clinical presentation of diabetes insipidus (or nephrogenic diabetes insipidus) and diagnostic workup, refer to Medscape:
- Online: [Pathway: www.medscape.org → Select "Reference" → Enter "Diabetes insipidus" into the search field → Select "Diabetes insipidus" → Review content under "Clinical Presentation"]
- On your mobile device, you can access the same information: [Pathway: Medscape → Enter "Diabetes insipidus" into the search field → Select "Diabetes insipidus" → Review content under "Clinical Presentation"]

Exercise 16-16: *True or false*

A major complication of the child with diabetes insipidus when experiencing extreme dehydration or hypernatremia is seizures.

_____ True
_____ False

Exercise 16-17: *Multiple-choice question*

Which endocrine disorder is the opposite of diabetes insipidus in which the child has increased urine osmolality, increased urine specific gravity, hyponatremia, and water intoxication?

- A. Adrenal insufficiency
- B. Syndrome of inappropriate antidiuretic hormone (SIADH)
- C. Hypothyroidism
- D. Hyperthyroidism

Answers to this chapter begin on page 255.

Exercise 16-18: *Select all that apply*

The various conditions responsible for causing SIADH include:

- ❏ Meningitis
- ❏ Brain tumors
- ❏ Chemotherapy
- ❏ Chest trauma
- ❏ Head trauma
- ❏ Barbiturates

Exercise 16-19: *True or false*

The treatment for correcting the hyponatremia in SIADH is intravenous (IV) D5W.

_____ True

_____ False

 eResource 16-13: To reinforce your understanding of the underlying causes and treatment of SIADH, refer to Medscape:

- ▇ Online: [Pathway: www.medscape.org → Select "Reference" → Enter "Syndrome of Inappropriate Antidiuretic Hormone" into the search field → Select "Syndrome of Inappropriate Antidiuretic Hormone" → Review content under the "Clinical Presentation" and "Treatment and Management" tab]
- ▇ On your mobile device: [Pathway: Medscape → Enter "Syndrome of Inappropriate Antidiuretic Hormone" into the search field → Select "Syndrome of Inappropriate Antidiuretic Hormone" → Review content under the "Clinical Presentation" and "Treatment and Management" tab]

Unfolding Case Study #16-4 ▇ Carmen

Carmen is a 4-year-old female living with her biological parents and older brother. For the past 3 or 4 months, she has been feeling extremely fatigued, requires 12 hours of sleep each night, has dry/scaly skin, has intolerance to cold, no appetite, and is constipated. Her parents took her to the health care provider and she was diagnosed with Hashimoto's thyroiditis.

 eResource 16-14: To learn more about the clinical presentation for Hashimoto's thyroiditis, refer to the following resources:

- ▇ Epocrates Online: [Pathway: online.epocrates.com → Under the "Diseases" tab, enter "thyroiditis" in the search field → Select "thyroiditis, Hashimoto" → Review "Highlights" and "Basics"]

Answers to this chapter begin on page 255.

■ Medscape:
   ■ Online: [Pathway: www.medscape.org → Enter "thyroiditis" into the search field → Select "Hashimoto Thyroiditis" → Review content under the "Overview" tab and "Presentation"]
   ■ On your mobile device: [Pathway: Medscape → Enter "thyroiditis" into the search field → Select "Hashimoto Thyroiditis" → Review content under the "Overview" tab and "Clinical Presentation"]

She was ordered to take Synthroid daily in the morning and her dose is being titrated according to the thyroid panel tests every month.

 eResource 16-15: To reinforce your understanding of Synthroid, refer to the following resources on your mobile device:
   ■ Skyscape's RxDrugs on your mobile device (www.skyscape.com): [Pathway: Skyscape → Select "RxDrugs" → Enter "Synthroid" into the search field → Select "Synthroid" to access content]
   ■ Epocrates: [Pathway: Epocrates → Enter "Synthroid" into the search field → Select "Synthroid" and review content]

The health care provider is concerned that Carmen's fluctuation in thyroid levels can cause her to have hyperthyroidism. Therefore, the health care provider must monitor the dose for restoration to a euthyroid (normal) state.

Exercise 16-20: *Multiple-choice question*
Which laboratory test is the best indicator for titrating medications in patients with hypothyroidism?
   A. T3 uptake study
   B. T4 uptake study
   C. Thyroid-stimulating hormone (TSH)
   D. Complete blood count

 eResource 16-16: To review the diagnostic tests for Hashimoto's thyroiditis, refer to Medscape:
   ■ Online: [Pathway: www.medscape.org → Enter "thyroiditis" into the search field → Select "Hashimoto Thyroiditis" → Review content under the "Workup" tab]
   ■ On your mobile device: [Pathway: Medscape → Enter "thyroiditis" into the search field → Select "Hashimoto Thyroiditis" → Review content under the "Workup" tab]

Exercise 16-21: *Fill-in*
Acquired hypothyroidism is categorized as primary, secondary, or tertiary and is commonly caused by a(n) _____ disorder.

Exercise 16-22: *True or false*

Hashimoto's thyroiditis is a primary acquired hypothyroidism also known as autoimmune chronic lymphocytic thyroiditis.

_____ True

_____ False

Exercise 16-23: *Matching*

Match the endocrine terms in Column A to the correct description in Column B.

Column A	Column B
A. Hypothyroidism	_____ Decreased rate of growth
B. Hyperthyroidism	_____ Increased rate of growth
	_____ Cold intolerance
	_____ Heat intolerance
	_____ Fatigue
	_____ Emotional lability
	_____ Dry skin
	_____ Warm, moist skin

e **eResource 16-17:** To reinforce your understanding of disorders of the thyroid, view the following videos:
- *Thyroid Physiology and Pathophysiology*: goo.gl/2tCs8X
- *Hyperthyroidism and Hypothyroidism*: goo.gl/E8XGjR
- *Thyroid Disease Symptoms and Treatments (Hypothyroidism, Hyperthyroidism and Goiter)* goo.gl/6LpGdi

Exercise 16-24: *Multiple-choice question*

A nurse is admitting a child suspected of having acquired hypothyroidism. Which assessment should the nurse understand as confirming that diagnosis?

    A. Thyroid goiter

    B. Hirsutism

    C. Exophthalmus

    D. Ptosis

Exercise 16-25: *Fill-in*

Hyperthyroidism is uncommon in children and adolescents and is known as _____ disease.

Exercise 16-26: *Multiple-choice question*

In which of the following groups is hyperthyroidism and hypothyroidism more common?

    A. Boys

    B. Girls

    C. Twins

    D. Triplets

Answers to this chapter begin on page 255.

Answers

Exercise 16-1: *Fill-in*

Type 1 DM is the **second** most common chronic disease of childhood in the United States and Europe.

Exercise 16-2: *True or false*

The increase in incidence of type 2 DM among children and adolescents is attributed to the increase in childhood obesity and decrease in physical activity.

   X   True

_____ False

Exercise 16-3: *Multiple-choice question*

When planning patient education for the parents of a young child with type 1 DM, which instructions should the nurse include in the teaching?

A. Limit the physical activity of the child—NO, children should stay active.

B. Rotate the insulin injection sites—Yes, to prevent hypertrophy of the skin.

C. Do not allow the child to do blood sugar testing—NO, children with DM are encouraged to check their glucose and participate in self-care.

D. Recommend a high-calorie, high- fat diet—NO, calories and carbohydrates need to be monitored.

Exercise 16-4: *Matching*

Match the endocrine terms in Column A to the correct description in Column B.

Column A	Column B
A. Acanthosis	__F__ Life-threatening medical emergency
B. Polyphagia	__L__ Conversion of glycogen to glucose
C. Polydipsia	__B__ Excessive hunger
D. Polyuria	__D__ Excessive urine output
E. Glyconeogenesis	__E__ Glycogen fixation from
F. Diabetic ketoacidosis	noncarbohydrates
G. Proteolysis	__K__ Localized fat under skin from insulin
H. Lipolysis	__H__ Fat breakdown
I. Hyperglycemia	__J__ Low blood glucose (insulin reaction)
J. Hypoglycemia	__I__ High blood glucose (low insulin)
K. Lipodystrophy	__C__ Excessive thirst
L. Glycogenolysis	__A__ Thickening and darkening of skin
	__G__ Protein breakdown

Exercise 16-5: *Select all that apply*

The clinical manifestations associated with hypoglycemia include:

☒ **Tachycardia**

☒ **Fatigue**

❑ Blurred vision

☒ **Headaches**

☒ **Dizziness**

❑ Dry skin

Exercise 16-6: *Select all that apply*

The clinical manifestations associated with hyperlycemia include:

☒ **Polyuria**

☒ **Polydispsia**

☒ **Fruity breath**

❑ Shakiness

☒ **Weak, slow pulse**

☒ **Dry skin**

Exercise 16-7: *Fill-in*

According to the American Diabetes Association, what is the treatment for type 1 DM?

Blood glucose control and insulin administration

According to the American Diabetes Association, what is the treatment for type 2 DM?

Weight loss, increased activity, blood glucose control, and oral antidiabetic medications

Exercise 16-8: *Multiple-choice question*

Which diabetic testing has the capacity to check compliance with blood sugars over a 2- to 3-month period?

A. Urine ketone testing—NO, this is used for short-term compliance.

B. C-peptide testing—NO, this is not used.

C. Blood glucose monitoring—NO, this is used for short-term compliance.

D. Hemoglobin A1c monitoring—YES, determines blood sugars for 8 to 12 weeks.

Exercise 16-9: *True or false*

In precocious puberty, the child develops sexual characteristics before the age of puberty, which include girls and boys at the age of 10 to 12 years.

_____ True

___**X**___ **False—Sexual characteristics occur in Caucasian girls before age 7, in African American girls before age 6, and boys younger than age 9.**

Exercise 16-10: *Select all that apply*

The clinical manifestations associated with precocious puberty include:

☒ **Facial acne**

☒ **Headaches**

☒ **Mood swings**

☒ **Accelerated growth**

☒ **Advanced bone age**

☒ **Early breast development**

❑ Pigmented skin

☒ **Adult body odor**

Exercise 16-11: *Multiple-choice question*

The newest treatment for precocious puberty is an implant for continuous and slow release of which medication?

A. Histrelin—YES, a GnRH agonist

B. Baclofen—NO, this is used to treat spasticity.

C. Morphine—NO, this is for discomfort.

D. Insulin—NO, this is for diabetes mellitus.

Exercise 16-12: *Fill-in*

Often, children with precocious puberty develop **self-esteem issues** and **anxiety** related to the body image disturbances and impaired social interactions.

Exercise 16-13: *Fill-in*

Diabetes insipidus or nephrogenic diabetes insipidus is caused by a hormone deficiency with **antidiuretic hormone (ADH)**.

Exercise 16-14: *Multiple-choice question*

Which diagnostic test is essential in diagnosing diabetes insipidus?
  A. Blood toxicology—NO, this is not used as it checks for chemicals in the blood.
  B. Urine toxicology—NO, this checks for chemicals in the urine.
  C. **Water deprivation test—YES, this will demonstrate the hormone imbalance.**
  D. Water intoxication test—NO, water is not retained.

Exercise 16-15: *Select all that apply*

The clinical manifestations associated with diabetes insipidus or nephrogenic diabetes insipidus include:

☒ **Decreased urine osmolality**

❑ Increased urine osmolality

☒ **Decreased urine specific gravity**

❑ Increased urine specific gravity

☒ **Hypernatremia**

❑ Hyponatremia

☒ **Extreme dehydration**

Exercise 16-16: *True or false*

A major complication of the child with diabetes insipidus when experiencing extreme dehydration or hypernatremia is seizures.

  X True
  ———— False

Exercise 16-17: *Multiple-choice question*

Which endocrine disorder is the opposite of diabetes insipidus in which the child has increased urine osmolality, increased urine specific gravity, hyponatremia, and water intoxication?
  A. Adrenal Insufficiency—NO, this does not produce water intoxication.
  B. **Syndrome of inappropriate antidiuretic hormone (SIADH)—YES, SIADH is the opposite of diabetes insipidus.**
  C. Hypothyroidism—NO, this effects activity.
  D. Hyperthyroidism—NO, this effects activity.

Exercise 16-18: *Select all that apply*
The various conditions responsible for causing SIADH include:

☒ **Meningitis**

☒ **Brain tumors**

☒ **Chemotherapy**

❏ Chest trauma

☒ **Head trauma**

☒ **Barbiturates**

Exercise 16-19: *True or false*
The treatment for correcting the hyponatremia in SIADH is intravenous (IV) D5W.

_____ True

___**X**___ **False—Intravenous fluids for increasing hyponatremia are normal saline (NS).**

Exercise 16-20: *Multiple-choice question*
Which laboratory test is the best indicator for titrating medications in patients with hypothyroidism?

A. T3 uptake study—NO, this does not demonstrate the imbalance.

B. T4 uptake study—NO, this does not demonstrate the imbalance.

C. **Thyroid-stimulating hormone (TSH)—YES, TSH is the best indicator for thyroid levels.**

D. Complete blood count—NO, this does not demonstrate the imbalance.

Exercise 16-21: *Fill-in*
Acquired hypothyroidism is categorized as primary, secondary, or tertiary and is commonly caused by a(n) **autoimmune** disorder.

Exercise 16-22: *True or false*
Hashimoto's thyroiditis is a primary acquired hypothyroidism also known as autoimmune chronic lymphocytic thyroiditis.

___**X**___ **True**

_____ False

Exercise 16-23: *Matching*

Match the endocrine terms in Column A to the correct description in Column B.

Column A		Column B
A. Hypothyroidism	**A**	Decreased rate of growth
B. Hyperthyroidism	**B**	Increased rate of growth
	A	Cold intolerance
	B	Heat intolerance
	A	Fatigue
	B	Emotional lability
	B	Warm, moist skin
	A	Dry skin

Exercise 16-24: *Multiple-choice question*

A nurse is admitting a child with a suspected diagnosis of acquired hypothyroidism. Which assessment should the nurse understand as confirming that diagnosis?

A. Thyroid goiter—YES, this is a common symptom.

B. Hirsutism—NO, this is not a common manifestation.

C. Exophthalmus—NO, this is hyperthyroidism.

D. Ptosis—NO, this is not a common manifestation.

Exercise 16-25: *Fill-in*

Hyperthyroidism is uncommon in children and adolescents and is known as **Graves'** disease.

Exercise 16-26: *Multiple-choice question*

In which of the following groups is hyperthyroidism and hypothyroidism more common?

A. Boys—NO

B. Girls—YES

C. Twins—NO

D. Triplets—NO

17

Children With Neurological
Health Care Needs

Vicki A. Martin

Unfolding Case Study #17-1 ▨ Donetta

Donetta is a 6-month-old female infant. She resides with her single mother and grandmother. Donetta's family survives with government assistance for housing and health care. She has been fussy and irritable for a few days. Her mother took her to the pediatrician for a check-up using her Medicaid card. The pediatrician could not find anything wrong with her. The next day, after seeing the health care provider, her temperature went from being normal to 103° F. She was taken to the emergency department. During the assessment, the temperature increased to 104° F and she started having febrile seizures. She was admitted to the pediatric intensive care unit (PICU) after the health care provider was suspicious of meningitis. A lumbar puncture and a septic workup were performed. Donetta was being treated now for bacterial meningitis until the diagnostic results rule it out.

Exercise 17-1: *Fill-in*
List five infectious processes common for causing febrile seizures in infants and children between 6 months and 5 years of age:

1. _____
2. _____
3. _____
4. _____
5. _____

e **eResource 17-1:** To learn more about fevers in children, refer to Medscape:
   ■ Online: [Pathway: www.medscape.org → Select "Reference" → Enter "fever" into the search field → Select "Fever in the Infant or Toddler" → Review content under "Differential Diagnosis" and "Workup"]

■ On your mobile device: [Pathway: Medscape → Enter "fever" into the search field → Select "Fever in the Infant or Toddler" → Review content under "Differential Diagnosis" and "Workup"]

Exercise 17-2: *True or false*

Febrile seizures are usually self-limiting and have a postictal period lasting for less than 10 to15 minutes.

_____ True

_____ False

Exercise 17-3: *Select all that apply*

The clinical manifestations associated with bacterial meningitis include:

❑ Malaise

❑ Myalgia

❑ Anorexia

❑ Skin rashes

❑ Nuchal rigidity

❑ Positive Kernig's pointed nose

❑ Negative Brudzinski

❑ Fevers more than 104° F

ⓔ **eResource 17-2:** To reinforce your understanding of the clinical presentation of bacterial meningitis, consult the following resources:
Epocrates Online: [Pathway: online.epocrates.com → Under the "Diseases" tab, enter "meningitis" in the search field → Select "bacterial meningitis" → Review "Highlights"]
■ Medscape Online: [Pathway: www.medscape.org → Select "Reference" → Enter "meningitis" into the search field → Select "meningitis" → Review content under "Overview" and "Presentation"]
■ On your mobile device: [Pathway: Medscape → Enter "meningitis" into the search field → Select "meningitis" → Review content under "Overview" and "Clinical Presentation"]

Exercise 17-4: *Multiple-choice question*

When a 6-month-old is admitted to the hospital with suspected meningitis and the infant is crying, irritable, and in an opisthotonic position, which nursing intervention is priority?

A. Educating the family on the prevention of meningitis in children.

B. Initiating isolation precautions and intravenous antibiotics.

C. Encouraging the parents to hold, feed, and care for their infant.

D. Assessing the infant's fontanels along with a head-to-toe assessment.

Answers to this chapter begin on page 271.

Exercise 17-5: *Matching*

Match the causative organism in Column A to the correct age affected in Column B.

Column A	Column B
A. *Escherichia coli*	_____ Children younger than 2 years and adolescents
B. *Streptococcus* group B	
C. *Haemophilus influenzae* type B	_____ Children older than 3 months and adults
D. *Streptococcus pneumoniae*	
E. *Neisseria meningitides*	_____ Children 3 months to 6 years
	_____ Infants younger than 1 month
	_____ Newborns and infants

Donetta's high fevers required treatment with intravenous fluids, intravenous antibiotics, and antipyretics. The antipyretics of choice for children with any type of infectious disease processes should not contain aspirin.

Exercise 17-6: *Multiple-choice question*

The nurse understands that children with infectious diseases require treatment with antipyretics for fever management to prevent febrile seizures, and that aspirin or aspirin by-products should not be administered to children. Which complication can be life-threatening to children when given aspirin during viral infections?

A. Cardiovascular disease
B. Upper respiratory infections
C. Urinary tract infections
D. Reye syndrome

Exercise 17-7: *Fill-in*

List five nursing interventions that are a priority for injury prevention and seizure precautions with children.

1. _____
2. _____
3. _____
4. _____
5. _____

 eResource 17-3: To assist in the development of a nursing care plan for Donetta, refer to the following nursing care plan resources:
- *Nursing Care Plan Index*: goo.gl/NKEJMM
- *Nursing Outcomes Index*: goo.gl/IxdH2o
- *Febrile Seizures Care Plan*: goo.gl/ygn7Mq
- *Fever*: goo.gl/33cCeW
- *Infection*: goo.gl/Lu1ykP

Answers to this chapter begin on page 271.

Unfolding Case Study #17-2 Malcolm

Malcolm is a 4-year-old who has returned home from a visit at his grandmother's home in Colorado. His mother has noticed that he is not his usual active and talkative self, but she is watching him closely. After his third day back home in the late afternoon, he starts to run a low-grade fever, has flu-like symptoms, and generally does not feel well. His mother takes him to the outpatient clinic in their community. The health care provider suspects encephalitis from an infected mosquito bite with the West Nile virus while visiting his grandmother.

 eResource 17-4: To learn more about West Nile virus, watch the following videos:
- *Killer Outbreaks—West Nile Virus*: goo.gl/kYqKTv
- *West Nile Virus: Treatment and Symptoms*: goo.gl/ooj6I8

The clinic refers them straight to the emergency department for admission to the pediatric intensive care unit (PICU) due to the possibility of cardiorespiratory complications, neurologic sequelae, seizures, and increased intracranial pressure. The health care provider informs the family that severe encephalitis cases can last up to 6 months. His family is very concerned and they remain by his bedside.

 eResource 17-5: To learn more about West Nile encephalitis, refer to Medscape:
- Online: [Pathway: www.medscape.org → Select "Reference" → Enter "West Nile" into the search field → Select "West Nile Encephalitis" → Review content]
- On your mobile device, you can access the same information: [Pathway: Medscape → Enter "West Nile" into the search field → Select "West Nile Encephalitis" → Review content]

Exercise 17-8: *Multiple-choice question*
Which explanation is an incorrect description of the acronym AVPU for assessing a child's level of consciousness (LOC)?

    A. A = Alert and awake
    B. V = Visual disturbances
    C. P = Responsive to painful stimuli
    D. U = Unresponsive

Exercise 17-9: *True or false*
Encephalitis can be caused by bacteria, viruses, fungi, or protozoa, but most are caused by protozoa.

_____ True
_____ False

Answers to this chapter begin on page 271.

Exercise 17-10: *Select all that apply*

The late signs of increased intracranial pressure include:

❏ Decreased systolic blood pressure

❏ Cushing's triad

❏ Papilledema

❏ Tachycardia

❏ Respiratory distress

❏ Deteriorating LOC

❏ Dilated pupil(s)

❏ Fixed pupil(s)

e   **eResource 17-6:** To learn more about intracranial pressure, view the following video: *ICP Management* goo.gl/sYI4vC

Exercise 17-11: *Fill-in*

List the ABCDE assessment of a neurologically injured child.

1. _____

2. _____

3. _____

4. _____

5. _____

Exercise 17-12: *Multiple-choice question*

Which symptom is not an early sign of increased intracranial pressure?

A. Sunsetting eyes

B. Vomiting episodes

C. Cheyne-Stokes respirations

D. Headache worse when awakening

Exercise 17-13: *Matching*

Match the cranial nerve in Column A to the reflex the nerve ennervates in Column B.

Column A	Column B
A. Cranial nerves II and III	_____ Gag
B. Cranial nerves II, IV, and VI	_____ Corneal
C. Cranial nerves III and VIII	_____ Oculocephalic
D. Cranial nerves V and VII	_____ Oculovestibular
E. Cranial nerves IX and X	_____ Pupillary

Answers to this chapter begin on page 271.

eResource 17-7: To aid in helping you remember the cranial nerves, use the *Cranial nerves mnemonic*: goo.gl/43Rbwa

Exercise 17-14: *Multiple-choice question*

When using the Glasgow Coma Scale (GCS) to determine the LOC with infants and children, which score should the nurse have when the child opens eyes with pain, responds verbally with cries to pain, and has abnormal flexion with motor response?

    A. Score of 8

    B. Score of 9

    C. Score of 10

    D. Score of 11

 eResource 17-8: To verify your answer, consult the following tools on your mobile device:

    ▪ Skyscape's Archimedes: [Pathway: Archimedes → Enter "Glasgow" into the search field → Select "Glasgow Coma Scale for Children" → Enter data from above]

    ▪ Medscape: [Pathway: Medscape → Enter "Glasgow" into the search field → Select "Glasgow Coma Scale—Pediatric" → Enter data from above]

Unfolding Case Study #17-3 Giselle

Giselle is a 3-week-old infant born to new parents. She has been a fussy, irritable infant since birth. Giselle experiences colic after breastfeeding constantly. Her mother became so exhausted and frustrated that she refrained completely from breastfeeding. Giselle is bottle fed at every feeding with a soy-based formula that is easily digested. She appears to tolerate the formula better but is still a difficult eater and feeder. The couple are young and do not have any family nearby to offer support. Both parents' mothers came to stay for 1 week each but the past week has been very difficult for Giselle's mother since Giselle's dad went back to work and she was alone to care for the fussy infant.

Exercise 17-15: *Multiple-choice question*

The emergency department has an infant brought in by both parents with assessment findings of vomiting, failure to thrive, and a decreased level of consciousness. Which occurrence should the nurse suspect?

    A. Immunization reaction

    B. Metabolic syndrome

    C. *Haemophilus influenzae*

    D. Shaken-baby syndrome

Answers to this chapter begin on page 271.

Exercise 17-16: *Fill-in*
List five risk factors associated with shaken-baby syndrome.

1. _____
2. _____
3. _____
4. _____
5. _____

Exercise 17-17: *True or false*
Many brain injuries with infants and children involve coup and contrecoup impact. The contrecoup injury results from secondary impact as the brain moves forward and then backward within the skull.

_____ True

_____ False

Exercise 17-18: *Matching*
Match the type of brain injury in Column A to the clinical manifestations in Column B.

Column A	Column B
A. Concussion or mild brain injury	_____ Coma, increased intracranial pressure with seizures
B. Moderate brain injury	_____ Easily irritated, changes in eating
C. Severe brain injury	_____ Loss of consciousness, amnesia

Exercise 17-19: *Select all that apply*
The common signs and symptoms of shaken-baby syndrome include:

❏ PERRLA

❏ Bulging fontanels

❏ Ecchymosis around eyes

❏ Vomiting without illness

❏ Respiratory distress

❏ Posturing

❏ Seizures

❏ Symmetrical pupils

ⓔ **eResource 17-9:** To learn more about traumatic brain injuries, read and view the following resources:
  ■ *A Journalist's Guide to Shaken Baby Syndrome: A Preventable Tragedy,* providing facts, figures, triggers, and prevention information: goo.gl/BrFsfl

Answers to this chapter begin on page 271.

■ Using Medscape on your mobile device, access Medscape's Educational Programs: [Pathway: Medscape → Select "Education" tab → Enter "shaken" into the search field → select and view these videos:
  ■ *Pediatric Brain Injuries: A Focus on Prevention*
  ■ *An Introduction to Pediatric Acquired Brain Injury*]
■ Centers for Disease Control and Prevention (CDC) Expert Commentary: *Shaken Baby Syndrome: Making the Diagnosis*: goo.gl/mtwwfR
■ *Preventing Shaken Baby Syndrome,* a component of the CDC's "Heads Up Series": goo.gl/Wyf0ce

Unfolding Case Study #17-4 ■ Benjamin

Benjamin is a 7-year-old boy born with a myelomeningocele, also referred to as spina bifida. He has a neurogenic bladder and requires intermittent catheterizations every 2 to 3 hours throughout the day. He also has a type II Chiari defect, which requires a ventriculoperitoneal (VP) shunt to prevent being hydrocephalic. A myelomeningocele can be located anywhere on the spinal cord but 75% are located in the lumbosacral area. Benjamin's spina bifida developed in the lumbosacral area.

 eResource 17-10: To reinforce your understanding of spina bifida, refer to MerckMedicus Online on your mobile device: [Pathway: www .merckmedicus.com → Select "Merck Manual" → Select "Merck Manual for Healthcare Professionals" → Enter "Spina Bifida" into the search field → Select "Spina Bifida" and review content]

His family has received patient education on numerous topics since this disease process affects multiple body systems. Some of the education included proper positioning to prevent skin breakdown, promoting urinary elimination through catheterization, preventing latex allergies, and identifying signs and symptoms of complications such as hydrocephalus and increased intracranial pressure.

Exercise 17-20: *Fill-in*
List three complications associated with ventriculoperitoneal shunts used for preventing hydrocephaly.

1. _____

2. _____

3. _____

 eResource 17-11: To learn more about the management of hydrocephalus and intracranial pressure:
■ Refer to Medscape on your mobile device: [Pathway: Medscape → Select "References" → Enter "shunt" into the search field → Select "Spina Bifida Hydrocephalus and Shunts" → Review content]

■ View *Shunt Surgery & Pediatric Hydrocephalus—What to Expect*: goo
.gl/6wXWi3
■ Review the video: *ICP Management* goo.gl/sYI4vC
■ View the surgical procedure: *Shunt for Hydrocephalus*: goo.gl/0YC2r7

Exercise 17-21: *Select all that apply*
The clinical manifestations common to ventriculoperitoneal shunt malfunction include:

❑ Changes or decreases in LOC

❑ Complaints of headaches

❑ Nausea and vomiting

❑ Visual disturbances

❑ Increased head circumference

❑ Bulging anterior fontanel

(e) **eResource 17-12:** To learn more about the complications associated
with a ventriculoperitoneal shunt, refer to:

■ Medscape on your mobile device: [Pathway: Medscape → Select
"References" → Enter "shunt" into the search field → Select "Spina
Bifida Hydrocephalus and Shunts" → Select "Shunt-Associated
Complications" and review content]
■ View *Hydrocephalus—Definition, treatment and complications*:
goo.gl/NBVIOh
■ View *Emergency Evaluation of Hydrocephalus and Shunts*:
goo.gl/63F5ov

Exercise 17-22: *Multiple-choice question*
During a well child visit in the pediatrician's office, the nurse would suspect hydrocephalus in an infant with which assessment finding?

A. Sunken fontanels

B. Narrow suture lines

C. Increase head circumference

D. Weight gain since last visit

Exercise 17-23: *True or false*
The signs of a shunt infection include negative blood cultures, decrease in white blood
cell count and protein, and an increase in glucose.

_____ True
_____ False

Answers to this chapter begin on page 271.

Exercise 17-24: *Matching*

Match the neural tube defect in Column A to the description in Column B.

Column A	Column B
A. Anencephaly	_____ Sac-like extrusion of spinal cord
B. Cranioschisis	_____ Sac-like herniation with meninges
C. Exencephaly	_____ Fissure of vertebral column
D. Encephalocele	_____ Failure of vertebral arches to fuse
E. Spina bifida occulata	_____ Absence of cranial vault
F. Rachischisis	_____ Skull defect with protruding nerves
G. Meningocele	_____ Malformation where brain exposed
H. Myelomeningocele	_____ Protrusion of brain and meninges

Answers to this chapter begin on page 271.

Answers

Exercise 17-1: *Fill-in*

List five infectious processes common for causing febrile seizures in infants and children between 6 months and 5 years of age:

1. **Urinary tract infections**
2. **Upper respiratory infections**
3. **Meningitis**
4. **Pneumonia**
5. **Otitis media**

Exercise 17-2: *True or false*

Febrile seizures are usually self-limiting and have a postictal period lasting for less than 10 to 15 minutes.

___**X**___ True

_____ False

Exercise 17-3: *Select all that apply*

The clinical manifestations associated with bacterial meningitis include:

☒ **Malaise**

☒ **Myalgia**

☒ **Anorexia**

☒ **Skin rashes**

☒ **Nuchal rigidity**

☒ **Positive Kernig's pointed nose**

❏ Negative Brudzinski

❏ Fevers greater than 104° F

Exercise 17-4: *Multiple-choice question*

When a 6-month-old is admitted to the hospital with suspected meningitis and the infant is crying, irritable, and in an opisthotonic position, which nursing intervention is priority?

A. Educating the family on the prevention of meningitis in children—NO, this is not the priority although it will be important for discharge teaching.

B. **Initiating isolation precautions and intravenous antibiotics—YES, this is the first thing that they will need to know about so they can assist in the care.**

C. Encouraging the parents to hold, feed, and care for their infant—NO, this is not the priority.

D. Assessing the infant's fontanels along with a head-to-toe assessment.—NO, this is important but not the first priority.

Exercise 17-5: *Matching*

Match the causative organism in Column A to the correct age affected in Column B.

Column A	Column B
A. *Escherichia coli*	__E__ Children younger than 2 years and adolescents
B. *Streptococcus* group B	
C. *Haemophilus influenzae* type B	__D__ Children older than 3 months and adults
D. *Streptococcus pneumoniae*	
E. *Neisseria meningitides*	__C__ Children 3 months to 6 years
	__B__ Infants younger than 1 month
	__A__ Newborns and infants

Donetta's high fevers required treatment with intravenous fluids, intravenous antibiotics, and antipyretics. The antipyretics of choice for children do not contain aspirin.

Exercise 17-6: *Multiple-choice question*

The nurse understands that children with infectious diseases require treatment with antipyretics for fever management to prevent febrile seizures, and that aspirin or aspirin by-products should not be administered to children. Which complication can be life-threatening to children when given aspirin during viral infections?

A. Cardiovascular disease—NO, this is not a complication of aspirin.

B. Upper respiratory infections—NO, this is not a complication of aspirin.

C. Urinary tract infections—NO, this is not a complication of aspirin.

D. **Reye syndrome—YES, this is a serious complication of administering aspirin to children.**

Exercise 17-7: *Fill-in*

List five nursing interventions that are a priority for injury prevention and seizure precautions with children.

1. Pad the side rails of the bed

2. Do not place anything in the mouth

3. Do not restrain a child

4. Maintain a patent airway

5. Keep the bed in a low and locked position

Exercise 17-8: *Multiple-choice question*
Which explanation is an incorrect description of the acronym AVPU for assessing a child's level of consciousness (LOC)?
A. A = Alert and awake—NO, this is correct.
B. V = Visual disturbances—YES, incorrect since responsive to verbal stimuli.
C. P = Responsive to painful stimuli—NO, this is correct.
D. U = Unresponsive—NO, this is correct.

Exercise 17-9: *True or false*
Encephalitis can be caused by bacteria, viruses, fungi, or protozoa, but most are caused by protozoa.
_____ True
___**X**___ **False—Mostly caused by viruses.**

Exercise 17-10: *Select all that apply*
The late signs of increased intracranial pressure include:
☐ Decreased systolic blood pressure
☒ **Cushing's triad**
☒ **Papilledema**
☐ Tachycardia
☒ **Respiratory distress**
☒ **Deteriorating LOC**
☒ **Dilated pupil(s)**
☒ **Fixed pupil(s)**

Exercise 17-11: *Fill-in*
List the ABCDE assessment of a neurologically injured child.
1. **A = Airway**
2. **B = Breathing**
3. **C = Circulation**
4. **D = Disability or neurological status**
5. **E = Exposure of body**

Exercise 17-12: *Multiple-choice question*
Which symptom is not an early sign of increased intracranial pressure?
A. Sunsetting eyes—NO, this is an early sign.
B. Vomiting episodes—NO, this is an early sign.
C. Cheyne-Stokes respirations—YES, this is a late and life-threatening sign.
D. Headache worse when awakening—NO, this is an early sign.

Exercise 17-13: *Matching*

Match the cranial nerve in Column A to the reflex the nerve ennervates in Column B.

Column A	Column B
A. Cranial nerves II and III	__D__ Gag
B. Cranial nerves II, IV, and VI	__E__ Corneal
C. Cranial nerves III and VIII	__B__ Oculocephalic
D. Cranial nerves V and VII	__C__ Oculovestibular
E. Cranial nerves IX and X	__A__ Pupillary

Exercise 17-14: *Multiple-choice question*

When using the Glasgow Coma Scale (GCS) to determine the level of consciousness with infants and children, which score should the nurse have when the child opens eyes with pain, responds verbally with cries to pain, and has abnormal flexion with motor response?

A. Score of 8—YES, this is a low GCS score that indicates poor brain function.

B. Score of 9—NO, a child with this score is serious but may be verbal.

C. Score of 10—NO, a child with this score is serious but may be verbal.

D. Score of 11—NO, a child with this score is serious but may be verbal.

Exercise 17-15: *Multiple-choice question*

The emergency department has an infant brought in by both parents with assessment findings of vomiting, failure to thrive, and a decreased level of consciousness. Which occurrence should the nurse suspect?

A. Immunization reaction—NO, these are not symptoms of a reaction; they are usually swelling and respiratory distress.

B. Metabolic syndrome—NO, these are not symptoms of a metabolic syndrome; they are usually obesity and glucose irregularity.

C. *Haemophilus influenzae*—NO, these are not symptoms of *influenzae;* they are usually flu-like symptoms.

D. Shaken-baby syndrome—YES, these are classic signs of shaken-baby syndrome.

Exercise 17-16: *Fill-in*

List five risk factors associated with shaken-baby syndrome.

1. **Single parent**

2. **Young parent**

3. **Substance abuse by a parent**

4. **Premature or sick infant**

5. **Infant with colic**

Exercise 17-17: *True or false*
Many brain injuries with infants and children involve coup and contrecoup impact. The contrecoup injury results from secondary impact as the brain moves forward and then backward within the skull.

___**X**___ True

_____ False

Exercise 17-18: *Matching*
Match the type of brain injury in Column A to the clinical manifestations in Column B.

Column A	Column B
A. Concussion or mild brain injury	___**C**___ Coma, increased intracranial pressure with seizures
B. Moderate brain injury	___**A**___ Easily irritated, changes in eating
C. Severe brain injury	___**B**___ Loss of consciousness, amnesia

Exercise 17-19: *Select all that apply*
The common signs and symptoms of shaken-baby syndrome include:

❑ PERRLA

☒ **Bulging fontanels**

☒ **Ecchymosis around eyes**

☒ **Vomiting without illness**

☒ **Respiratory distress**

☒ **Posturing**

☒ **Seizures**

❑ Symmetrical pupils

Exercise 17-20: *Fill-in*
List three complications associated with ventriculoperitoneal shunts used for preventing hydrocephaly.

1. **Infections**

2. **Obstruction**

3. **Need for revision with growth**

Exercise 17-21: *Select all that apply*

The clinical manifestations common to ventriculoperitoneal shunt malfunction include:

☒ **Changes or decreases in LOC**

☒ **Complaints of headaches**

☒ **Nausea and vomiting**

☒ **Visual disturbances**

☒ **Increased head circumference**

☒ **Bulging anterior fontanel**

Exercise 17-22: *Multiple-choice question*

During a well child visit in the pediatrician's office, the nurse would suspect hydrocephalus in an infant with which assessment finding?

A. Sunken fontanels—NO, this is a sign of dehydration.

B. Narrow suture lines—NO, this may be a sign of premature closure.

C. **Increase in head circumference—YES, this is due to the fact that cerebral spinal fluid is unable to drain and is backing up in the brain cavity.**

D. Weight gain since last visit—NO, this is not a normal sign.

Exercise 17-23: *True or false*

The signs of a shunt infection include negative blood cultures, decrease in white blood cell count and protein, and an increase in glucose.

_____ True

___**X**___ **False—All variables would be the opposite.**

Exercise 17-24: *Matching*

Match the neural tube defect in Column A to the description in Column B.

Column A		Column B
A. Anencephaly	__H__	Sac-like extrusion of spinal cord
B. Cranioschisis	__G__	Sac-like herniation with meninges
C. Exencephaly	__F__	Fissure of vertebral column
D. Encephalocele	__E__	Failure of vertebral arches to fuse
E. Spina bifida occulata	__A__	Absence of cranial vault
F. Rachischisis	__B__	Skull defect with protruding nerves
G. Meningocele	__C__	Malformation where brain exposed
H. Myelomeningocele	__D__	Protrusion of brain and meninges

18

Children With Mental and Cognitive Health Care Needs

Vicki A. Martin

Unfolding Case Study #18-1 ▨ Trey

Trey is a 9-year-old living in a single-family dwelling with a younger and older sibling and both biological parents. He has not had any medical issues but has communication problems that were identified when he was 3 years old. At that age, he presented with tendencies that included poor eye contact, bizarre behaviors, delayed language acquisition, poor social interactions, impairment of self-care skills, and altered sensory responses. The pediatrician diagnosed him with autism by the Denver Developmental Screening Test II (DDST-II). He attends a special needs school that is able to accommodate his learning and social needs. He also attends the after-school program for special needs children while both of his parents work, and he is doing well.

 eResource 18-1: Materials that have been provided to Trey's parents include:
- National Institute of Mental Health's (NIMH), *A Parent's Guide to Autism*: goo.gl/5PA1xV
- Centers for Disease Control's (CDC), Autism Spectrum Disorder Fact Sheet: goo.gl/yIh3u9

Exercise 18-1: *Fill-in*
The five autistic spectrum disorders are these pervasive developmental disorders:

1. _____
2. _____
3. _____
4. _____
5. _____

 eResource 18-2: To learn more about autism, early diagnosis and treatment, watch the following videos from the Healthy Minds series:
- *Autism—Part One: Discovery and Diagnosis*: goo.gl/TPcHDd
- *Autism—Part Two: Treatment and Early Intervention*: goo.gl/jT4FuW

Answers to this chapter begin on page 286.

Exercise 18-2: *True or false*

Autism is sometimes associated with other syndromes or diseases such as fragile X syndrome, Tourette's syndrome, or intellectually disabled children.

_____ True

_____ False

 eResource 18-3: To learn more about Tourette's syndrome, refer to Medscape:
- Online: [Pathway: www.medscape.org → Select "Reference" → Enter "Tourette" into the search field → Select "Tourette's syndrome" → Review content; be sure to view media files under "Clinical Presentation"; review "Treatment and Management" as well]
- On your mobile device, you can access the same information: [Pathway: Medscape → Enter "Tourette" into the search field → Select "Tourette's syndrome" → Review content; be sure to view media files under "Clinical Presentation"; review "Treatment and Management" as well]

Exercise 18-3: *Multiple-choice question*

What is the DDST-II that makes it useful in working with children?

    A. It is a test used to rule out intellectually disabled children.

    B. It is an intelligence quotient (IQ) test that is age-scaled to 6 years old.

    C. It is a method for measuring healthy, normal pediatric adaptation.

    D. It is a measurement of the abilities of children across five spectra.

eResource 18-4: To learn more about autism, visit the American Psychiatric Association website: [Pathway: www.psychiatry.org → Select "Public" tab at the top of the screen → Select "autism" from the dropdown tab and review content]

Exercise 18-4: *Select all that apply*

Clinical manifestations associated with autism spectrum disorder (ASD) include:

❑ Lack of eye contact

❑ Poor communication skills

❑ Shared play activities

❑ Responsiveness to auditory stimuli

❑ Sensitivity to tactile stimuli

❑ Receptive to usual teaching methods

❑ Repetitive actions or movements

eResource 18-5: To reinforce your understanding of autism, refer to Medscape:
- Online: [Pathway: www.medscape.org → Select "Reference" → Enter "autism" into the search field → Select "autism" → Review content; be sure to view media files under "Clinical Presentation"; review "Treatment and Management" as well]

Answers to this chapter begin on page 286.

■ On your mobile device, you can access the same information: [Pathway: Medscape → Enter "autism" into the search field → Select "autism" → Review content; be sure to view media files under "Clinical Presentation"; review "Treatment and Management" as well]

Unfolding Case Study #18-2 Alexis

Alexis was born to a 40-year-old mother and a 55-year-old father. Her mother had a normal pregnancy and delivery without any complications. Alexis was diagnosed at birth with Down syndrome. She has numerous medical issues and requires frequent health care along with an individualized educational plan in kindergarten. She is a loving and happy young child. She appears to be doing the best the pediatrician can expect with a known diagnosis of Down syndrome. Her health care issues are being managed and her learning disabilities are being adjusted as needed to meet her developmental needs for having a moderate disability.

 eResource 18-6: Alexis's parents frequently refer to Children with Down Syndrome: Health Care Information for Families from HealthyChildren .org: [Pathway: www.healthychildren.org or on your mobile device → Enter "Down syndrome" into the search field → Select "Children with Down Syndrome: Health Care Information for Families" → Read or listen to content; be sure to download a copy of the complete guide, *Health Care Information for Families of Children with Down Syndrome*. Review content, focusing on age-related content for Alexis]

Exercise 18-5: *True or false*
Down syndrome is an uncommon and rare chromosomal abnormality seen in children that is usually caused by the presence of one X chromosome being deficient.
_____ True
_____ False

Exercise 18-6: *Multiple-choice question*
Definitive diagnosing for Down syndrome is based on which type of test?
    A. Amniocentesis
    B. Developmental testing
    C. Quadruple screening
    D. Karyotyping

 eResource 18-7: To learn more about diagnostic procedures for Down syndrome, refer to MerckMedicus Online on your mobile device: [Pathway: www.merckmedicus.com → Select "Merck Manual" → Select "Merck Manual for Healthcare Professionals" → Enter "Down syndrome" into the search field → Select "Down syndrome" → Scroll down and select "Diagnosis" and review content]

Answers to this chapter begin on page 286.

Exercise 18-7: *Fill-in*

Down syndrome also has another name known as trisomy _____.

Exercise 18-8: *Select all that apply*

Common features of Down syndrome include:

- ❏ Hypertonia
- ❏ Epicanthic folds
- ❏ Palpebral fissures
- ❏ Longer great toe
- ❏ Enlarged tongue
- ❏ Depressed nasal bridge

Exercise 18-9: *Matching*

Match the disability in Column A to the correct description in Column B.

Column A	Column B
A. Mild disability	_____ IQ below 20
B. Moderate disability	_____ IQ of 20 to 35
C. Severe disability	_____ IQ of 35 to 50
D. Profound disability	_____ IQ of 50 to 70
E. Dyslexia	_____ Difficulty with mathematics
F. Dyspraxia	_____ Difficulty with written word
G. Dyscalculia	_____ Difficulty with reading
H. Dysgraphia	_____ Difficulty with coordination

Exercise 18-10: *True or false*

Down syndrome does not have a cure.

_____ True

_____ False

Exercise 18-11: *Multiple-choice question*

Which causes of intellectual disabilities are not preventable?

- A. Genetic
- B. Prenatal
- C. Perinatal
- D. Postnatal

e **eResource 18-8:** To reinforce your understanding of Down syndrome and the long-term care required for Alexis, refer to Medscape:
- ■ Online: [Pathway: www.medscape.org → Select "Reference" → Enter "Down Syndrome" into the search field → Select "Down Syndrome" → Review "Treatment and Management"]

Answers to this chapter begin on page 286.

■ On your mobile device, you can access the same information: [Pathway: Medscape → Enter "Down Syndrome" into the search field → Select "Down Syndrome" → Review "Treatment and Management"]

Unfolding Case Study #18-3 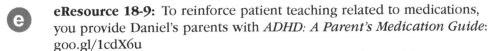 Daniel

Daniel is a 7-year-old first grader who has numerous problems at school related to his attention deficit/hyperactivity disorder (ADHD) diagnosis. His mother quit her job to volunteer at the school to assist him when it is necessary. Daniel experiences episodes characterized by impulsivity, inattention, hyperactivity, and distractibility. His parents were called to the school constantly and were very frustrated until his mother developed an individualized educational plan (IEP) for his learning disability while at school. Part of the plan was for his mother to be available to work with him in the classroom one-on-one to assist the teacher. This intervention has helped Daniel stay on target with the class.

Exercise 18-12: *True or false*
ADHD affects 25% of all children and 10% of all adults.

_____ True

_____ False

Exercise 18-13: *Fill-in*
List four common contributing factors for a child in developing ADHD.

1. _____

2. _____

3. _____

4. _____

Exercise 18-14: *Multiple-choice question*
Children with moderate to severe ADHD are treated with medications and often methylphenidate (Ritalin) is prescribed. Which side effects are common with Ritalin?

A. Increased appetite and weight gain

B. Insomnia and nervousness

C. Subnormal temperature

D. Increased saliva production

eResource 18-9: To reinforce patient teaching related to medications, you provide Daniel's parents with *ADHD: A Parent's Medication Guide*: goo.gl/1cdX6u

Answers to this chapter begin on page 286.

Exercise 18-15: *Select all that apply*

Common treatments effective in managing ADHD include:

❑ Pharmacotherapy

❑ Growth plotting

❑ Baseline cardiac monitoring

❑ Monitoring vital signs

❑ Behavior modification programs

❑ Increased environmental stimuli

ⓔ **eResource 18-10:** To learn more about ADHD refer to:
■ PDR Health: [Pathway: www.pdrhealth.com → Enter "ADHD" into the search field → Select "Attention Deficit/Hyperactivity Disorder" → Review content]
■ American Psychiatric Association: [Pathway: www.psychiatry.org → Select "Public" tab at the top of the screen → Select "ADHD" from the dropdown tab and review content]

Exercise 18-16: *Fill-in*

Comorbid conditions such as ADHD and obsessive-compulsive disorder (OCD) occur in _____% of children with Tourette's syndrome.

Exercise 18-17: *Multiple-choice question*

Tourette's syndrome is accompanied by which clinical manifestation?

A. Flat facial affect

B. Hallucinations

C. Motor and vocal tics

D. Inattentiveness

Exercise 18-18: *Select all that apply*

Disruptions in the levels of the brain that are associated with tic disorders include:

❑ Catecholamines

❑ Dopamine

❑ Epinephrine

❑ Neurotransmitters

❑ Neuropeptides

❑ Serotonin

❑ Norepineprine

ⓔ **eResource 18-11:** You refer Daniel's parents to HealthyChildren.org for additional parenting resources for children with ADHD: [Pathway: or on your mobile device → Enter "ADHD" into the search field → Select "ADHD" → Review list of resources available]

Answers to this chapter begin on page 286.

Unfolding Case Study #18-4 ▓ Terry

Terry is a 16-year-old female who has been being bullied at school. She is very thin, wears glasses, has social anxiety, and does not have many friends at school or in the community. Her parents are very concerned about her and took her to the health care provider for assessment.

 eResource 18-12: To learn more about bullying:
- American Psychiatric Association: [Pathway: www.psychiatry.org → Select "Public" tab at the top of the screen → Select "ADHD" from the dropdown tab and review content]
- American Academy of Child and Adolescent Psychiatry's Bullying Resource Center: goo.gl/ejIufJ

The health care provider referred her to a psychologist for evaluation. The evaluation revealed anorexia nervosa and depression diagnoses. She is being monitored closely by both health care providers and is being treated with family therapy, nutrition therapy, atypical antipsychotics, and antidepressants.

 eResource 18-13: To learn more about these diagnoses, refer to:
- American Psychiatric Association: [Pathway: www.psychiatry.org → Select "Public" tab at the top of the screen → Select "eating disorders" from the dropdown tab and review content; repeat with "Depression" and "Teens" and review content. Be sure to view videos under "Teens"]

Exercise 18-19: *Fill-in*
Clinical manifestations that accompany anorexia nervosa include a history of which type of symptoms?
1. _____
2. _____
3. _____
4. _____
5. _____
6. _____
7. _____
8. _____

 eResource 18-14: To supplement your understanding of anorexia nervosa, you watch Healthy Minds streaming video about *Eating Disorders*: goo.gl/SSXtzl

Exercise 18-20: *True or false*
The anorexic adolescent is usually underweight and presents with a body mass index (BMI) of 20.
_____ True
_____ False

Answers to this chapter begin on page 286.

Exercise 18-21: *Matching*

Match the mental health terms in Column A to the correct description in Column B.

Column A	Column B
A. Bingeing	_____ Mild to severe psychological distress
B. Purging	_____ Consumption of nonnutritive materials
C. Cachexia	_____ Excessive consumption of foods
D. Pica	_____ Malnutrition and muscle wasting
E. Anorexia nervosa	_____ Eating disorder with near-normal weight
F. Bulimia	_____ Forced vomiting after food consumption
G. Depression	_____ Eating disorder with weight loss

Exercise 18-22: *Multiple-choice question*

Which actions by the nurse would be a priority intervention for a child or adolescent having suicidal ideations?

    A. Implement suicide precautions and prompt referral to the emergency department.

    B. Discuss the feelings causing these thoughts to occur.

    C. Obtain a history and perform a nursing assessment.

    D. No cause for immediate concern but monitor the situation.

 eResource 18-15: To learn more about the signs of mental illness, early warning signs of teen depression, and suicide prevention, watch:
- *Teens: Typical or Troubled? Part One—What You Need to Know*: goo.gl/iHdkZm
- *Teens: Typical or Troubled? Part Two—Suicide Prevention*: goo.gl/7RZCDT

Exercise 18-23: *Select all that apply*

Treatment options for children and adolescents with eating disorders and mental health issues include:

❑ Family counseling

❑ Nutrition referrals

❑ Tricyclic antidepressants

❑ Selective serotonin reuptake inhibitors

❑ Depression and suicide monitoring

❑ Assessment for substance abuse

❑ Group therapy with support resources

❑ Sporadic medical follow-up

Answers to this chapter begin on page 286.

eResource 18-16: To reinforce the medication teaching you provide to Terry and her parents, you give them, *The Use of Medication in Treating Childhood and Adolescent Depression: Information for Patients and Families*: goo.gl/cO7X0K

Exercise 18-24: *True or false*

Children and adolescents experiencing depressive episodes may harm themselves purposefully without the intent to kill themselves. This action is known as self-mutilation.

_____ True

_____ False

Answers

Exercise 18-1: *Fill-in*

The five autistic spectrum disorders are these pervasive developmental disorders:

1. <u>**Autism**</u>
2. <u>**Asperger's syndrome**</u>
3. <u>**Childhood disintegrative disorder**</u>
4. <u>**Rett syndrome**</u>
5. <u>**Pervasive developmental disorder not specified (PDD-NOS)**</u>

Exercise 18-2: *True or false*

Autism is sometimes associated with other syndromes or diseases such as fragile X syndrome, Tourette's syndrome, or mentally challenged children.

___**X**___ **True**

_____ False

Exercise 18-3: *Multiple-choice question*

What is the DDST-II that makes it useful in working with children?

A. It is a test used to rule out intellectually challenged children—NO, this is not the purpose of the tool.

B. It is an intelligence quotient (IQ) test that is age-scaled to 6 years old—YES, this is the purpose of the tool.

C. It is a method for measuring healthy, normal pediatric adaptation—NO, this is not the purpose of the tool.

D. It is a measurement of the abilities of children across five spectra—NO, this is not the purpose of the tool.

Exercise 18-4: *Select all that apply*

Clinical manifestations associated with autism spectrum disorder (ASD) include:

☒ **Lack of eye contact**

☒ **Poor communication skills**

❑ Shared play activities

❑ Responsiveness to auditory stimuli

☒ **Sensitivity to tactile stimuli**

⊠ **Receptive to usual teaching methods**
⊠ **Repetitive actions or movements**

Exercise 18-5: *True or false*
Down syndrome is an uncommon and rare chromosomal abnormality seen in children that is usually caused by the presence of one X chromosome being deficient.
_____ True
___**X**___ **False**

Exercise 18-6: *Multiple-choice question*
Definitive diagnosing for Down syndrome is based on which type of test?
 A. Amniocentesis—NO, this is a genetic test done in utero.
 B. Developmental testing—NO, this differentiates delays of many causes.
 C. Quadruple screening—NO, this is a prenatal test.
 D. Karyotyping—YES, this will provide genetic diagnosis of the syndrome.

Exercise 18-7: *Fill-in*
Down syndrome also has a medical name known as trisomy ___**21**___.

Exercise 18-8: *Select all that apply*
Common features of Down syndrome include:
❑ Hypertonia
⊠ **Epicanthic folds**
⊠ **Palpebral fissures**
❑ Longer great toe
⊠ **Enlarged tongue**
⊠ **Depressed nasal bridge**

Exercise 18-9: *Matching*
Match the disability in Column A to the correct description in Column B.

Column A	Column B	
A. Mild disability	**D**	IQ below 20
B. Moderate disability	**C**	IQ of 20 to 35
C. Severe disability	**B**	IQ of 35 to 50
D. Profound disability	**A**	IQ of 50 to 70
E. Dyslexia	**G**	Difficulty with mathematics
F. Dyspraxia	**H**	Difficulty with written word
G. Dyscalculia	**E**	Difficulty with reading
H. Dysgraphia	**F**	Difficulty with coordination

Exercise 18-10: *True or false*

Down syndrome does not have a cure.

___**X**___ True

_____ False

Exercise 18-11: *Multiple-choice question*

Which causes of intellectual disability are not preventable?

A. Genetic—YES, these are inherited.

B. Prenatal—NO, these have to do with fetal oxygenation.

C. Perinatal—NO, these have to do with prenatal, intrapartum, or postnatal oxygenation issues.

D. Postnatal—NO, these have to do with postnatal oxygenation.

Exercise 18-12: *True or false*

ADHD affects 25% of all children and 10% of adults.

_____ True

___**X**___ **False**

Exercise 18-13: *Fill-in*

List four common contributing factors for a child in developing ADHD.

1. **Childhood exposure to high levels of lead or mercury.**

2. **Prenatal exposure to alcohol or tobacco smoke.**

3. **Prenatal factors including preterm labor.**

4. **Any episode resulting in impaired oxygenation.**

Exercise 18-14: *Multiple-choice question*

Children with moderate to severe ADHD are treated with medications and often methylphenidate (Ritalin) is prescribed. Which side effects are common with Ritalin?

A. Increased appetite and weight gain—NO, these children often lose weight due to the hyperactivity.

B. Insomnia and nervousness—YES, these are classic side effects of the medication.

C. Subnormal temperature—NO, this thermoregulation is not affected.

D. Increased saliva production—NO, this is usually not affected.

Exercise 18-15: *Select all that apply*

Common treatments effective in managing ADHD include:

☒ **Pharmacotherapy**

☒ **Growth plotting**

☒ **Baseline cardiac monitoring**

☒ **Monitoring vital signs**

☒ **Behavior modification programs**

❏ Increased environmental stimuli

Exercise 18-16: *Fill-in*
Comorbid conditions such as ADHD and obsessive-compulsive disorder (OCD) occur in **50%** of children with Tourette's syndrome.

Exercise 18-17: *Multiple-choice question*
Tourette's syndrome is accompanied by which clinical manifestation?
  A. Flat facial affect—NO, facial tics are common.
  B. Hallucinations—NO, this does not occur.
  C. Motor and vocal tics—YES, these are common.
  D. Inattentiveness—NO, this is not affected.

Exercise 18-18: *Select all that apply*
Disruptions in the levels of the brain that are associated with tic disorders include:
❑ Catecholamines
☒ **Dopamine**
❑ Epinephrine
☒ **Neurotransmitters**
☒ **Neuropeptides**
☒ **Serotonin**
❑ Norepineprine

Exercise 18-19: *Fill-in*
Clinical manifestations that accompany anorexia nervosa include a history of which type of symptoms?
  1. **Constipation**
  2. **Secondary amenorrhea**
  3. **Syncope**
  4. **Weight loss**
  5. **Low self-esteem**
  6. **Distorted body image**
  7. **Abdominal pain**
  8. **Complaints of cold hands and feet**

Exercise 18-20: *True or false*
The anorexic adolescent is usually underweight and presents with a body mass index (BMI) of 20.
_____ True
__**X**__ False

Exercise 18-21: *Matching*

Match the mental health terms in Column A to the correct description in Column B.

Column A		Column B
A. Bingeing	_G_	Mild to severe psychological distress
B. Purging	_D_	Consumption of nonnutritive materials
C. Cachexia	_A_	Excessive consumption of foods
D. Pica	_C_	Malnutrition and muscle wasting
E. Anorexia nervosa	_F_	Eating disorder with near-normal weight
F. Bulimia	_B_	Forced vomiting after food consumption
G. Depression	_E_	Eating disorder with weight loss

Exercise 18-22: *Multiple-choice question*

Which actions by the nurse would be a priority intervention for a child or adolescent having suicidal ideations?

A. **Implement suicide precautions and prompt referral to the emergency department—YES, this is an emergency and should be a priority.**

B. Discuss the feelings causing these thoughts to occur—NO, this may create an unsafe environment if the child is in crises and has a plan.

C. Obtain a history and perform a nursing assessment—NO, this is not a priority.

D. No cause for immediate concern but monitor the situation—NO, this may create an unsafe environment if the child is in crises and has a plan.

Exercise 18-23: *Select all that apply*

Treatment options for children and adolescents with eating disorders and mental health issues include:

☒ **Family counseling**

☒ **Nutrition referrals**

☒ **Tricyclic antidpressants (TCAs)**

☒ **Selective serotonin reuptake inhibitors (SSRIs)**

☒ **Depression and suicide monitoring**

☒ **Assessment for substance abuse**

☒ **Group therapy with support resources**

❏ Sporadic medical follow-up

Exercise 18-24: *True or false*

Children and adolescents experiencing depressive episodes may harm themselves purposefully without the intent to kill themselves. This action is known as self-mutilation.

___X___ True

_____ False

19

Children With Cancer

Susan Parnell Scholtz

Unfolding Case Study #19-1 ▒ Ellie

You are working on an oncology unit in a large regional health care organization. Many of the patients are transferred from smaller community hospitals that do not have pediatric oncologists to care for them. Unfortunately, over the past year you have seen many different types of childhood cancer. Although it is a stressful unit to work on, it is also very rewarding when children get well enough to go home. Parents are always thankful for the care you provide.

Exercise 19-1: *Matching*
Match the term Column A with the correct definition of a common finding in pediatric oncology in Column B.

Column A	Column B
A. Leukocytosis	_____ A measure of the body's ability to fight infection that uses the mature and immature neutrophils as an index
B. Polycythemia	
C. Blast cells	
D. Thrombocytopenia	
E. Absolute neutrophil count (ANC)	_____ Absolute neutrophil count (ANC) less than 1,500/mcL
F. Neutropenia	
	_____ Significant increase in red blood cells
	_____ Decreased platelet count of less than 50,000 mcL.
	_____ Immature white cells found in the bone marrow
	_____ Significant increase in white blood cells

Last week, Ellie, age 3, was seen by the pediatrician with chief complains of a sore throat, fever, and "pain over both shins." Her strep test was negative and she was started on a course of antibiotics. The sore throat and pyrexia did not resolve and was sent for a complete blood count (CBC) with differential. Her platelet count was 100,000/mcL, white blood count (WBC) 30,000/mcL and hemoglobin 7g/dL. Ellie and her parents are scheduled to meet with the pediatrician to discuss the findings.

Exercise 19-2: *Multiple-choice question*
A review of the diagnostic findings can be interpreted as:

    A. Decreased platelets and increased WBC count

    B. Blood work is within normal limits

    C. Platelet count and WBC are normal; hemoglobin decreased

    D. Platelet and WBC count elevated; hemoglobin slightly decreased

The pediatrician reviews the physical assessment findings as well as the results of the preliminary blood work and orders a bone marrow biopsy to rule out acute lymphocytic leukemia.

 eResource 19-1: To reinforce your assessment of the blood results, refer to Sutter Health's *Health Information*: goo.gl/IBEMyi

Exercise 19-3: *Multiple-choice question*
Which of the following statements best describes the rationale for use of the bone marrow test to diagnose acute lymphocytic leukemia?

    A. It provides valuable information about DNA analysis.

    B. It tests for immature and abnormal blast cells found in leukemia.

    C. It measures very small numbers of leukemic cells.

    D. It classifies French-American British (FAB) cell type.

A diagnosis of acute lymphocytic leukemia is made. You have the opportunity to examine Ellie for additional symptoms related to acute lymphocytic leukemia.

Exercise 19-4: *Select all that apply*
Other manifestations that may be seen in the child with acute lymphocytic leukemia are:

    ❑ Inability to move the eye to the side

    ❑ Bone pain

    ❑ Hepatosplenomegaly

    ❑ Headache

    ❑ Enlarged sentinel node

eResource 19-2: To supplement your understanding of the clinical manifestations of a child with acute lymphocytic leukemia,
    ■ View the following video, *What is Acute Lymphoblastic Leukemia (ALL)?* goo.gl/axLb5S

Answers to this chapter begin on page 298.

■ Refer to Epocrates Online: [Pathway: online.epocrates.com → Under the "Diseases" tab, enter "Acute Lymphocytic Leukemia" in the search field → Select "Acute Lymphocytic Leukemia" → Review "Highlights," "Basics," and "Diagnosis"]

Ellie is scheduled to receive four phases of chemotherapy as an inpatient on your unit.

Exercise 19-5: *Ordering*

Place the phases of chemotherapy in the order from 1 to 4 in which it will be administered from initiation to end.

_____ Consolidation

_____ Maintenance

_____ Induction

_____ Delayed intensification

Exercise 19-6: *Select all that apply*

Ellie is scheduled to receive cyclophosphamide. Based on an understanding of this medication, which of the following nursing interventions should be implemented?

❏ Monitor specific gravity to ensure it is greater than 1.015

❏ Administer intravenous fluids at 1.5 times maintenance 6 to 8 hours prior to medication infusion

❏ Daily weights

❏ Assess urine for gross hematuria

eResource 19-3: To reinforce your understanding of the medication, cyclophosphamide, consult:

■ Skyscape's RxDrugs: [Pathway: Skyscape → Select "RxDrugs" → Enter "Cyclophosphamide" into the search field → Select "Cyclophosphamide" to review content]

■ Epocrates: [Pathway: Epocrates → Enter "Cyclophosphamide" in the search field → Select "Cyclophosphamide" → Review content]

■ Medscape: [Pathway: Medscape → Enter "Cyclophosphamide" in the search field → Select "Cyclophosphamide" → Review content]

The nurse assesses Ellie's mouth and finds oral thrush and she also has thrombocytopenia and neutropenia.

Exercise 19-7: *Multiple-choice question*

Which of the following measures should be instituted for Ellie's thrush?

A. Use a medium bristle toothbrush to remove the white coating.

B. Encourage the child to swish and swallow with mycostatin as ordered.

C. Request that an oral antibiotic be ordered.

D. Encourage the child to floss daily to remove plaque.

Answers to this chapter begin on page 298.

eResource 19-4: To learn more about thrush, review the following:
- Medscape: [Pathway: Medscape → Enter "Thrush" in the search field → Select "Thrush" → Review content, focusing on "Clinical Presentation." Be sure to view images under "Physical"]
- View video, *Oral candidiasis (thrush) before and 18 hours after treatment* goo.gl/BJDnOG

Ellie tolerates the chemotherapy fairly well and after her treatment is discharged home with very specific instructions to avoid crowds and people with colds or flu. You help her parents arrange for follow-up with the pediatric oncologist. Her parents want to do what is best for Ellie and continue to have questions. You sit down and spend some time answering their questions.

eResource 19-5: To supplement your teaching, you provide Ellie's parents with a link to the Centers for Disease Control and Prevention's (CDC) Mobile Health and Safety topics and direct them to *Preventing Infections in Cancer Patients*: goo.gl/Xob49D [source CDC: m.cdc.gov/en]

As you are having Ellie's room cleaned, your colleague is admitting a young boy who has symptoms of a hydrocele.

Exercise 19-8: *Multiple-choice question*
Knowing the child has a probable diagnosis of a hydrocele, you know the following implications should be considered given his history:

A. The child may have an infection of the testicles.
B. Leukemic cells may be harbored in the scrotal sac.
C. A tumor may be causing an obstruction.
D. There is bleeding into the scrotal sac.

eResource 19-6: To learn more about hydrocele, refer to the following resources:
- MerckMedicus Online on your mobile device: [Pathway: www.merckmedicus.com → Select "Merck Manual" → Select "Merck Manual for Healthcare Professionals" → Enter "hydrocele" into the search field → Select "hydrocele" to access and review content]
- Medscape Online: [Pathway: www.medscape.org → Select "Reference" → Enter "hydrocele" into the search field → Select "hydrocele" → Review content. On your mobile device, you can access the same information: [Pathway: Medscape → Enter "hydrocele" into the search field → Select "hydrocele" → review content]

Unfolding Case Study #19-2 Tom

Sixteen-year-old Tom is admitted with a diagnosis of stage III Hodgkin's disease. You are the admitting nurse and review his past medical history.

Exercise 19-9: *Multiple-choice question*
Which of the following factors are used to determine that Tom has stage III Hodgkin's disease?
  - A. Radionuclide scan with gallium
  - B. Presence of Reed-Sternberg cells
  - C. Biopsy of the spleen
  - D. Presence of small noncleaved cells

Tom is scheduled to have a test that will use radioactive imaging to determine the functional capacity of organs within the human body.

Exercise 19-10: *Fill-in*
You know the test Tom will have is frequently used in staging a child with cancer. This test is called ————.

Exercise 19-11: *Multiple-choice question*
In an attempt to learn more about the disease, Tom has been searching the Internet. He asks you, "What is the difference between non-Hodgkin's lymphoma and what I have (Hodgkin's disease)?" Based on an understanding of pathophysiology, the best response would be:
  - A. "Basically, they have the same course but are caused by different cell types."
  - B. "The cell types identified in biopsy are vastly different."
  - C. "The symptoms of both malignancies are very different."
  - D. "Hodgkin's disease is a more disseminated, aggressive disease than non-Hodgkin's lymphoma."

eResource 19-7: To reinforce your patient teaching, you review the following materials with Tom:
  - ■ A patient education booklet, *Hodgkin Lymphoma*: goo.gl/0V3eFd [Source: The Epocrates Patient Reference Library goo.gl/OBBw2X]
  - ■ A video tutorial, *Hodgkin's Disease or Non-Hodgkin's Lymphoma Diagnosis and Treatment*: goo.gl/0V3eFd

Tom has completed his first phase of chemotherapy and is about to be discharged. You are concerned about his ability to cope with the disease and its treatment once he goes home.

Answers to this chapter begin on page 298.

Exercise 19-12: *Multiple-choice question*

Based on your understanding of growth and development, identify the stressor that Tom may face upon discharge.

    A. Fear of the ability to feel intimacy

    B. Loss of autonomy

    C. Altered body image

    D. Regressive behaviors

You make a referral for Tom to talk to a neutral person, a clinical psychologist, about what is going on with him. His parents agree that this intervention may be helpful and they can transport him back and forth for weekly visits.

 eResource 19-8: In addition, you develop an individualized care plan to put into place supports that will help Tom and link him with the following resources:

    ■ Coping with Cancer: *Managing Emotional Effects* goo.gl/naLFnP [Source: www.cancer.gov]

    ■ *Cancer Resources for Teens*: goo.gl/Z9Dg6v [Source: www.Cancer.net]

Unfolding Case Study #19-3   Tammy

Four-year-old Tammy was brought into the well child clinic for a routine examination. During the visit, her mother notes that she has been irritable and that her "belly seems to be distended." It was noted by the nurse that she has lost weight since her last visit, which may be due to a poor appetite. After a thorough history and physical examination, blood work is ordered. Her findings indicated anemia and thrombocytopenia. Tammy is now admitted to your unit and diagnostic tests are ordered to rule out neuroblastoma.

Exercise 19-13: *Multiple-choice question*

Which of the following tests would be done first to diagnose neuroblastoma?

    A. Bone marrow aspirate

    B. Radiolabeled scanning with metaoidobenzylguanidine (MIBG)

    C. Lumber puncture

    D. Biopsy of tumor cells and tests for increased serum catecholamines

 eResource 19-9: To learn more about the tests to confirm the diagnosis of neuroblastoma, refer to Medscape:

    ■ Online: [Pathway: www.medscape.org → Select "Reference" → Enter "neuroblastoma" into the search field → Select "pediatric neuroblastoma" → Review content]

    ■ On your mobile device, you can access the same information: [Pathway: Medscape → Enter "neuroblastoma" into the search field → Select "neuroblastoma" → Review content]

Answers to this chapter begin on page 298.

A diagnosis of neuroblastoma has been made. Tammy's parents are told the news and now it is time to sit down with them and discuss the nursing care that will be needed.

Exercise 19-14: *Select all that apply*

Identify the nursing diagnoses that would be appropriate for Tammy's care.

❏ Acute pain related to surgery

❏ Infection: Risk for, due to surgery and effects from chemotherapy

❏ Family grieving related to potential loss of child

❏ Nutrition: Imbalanced, greater than body requirements due to side effects of chemotherapy

e **eResource 19-10:** To reinforce your understanding of neuroblastoma in children, you do a little research and watch the following video, *What Is Neuroblastoma?* goo.gl/p7Tq1C

Tammy's parents have a lot of questions. You sit down with them and you do your best to answer their questions. Tammy's parents seem to be reassured. You recognize that your teaching needs to be reinforced with written materials.

e **eResource 19-11:** You provide supplemental materials from the National Cancer Institute:

■ A patient education booklet, *Hodgkin Lymphoma*: goo.gl/0V3eFd

■ *General Information About Neuroblastoma* goo.gl/KVGuw3

■ *Treatment Options Overview*: goo.gl/VRwPDR

Tammy is expected to be on your unit for a number of days. Her parents make arrangements to stay with her. You become her primary nurse and take charge of her plan of care in coordination with the interprofessional team members and her parents.

Answers to this chapter begin on page 298.

Answers

Exercise 19-1: *Matching*

Match the term Column A with the correct definition of a common finding in pediatric oncology in Column B.

Column A	Column B
A. Leukocytosis	**E** A measure of the body's ability to fight infection that uses the mature and immature neutrophils as an index
B. Polycythemia	
C. Blast cells	
D. Thrombocytopenia	**F** Absolute neutrophil count (ANC) less than 1,500/mcL
E. Absolute neutrophil count (ANC)	**B** Significant increase in red blood cells
F. Neutropenia	**D** Decreased platelet count of less than 50,000 mcL
	C Immature white cells found in the bone marrow
	A Significant increase in white blood cells

Exercise 19-2: *Multiple-choice question*

A review of the diagnostic findings can be interpreted as:

A. **Decreased platelets and increased WBC count—YES, normal values are: WBC 4,500 to 10,000/mcL; platelets 150,000 to 400,000; HgB 12 to 16 g/dL.**

B. Blood work is within normal limits—NO, normal values are: WBC 4,500 to 10,000/ mcL; platelets 150,000 to 400,000; HgB 12 to 16 g/dL.

C. Platelet count and WBC are normal; hemoglobin decreased—NO, normal values are: WBC 4,500 to 10,000/mcL; platelets 150,000 to 400,000; HgB 12 to 16 g/dL.

D. Platelet and WBC count elevated; hemoglobin slightly decreased—NO, normal values are: WBC 4,500 to 10,000/microliter; platelets 150,000 to 400,000; HgB 12 to 16 g/dL.

Exercise 19-3: *Multiple-choice question*

Which of the following statements best describes the rationale for use of the bone marrow test to diagnose acute lymphocytic leukemia?

A. It provides valuable information about DNA analysis—NO, this information is obtained by a rapid flow cytometric assay test.

B. It tests for immature and abnormal blast cells found in leukemia—YES, it also detects hypercellular marrow and is a definitive test for acute lymphocytic leukemia.

C. It measures very small numbers of leukemic cells—NO, this information is obtained by a rapid flow cytometric assay test.

D. It classifies French-American British (FAB) cell type—NO, the bone marrow aspiration detects hyperceullar marrow, and immature and/or abnormal blast cells.

Exercise 19-4: *Select all that apply*

Other manifestations that may be seen in the child with acute lymphocytic leukemia are

☒ **Inability to move the eye to the side—YES, this finding is seen when there is a palsy of the 6th cranial nerve due to infiltration of leukemic cells.**

☒ **Bone pain—YES, leukemic cells have the ability to infiltrate joint spaces and bone.**

☒ **Hepatosplenomegaly—YES, enlargement of the liver and spleen is a common finding in childhood leukemia.**

☒ **Headache—YES, headache occurs when the central nervous system has been invaded.**

☐ Enlarged sentinel node—NO, this is a hallmark sign of Hodgkin's disease.

Exercise 19-5: *Ordering*

Place the phases of chemotherapy in the order from 1 to 4 in which it will be administered from initiation to end.

_2_ Consolidation. **Medications include L-asparaginase and doxorubicin**

_4_ Maintenance. **Medications include 6MP, 6-thioguanine, methotrexate**

_1_ Induction. **Medications include vincristine, prednisone, L-asparaginase, daunorubicin**

_3_ Delayed intensification. **Vincristine, Ara C, cyclophosphamide**

Exercise 19-6: *Select all that apply*

Ellie is scheduled to receive cyclophosphamide. Based on an understanding of this medication, which of the following nursing interventions should be implemented?

☐ Monitor specific gravity to ensure it is greater than 1.015—NO, fluids should be administered to keep the urine specific gravity less than 1.010 in order to flush the by-products of the tumor breakdown.

☒ **Administer intravenous fluids at 1.5 times maintenance 6 to 8 hours prior to medication infusion—YES, this rate is maintained 6 to 8 hours before the infusion, throughout the infusion, and at least 2 hours postmedication.**

☒ **Daily weights—YES, fluctuations can detect hydration and nutritional concerns.**

☒ **Assess urine for gross hematuria—YES, hematuria is a common effect of cyclophosphamide.**

Exercise 19-7: *Multiple-choice question*

Which of the following measures should be instituted for Ellie's thrush?

A. Use a medium bristle toothbrush to remove the white coating—NO, a medium bristle toothbrush predisposes the child to oral bleeding and the coating is due to a fungal infection and must be treated with an antifungal medication.

B. **Encourage the child to swish and swallow with mycostatin as ordered—YES, oral thrush is caused by a fungus and must be treated with an antifungal.**

C. Request that an oral antibiotic be ordered—NO, oral antifungals are the drug of choice to manage thrush.

D. Encourage the child to floss daily to remove plaque—NO, floss could cut the gums and cause bleeding. Also, the problem is a fungus not plaque.

Exercise 19-8: *Multiple-choice question*

Knowing the child has a probable diagnosis of a hydrocele, you know the following implications should be considered given his history:

A. The child may have an infection of the testicles—NO, this is not associated with leukemic cells.

B. **Leukemic cells may be harbored in the scrotal sac—YES, leukemic cells often infiltrate the scrotal sac and use it as a sanctuary.**

C. A tumor may be causing an obstruction—NO, although an enlargement of the testicles can occur due to infiltration of the scrotal sac, it is not associated with obstruction.

D. There is bleeding into the scrotal sac—NO, there is no bleeding; rather, infiltration of leukemic cells into the scrotal sac.

Exercise 19-9: *Multiple-choice question*

Which of the following factors are used to determine that Tom has stage III Hodgkin's disease?

A. **Radionuclide scan with gallium—YES, this scan will identify the extent of nodal involvement.**

B. Presence of Reed-Sternberg cells—NO, these cells will be present on biopsy but do not identify the extent of the disease. They are also present in mononucleosis.

C. Biopsy of the spleen—NO, if done, it would only identify involvement of the spleen.

D. Presence of small noncleaved cells—NO, these cells are found in non-Hodgkin's lymphoma.

Exercise 19-10: *Fill-in*

You know the test Tom will have is frequently used in staging a child with cancer. This test is called **positron emission tomography scan (PET scan)**.

Exercise 19-11: *Multiple-choice question*

In an attempt to learn more about the disease, Tom has been searching the Internet. He asks his nurse, "What is the difference between non-Hodgkin's lymphoma and what I have (Hodgkin's disease)? Based on an understanding of pathophysiology, the best response would be:

A. "Basically, they have the same course but are caused by different cell types."—NO, it is true that they are caused by different cell types; however, non-Hodgkin's lymphoma is usually more aggressive and highly disseminated.

B. **"The cell types identified in biopsy are vastly different."—YES, non-Hodgkin's lymphoma is caused by T and B cell abnormalities, whereas Reed-Sternberg cells are present in Hodgkin's disease.**

C. "The symptoms of both malignancies are very different."—NO, there are many similar symptoms such as weight loss, fever, and lymph node involvement; however, there are differences as well.

D. "Hodgkin's disease is a more disseminated aggressive disease than non-Hodgkin's lymphoma.—NO, non-Hodgkin's disease often is more aggressive in its progression as well as diffuse and disseminated.

Exercise 19-12: *Multiple-choice question*

Based on your understanding of growth and development, identify the stressor that Tom may face upon discharge.

A. Fear of the ability to feel intimacy—NO, the desire to form long-term intimate relationships typically begins in young adulthood.

B. Loss of autonomy—NO, this period of psychosocial development is most prominent during toddlerhood.

C. **Altered body image—YES, his altered appearance secondary to chemotherapy may threaten his sense of identity.**

D. Regressive behaviors—NO, regressive behaviors typically occur in the toddler and preschooler as a reaction to hospitalization.

Exercise 19-13: *Multiple-choice question*

Which of the following tests would be done first to diagnose neuroblastoma?

A. Bone marrow aspirate—NO, this test may be done to determine if metastasis has occurred but not for an initial diagnosis.

B. Radiolabeled scanning with metaoidobenzylguanidine (MIBG)—NO, this test may be done to determine if metastasis has occurred but not for an initial diagnosis.

C. Lumber puncture—NO, a lumbar puncture is not done for the initial diagnosis or staging.

D. **Biopsy of tumor cells and tests for increased serum catecholamines—YES, biopsy of the tumor tissue and laboratory evaluation of catecholamines are used to initially diagnose a neuroblastoma.**

Exercise 19-14: *Select all that apply*

A diagnosis of neuroblastoma has been made. Identify the nursing diagnoses that would be appropriate for her care.

☒ **Acute pain related to surgery—YES, surgical removal of the abdominal mass will be indicated once the diagnosis is confirmed.**

☒ **Infection: Risk for, due to surgery and effects from chemotherapy—YES, there is always the potential for sepsis secondary to surgery and the side effects of chemotherapy.**

☒ **Family grieving related to potential loss of child—YES, this is a normal reaction to the diagnosis of cancer.**

❑ Nutrition: Imbalanced, greater than body requirements due to side effects of chemotherapy—NO, the chemotherapeutic agents used to treat a neuroblastoma do not increase appetite. Prednisone, which increases appetite, is not typically used in the treatment of a neuroblastoma.

20

Pain Management in Children

Susan Parnell Scholtz

Unfolding Case Study #20-1 Andy

Andy is a patient in the neonatal intensive care unit (NICU) who was born at 32 weeks gestation with a grade IV interventricular hemorrhage. Throughout the duration of his hospitalization, Andy has undergone many invasive procedures in which he cries incessantly, experiences oxygen desaturation, and tachycardia. Andy's father is concerned that his son is experiencing too much pain.

Exercise 20-1: *Multiple-choice question*

Andy's father asks you, "Do you think he will have long-term effects from these painful experiences?" Based on an understanding of a child's understanding of pain, you state:

    A. "There is no scientific evidence that babies experience pain. He most likely does not like the fact that he is restrained."

    B. "Although he does not understand pain, babies who have long-term exposure to pain may experience an increased response to pain."

    C. "He is most likely reacting to parental anxiety, which can be disruptive to attachment behaviors."

    D. "He may demonstrate aggressive behaviors later in his childhood."

You are careful to assess and document Andy's cues that he is experiencing pain.

eResource 20-1: To review your understanding of pain assessment, refer to the following resources:
- Medscape:
  - Online [Pathway: www.medscape.org → Select "Reference" → Enter "Pain" into the search field → Select "Pain Assessment" → Review content under the "Practice Essentials" and "Technique"; be sure to focus on content related to pain assessment in infants]
  - On your mobile device, you can access the same information: [Pathway: Medscape → Enter "Pain" into the search field → Select "Pain Assessment" → Review content under the "Practice Essentials"

Answers to this chapter begin on page 312.

and "Technique"; be sure to focus on content related to pain assessment in infants]

■ Skyscape's Outline in Clinical Medication on your mobile device: [Pathway: Outline in Clinical Medication → Enter "Pain" → Select "Pain Management" → Review content under "Pain Management in Children"]

Exercise 20-2: *Select all that apply*

Which of the following signs are noted when an infant experiences pain?

❑ Bradycardia

❑ Rapid extension and flexion of the arms

❑ Increased breathing or breath holding

❑ Two percent to 4% decrease in oxygen saturation

❑ Occasional random movements of the extremities

Exercise 20-3: *Matching*

Select the pain scale in Column A used in children that best matches its definition in Column B.

Column A	Column B
A. Neonatal Infant Pain Scale (NIPS)	_____ This scale was developed to measure pain in the neonate experienced during a procedure.
B. Behavioral Indicators of Infant Pain (BIIP)	
C. CRIES Scale	_____ This scale measures the neonate's pain perception postoperatively.
D. Noncommunicating Children's Pain Checklist (NCCPC)	_____ This assessment scale measures acute pain in the neonate and focuses on behavioral indices of pain.
E. Face, Legs, Activity and Consolability Pain Scale (FLACC)	_____ This assessment tool measures pain in infants older than 2 months and focuses on face, legs, activity, cry, and consolability.
	_____ This pain scale was developed specifically to meet the needs of cognitively impaired children who are experiencing pain.

eResource 20-2: To learn more about pain assessment scales, you do a review of the literature and locate the following information related to infants:

■ National Initiative on Pain Control's Pain Assessment Scales: goo.gl/ EAMgES

Answers to this chapter begin on page 312.

- Overview of Pediatric Pain Assessment Scales: goo.gl/NY0jvJ
- Specific Pain Assessment Scales for infants:
  - Neonatal/Infants Pain Scale (NIPS): goo.gl/y3oh1x
  - Neonatal Pain, Agitation, & Sedation Scale (NPASS): goo.gl/0tztrF

During painful and invasive procedures, you encourage Andy's parents to execute kangaroo care and this seems to alleviate some of the crying during the procedure. Other techniques you teach them are baby massage and using gentle music. Again your pediatric experience is needed and there is an admission on the pediatric inpatient unit that warrants your care. The evening nurse supervisor asks you to go to pediatrics and admit a patient. You agree since you love all aspects of pediatric nursing. The pediatric unit is busy; there are admissions and postoperative patients. The charge nurse asks you to be the pain management nurse and you agree.

Unfolding Case Study #20-2 ██ Bonnie

Bonnie is a 6-year-old who is being admitted to the pediatric unit with a diagnosis of acute appendicitis. Upon admission, she is experiencing severe pain and an order for parenteral morphine is written. She weighs 40 pounds. The recommended dose of parenteral morphine for a child is 0.05 to 0.1 mg/kg every 3 to 4 hours.

Exercise 20-4: *Calculation*
What is the highest dose Bonnie can receive on admission?

You give Bonnie a dose of morphine and she is now complaining of itchiness; however, there are no hives associated with it. Her vital signs are:

- Temperature 101° F
- Pulse 90
- Respirations 38
- BP 88/58
- She appears drowsy
- Pain rating is a 2 on the FACES rating scale

 eResource 20-3: Verify your understanding of pediatric dosing for morphine by referring to Epocrates:

- Online [Pathway: online.epocrates.com → Under the "Drugs" tab, enter "Morphine" in the search field → Select "morphine sulfate" → Review "Peds Dosing"]
- On your mobile device: (download from Android: goo.gl/qZ2zB; and iOS: goo.gl/mL3Hya) [Pathway: Epocrates → Enter "Morphine" in the search field → Select "morphine sulfate" → Review "Peds Dosing"]

Answers to this chapter begin on page 312.

Exercise 20-5: *Multiple-choice question*

Based on these findings, you determine:

    A. Bonnie is experiencing an allergic reaction to morphine and you must notify the physician.

    B. Pain management has been achieved and she is experiencing a typical side effect of morphine.

    C. Bonnie is experiencing an adverse reaction to morphine as evidenced by her vital signs.

    D. Morphine has been ineffective and a higher dose may be warranted.

When you return to work on Saturday, Bonnie is 2 days post-appendectomy and no longer needs morphine for pain because her pain has significantly decreased. She still has mild pain when she ambulates and requires acetaminophen. The recommended dose for acetaminophen for a child is 10 to 15 mg/kg; she weighs 40 pounds.

 eResource 20-4: Refer back to Epocrates to learn more about the side effects of morphine:

    ■ Online [Pathway: online.epocrates.com → Under the "Drugs" tab, enter "Morphine" in the search field → Select "morphine sulfate" → Review "adverse reactions" and "contraindications/cautions"]

    ■ On your mobile device: [Pathway: Epocrates → Enter "Morphine" in the search field → Select "morphine sulfate" → Review "adverse reactions" and "contraindications/cautions"]

You are curious about other pain assessment tools for children Bonnie's age and decide to do a bit of research online.

 eResource 20-5: In doing a review of the literature, you discover that there is another pain assessment tool intended for children 1 to 7 years old developed by the Children's Hospital of Eastern Ontario (Children's Hospital of Eastern Ontario Pain Scale: goo.gl/mFqmMC)

Exercise 20-6: *Calculation*

Based on the aforementioned parameters, what is the dosage of acetaminophen Bonnie should receive per dose?

Exercise 20-7: *Calculation*

Children's Tylenol is dispensed in a suspension of 160 mg/5 mL and the order is for 250 mg by mouth every 3 to 4 hours for pain. How much Tylenol should Bonnie receive?

You provide Bonnie's family with discharge instructions and they are relieved that this episodic ordeal is over. You make an appointment for Bonnie to see her regular pediatrician in a week.

Answers to this chapter begin on page 312.

eResource 20-6: To supplement your discharge teaching, you show Bonnie's parents the discharge video, *Pediatric Appendectomy Surgery Discharge Instructions for Parents:* goo.gl/YRVhuv

Unfolding Case Study #20-3 Gregg

Gregg is a 10-year-old boy admitted to the pediatrics department in sickle cell crisis. His pain is reported as a 10 on the Wong-Baker FACES Pain Rating Scale. In order to manage his pain he received oxycodone. He weighs 39 kg.

Exercise 20-8: *Multiple-choice question*
Which of the following signs may indicate serious complications of oxycodone?

    A. Tachycardia

    B. Hyperactive deep tendon reflexes

    C. Respiratory depression

    D. Nausea

 eResource 20-7: To access the pain assessment tool for Face, Legs, Activity, Crying, Consolability scale (FLACC), go to: goo.gl/gn3FXS

Gregg's respiratory rate is now 16 respirations/min and his breathing is shallow. The primary care provider is concerned that he is beginning to show signs of respiratory distress secondary to the opioid administration.

Exercise 20-9: *Multiple-choice question*
Which of the following actions should you perform first when there is a suspicion of respiratory distress secondary to opioid administration?

    A. Do not give the next scheduled dosage of oxycodone.

    B. Closely monitor ventilation via a pulse oximeter.

    C. Administer naloxone to reverse the adverse effects of oxycodone.

    D. Administer oxygen via a nasal cannula.

After the naloxone Gregg is alert and a nonnarcotic is administered for pain. His joint is placed on ice and he is monitored the entire night.

eResource 20-8: To reinforce your understanding of naloxone, consult the following resources:

    ■ Skyscape's RxDrugs on your mobile device [Pathway: Skyscape → Select "RxDrugs" → Enter "Naloxone" into the search field → Select "Naloxone" to review content]

    ■ Epocrates

        ■ Online [Pathway: online.epocrates.com → Under the "Drugs" tab, enter "Naloxone" into the search field → Select "Naloxone" to review content]

        ■ On your mobile device: [Pathway: Epocrates → Enter "Naloxone" into the search field → Select "Naloxone" to review content]

Answers to this chapter begin on page 312.

Unfolding Case Study #20-4 Kate

Kate is a 7-year-old child who was involved in a motor vehicle accident and returned from the operating room following an open reduction of her femur. She is in moderate pain and the decision was made to place her on patient-controlled analgesia (PCA).

Exercise 20-10: *Select all that apply*
Identify statements that accurately describe the use of patient-controlled analgesia in children.

❑ The child should have the cognitive ability to understand the cause and effect of pushing the patient-controlled analgesia button.

❑ Programming an incorrect lower concentration of the analgesic can cause an overdose.

❑ The child has the ability to control the basal infusion of the narcotic.

❑ Both the parent and the child should operate the patient-controlled analgesia pump.

❑ The child should be cautioned against pressing the patient-controlled analgesia pump frequently in order to prevent an overdose.

After you get Kate settled, the charge nurse asks you to go and assess Ken. Ken is a "frequent flyer" on the pediatric unit because of his chronic condition, juvenile rheumatoid arthritis (JRA).

e **eResource 20-9:** Prior to starting your teaching, you download the Patient Safety Council's *Toolkit for Patient Controlled Analgesia (PCA) Guidelines of Care For the Opioid Naïve Patient*: goo.gl/Bo882J

Unfolding Case Study #20-5 Ken

Ken is being admitted for pain control. He has been diagnosed with juvenile rheumatoid arthritis (JRA) and has severe pain and stiffness when he awakens in the morning. It is especially bad today so the pediatrician told his mother to bring him to the unit so he could be seen.

Exercise 20-11: *Multiple-choice question*
Which of the following treatments may help to alleviate the pain in Ken's joints upon arising?

A. Place hot, dry heat packs on the affected joints upon awakening.

B. Place ice packs directly on the joint after exercise.

C. Place warm, moist heat on the affected joints.

D. Cold pack should never be used for pain control.

Answers to this chapter begin on page 312.

In addition to heat and cold therapy, Ken is receiving Percocet to control his pain.

Exercise 20-12: *Select all that apply*

You know the typical side effects of Percocet and design a plan of care to prevent these side effects. Which of the following interventions would be appropriate to meet the physiological needs of the child receiving an opioid?

- ❑ Encourage the child to eat a diet high in fiber.
- ❑ Assess the bowel sounds for hyperactivity, which is associated with opioids.
- ❑ Request an order for a stool softener.
- ❑ Encourage increased fluid intake.
- ❑ Request an order for Imodium to slow the transit of stool through the bowel.

You barely have time to say hello to Ken's parents who you have interacted with many times when the charge nurse asks you to see Eddie.

Unfolding Case Study #20-6 ▨ Eddie

Eight-week-old Eddie was admitted to the pediatric unit 2 days ago with a diagnosis of "rule out sepsis." His primary nurse is about to draw his daily blood work but knows that even though the length of the procedure is short it causes Eddie distress.

Exercise 20-13: *Multiple-choice question*

Which of the following interventions will help decrease pain during this procedure?

- A. Apply eutectic mixture of local anesthetics (EMLA) cream topically immediately before the procedure.
- B. Administer cold packs immediately following the procedure.
- C. Give the infant concentrated sucrose 2 to 3 minutes before the procedure.
- D. Swaddle the infant throughout the procedure.

You help the primary nurse with Eddie, then continue on your "pain relief rounds."

Unfolding Case Study #20-7 ▨ Annie

Annie, age 5, is being evaluated by the play therapist. The concern is that she has experienced multiple invasive and painful procedures over the past month. Since her diagnosis of acute lymphocytic leukemia (ALL), she has received lumbar punctures, bone marrow aspirations, and venipuncture. You discuss this privately with the play therapist and collaboratively you both decide on some play interventions.

Answers to this chapter begin on page 312.

Exercise 20-14: *Multiple-choice question*

Which of the following play activities would therapeutically enable Annie to deal with her feelings regarding prolonged pain?

    A. Watch age-appropriate videos that deal with hospitalization.

    B. Encourage the child to play with puppets to address any fears/anxieties she may have experienced.

    C. Play board games with the child.

    D. Encourage her to play interactive games on her iPad.

In the room next to Annie is Maria.

Unfolding Case Study #20-8 Maria

Maria is a 15-year-old girl who has been hospitalized for treatment of bone pain due to osteogenic sarcoma. She is scheduled for another biopsy and received fentanyl for the procedure.

 eResource 20-10: To reinforce your understanding of osteosarcoma, refer to Medscape:

    ■ Online [Pathway: www.medscape.org → Select "Reference" → Enter "osteosarcoma" into the search field → Select "osteosarcoma" → Review content]

    ■ On your mobile device: [Pathway: Medscape → Enter "osteosarcoma" into the search field → Select "osteosarcoma" → Review content]

Exercise 20-15: *Multiple-choice question*

Which of the following statements is most accurate about fentanyl administration?

    A. Rapid infusion of fentanyl may lead to chest rigidity and bradycardia.

    B. Fentanyl is typically administered for procedures that require a long-acting sedative.

    C. Fentanyl is contraindicated for use in children.

    D. Fentanyl is a barbiturate used to produce hypnosis.

 eResource 20-11: To reinforce your understanding of fentanyl, its effects and potential side effects, refer to

    ■ Skyscape's RxDrugs on your mobile device [Pathway: Skyscape → Select "RxDrugs" → Enter "Fentanyl" into the search field → Select "Fentanyl" to review content]

    ■ Epocrates

        ■ Online [Pathway: online.epocrates.com → Under the "Drugs" tab, enter "Fentanyl" into the search field → Select "Fentanyl" to review content]

Answers to this chapter begin on page 312.

■ On your mobile device: [Pathway: Epocrates → Enter "Fentanyl" into the search field → Select "Fentanyl" to review content]

Maria is being discharged; however, she states, "I am having difficulty processing all that has happened to me during this past hospitalization. I never thought I could be as strong as I was throughout all of the pain."

Exercise 20-16: *Multiple-choice question*

Which of the following activities should the play therapist suggest to help Maria process these feelings related to ineffective pain management?

    A. Suggest that she keep herself distracted with projects.

    B. Encourage her to reflect on her feelings and experiences and write these in a personal journal.

    C. Remind her that these experiences, albeit painful, are in the past and should not be dwelled upon.

    D. Encourage her to discuss these feelings with her oncologist.

After talking to Maria you realize how important pain relief and understanding is on a pediatric unit and that a painful experience can alter a child's life.

Answers to this chapter begin on page 312.

Answers

Exercise 20-1: *Multiple-choice question*

Andy's father asks you, "Do you think he will have long-term effects from these painful experiences?" Based on an understanding of a child's understanding of pain, you state:

A. "There is no scientific evidence that babies experience pain. He most likely does not like the fact that he is restrained."—NO, there is scientific evidence that neonates have specific physiologic responses to pain.

B. **"Although he does not understand pain, babies who have long-term exposure to pain may experience an increased response to pain."—YES, prior to 6 months of age, there is no evidence of memory recall; however, there may be increased response to pain as well as a hypersensitivity to light touch.**

C. "He is most likely reacting to parental anxiety, which can be disruptive to attachment behaviors."—NO, although there is perception of parental anxiety, there are also physiologic pain perceptions. There is no direct correlation between parental anxiety and attachment behaviors.

D. "He may demonstrate aggressive behaviors later in his childhood."—NO, although an older child may demonstrate aggressive behaviors during the procedure, there are no data to support the premise that the child is at risk for long-term aggression.

Exercise 20-2: *Select all that apply*

Which of the following signs are noted when an infant experiences pain?

❏ Bradycardia—NO, the typical response to pain in the neonate is an increase in heart rate.

☒ **Rapid extension and flexion of the arms—YES, the infant will become tense and rapidly extend and flex the arms and legs.**

☒ **Increased breathing or breath holding—YES, there will be a change in breathing and possible gagging.**

☒ **Two percent to 4% decrease in oxygen saturation—YES, the lungs may not adequately inflate due to the response in pain; therefore, inadequate oxygen saturation will occur.**

❏ Occasional random movements of the extremities—NO, typically the neonate will respond with rapid, rhythmical extension and flexion of the extremities.

Exercise 20-3: *Matching*

Select the pain scale in Column A used in children that best matches its definition in Column B.

Column A	Column B
A. Neonatal Infant Pain Scale (NIPS)	__A__ This scale was developed to measure pain in the neonate experienced during a procedure.
B. Behavioral Indicators of Infant Pain (BIIP)	
C. CRIES Scale	__C__ This scale measures the neonate's pain perception postoperatively.
D. Noncommunicating Children's Pain Checklist (NCCPC)	
E. Face, Legs, Activity and Consolability Pain Scale (FLACC)	__B__ This assessment scale measures acute pain in the neonate and focuses on behavioral indices of pain.
	__E__ This assessment tool measures pain in infants older than 2 months and focuses on face, legs, activity, cry, and consolability.
	__D__ This pain scale was developed specifically to meet the needs of cognitively impaired children who are experiencing pain.

Exercise 20-4: *Calculation*

What is the highest dose Bonnie can receive on admission?
<u>Bonnie's weight in kg = 18.14 kg; dose 1.18 mg</u>

Exercise 20-5: *Multiple-choice question*

Based on these findings, you determine:

A. Bonnie is experiencing an allergic reaction to morphine and you must notify the physician—NO, itching a is a common side effect of morphine and is not an adverse reaction.

B. **Pain management has been achieved and she is experiencing a typical side effect of morphine—YES, a rating of 2 on the FACES scale indicates that "It hurts a little" and itching is a common side effect of morphine.**

C. Bonnie is experiencing an adverse reaction to morphine as evidenced by her vital signs—NO, itching a is a common side effect of morphine and is not an adverse reaction.

D. Morphine has been ineffective and a higher dose may be warranted—NO, a pain rating of 2 on the FACES indicates pain control has been attained. Also, the highest dosage of morphine appropriate for this age is 0.1 mg/kg every 3 to 4 hours.

Exercise 20-6: *Calculation*
Based on the aforementioned parameters, what is the dosage of acetaminophen Bonnie should receive per dose?
Bonnie's weight in kg = 18.14 kg; the range of Tylenol is 180 mg to 270 mg

Exercise 20-7: *Calculation*
Children's Tylenol is dispensed in a suspension of 160 mg/5 mL and the order is for 250 mg by mouth every 3 to 4 hours for pain. How much Tylenol should Bonnie receive?
7.8 mL

Exercise 20-8: *Multiple-choice question*
Which of the following signs may indicate serious complications of oxycodone?
A. Tachycardia—NO, a typical side effect may be a decrease in pulse.
B. Hyperactive deep tendon reflexes—NO, this is a sign of opioid withdrawal in long-term use of this drug.
C. Respiratory depression—YES, this is a major life-threatening complication of opiates.
D. Nausea—NO, this is a common side effect of opiates.

Exercise 20-9: *Multiple-choice question*
Which of the following actions should you perform first when there is a suspicion of respiratory distress secondary to opioid administration?
A. Do not give the next scheduled dosage of oxycodone—NO, while this is an important step, the child needs immediate attention to reverse his respiratory distress secondary to opioid administration.
B. Closely monitor ventilation via a pulse oximeter—NO, pulse oximeter measures oxygenation but does not measure ventilation.
C. Administer naloxone to reverse the adverse effects of oxycodone—YES, naloxone is the medication used to reverse adverse effects of opioids.
D. Administer oxygen via a nasal cannula—NO, the first step in this medical emergency is to administer naloxone to reverse the adverse reaction of oxycodone.

Exercise 20-10: *Select all that apply*
Identify statements that accurately describe the use of patient-controlled analgesia in children.
☒ **The child should have the cognitive ability to understand the cause and effect of pushing the patient-controlled analgesia button—YES, a child**

who is age 7 or older typically has the cognitive ability to understand the cause and effect involved in the use of patient-controlled analgesia.

☒ **Programming an incorrect lower concentration of the analgesic can cause an overdose—YES, when there is an incorrect concentration programmed into the pump, there is a chance for an overdose or fatality.**

❏ The child has the ability to control the basal infusion of the narcotic—NO, the basal dose is administered with a continuous infusion of the drug by the registered nurse.

❏ Both the parent and the child should operate the patient-controlled analgesia pump—NO, only the child should assume responsibility for identification and control of pain via the patient-controlled analgesia device.

❏ The child should be cautioned against pressing the patient-controlled analgesia pump frequently in order to prevent an overdose—NO, the patient-controlled analgesia pump will not deliver any more medication than it is programmed to deliver.

Exercise 20-11: *Multiple-choice question*

Which of the following treatments may help to alleviate the pain in Ken's joints upon arising?

A. Place hot, dry heat packs on the affected joints upon awakening—NO, when heat is applied, moist heat is recommended to control pain.

B. Place ice packs directly on the joint after exercise—NO, although ice can be used for acute pain, it must not directly touch the skin and should be applied for 15 20 minutes.

C. **Place warm, moist heat on the affected joints—YES, moist heat is effective for pain control in children with juvenile rheumatoid arthritis.**

D. Cold pack should never be used for pain control— NO, acute pain can be controlled by wrapped ice packs.

Exercise 20-12: *Select all that apply*

You know the typical side effects of Percocet and design a plan of care to prevent these side effects. Which of the following interventions would be appropriate to meet the physiological needs of the child receiving an opioid?

☒ **Encourage the child to eat a diet high in fiber—YES, a side effect of opioids is constipation and a diet high in fiber will promote elimination.**

❏ Assess the bowel sounds for hyperactivity, which is associated with opioids— NO, although it is important to assess bowel sounds, it is more common to hear hypotonic bowel sounds following opioid ingestion.

☒ **Request an order for a stool softener—YES, a common side effect of opioids is constipation.**

☒ **Encourage increased fluid intake—YES, extra fluids will promote motility and passage of stool.**

❑ Request an order for Imodium to slow the transit of stool through the bowel—NO, Imodium is indicated for diarrhea and a side effect of opioids is constipation.

Exercise 20-13: *Multiple-choice question*

Which of the following interventions will help decrease pain during this procedure?

A. Apply eutectic mixture of local anesthetics (EMLA) cream topically immediately before the procedure—NO, while EMLA is a dermal anesthetic, application of it immediately prior to the invasive procedure will not provide pain relief. It must be applied 1 to 2 hours or prior to the procedure for effectiveness.

B. Administer cold packs immediately following the procedure— NO, typically the pain is short-lived and occurs during the procedure and during the restraint.

C. **Give the infant concentrated sucrose 2 to 3 minutes before the procedure— YES, there is evidence to support that concentrated sucrose has a analgesic effect.**

D. Swaddle the infant throughout the procedure—NO, while swaddling and touch may comfort the child postprocedure, there is no evidence to support that it decreases pain during the procedure.

Exercise 20-14: *Multiple-choice question*

Which of the following play activities would therapeutically enable Annie to deal with her feelings regarding prolonged pain?

A. Watch age-appropriate videos that deal with hospitalization—NO, this activity is passive and does not encourage expression of Annie's feelings. Videos may be effective to prepare children for upcoming procedures.

B. **Encourage the child to play with puppets to address any fears/anxieties she may have experienced—YES, puppets are particularly useful projective techniques used in the preschool child to deal with fears and anxieties.**

C. Play board games with the child—NO, board games will create a diversion for the child; however, it is not a projective technique and will not alleviate fears or anxieties.

D. Encourage her to play interactive games on her iPad—NO, this activity is passive and does not encourage expression of Annie's feelings.

Exercise 20-15: *Multiple-choice question*

Which of the following statements is most accurate about fentanyl administration?

A. **Rapid infusion of fentanyl may lead to chest rigidity and bradycardia—YES, it is important that this opioid is infused slowly.**

B. Fentanyl is typically administered for procedures that require a long-acting sedative—NO, fentanyl is used for its short-acting properties.

C. Fentanyl is contraindicated for use in children—NO, fentanyl is used in children.

D. Fentanyl is a barbiturate used to produce hypnosis—NO, it is a short-acting opioid.

Exercise 20-16: *Multiple-choice question*

Which of the following activities should the play therapist suggest to help Maria process these feelings related to ineffective pain management?

A. Suggest that she keep herself distracted with projects—NO, this intervention encourages her to avoid the thoughts that have been plaguing her.

B. Encourage her to reflect on her feelings and experiences and write these in a personal journal—YES, reflective writing will help her identify her fears and process them through reflective thought.

C. Remind her that these experiences, albeit painful, are in the past and should not be dwelled upon—NO, this response would negate the importance and value of her feelings.

D. Encourage her to discuss these feelings with her oncologist—NO, this statement would dismiss her concerns and anxieties.

Bibliography

Ball, J. W., Bindler, R. C., & Cowen, K. J. (2014). *Child health nursing: Partnering with children and families* (3rd ed.). Upper Saddle River, NJ: Pearson Education.

Hogan, M. (2013). *Child health nursing: Pearson reviews & rationales for NCLEX* (3rd ed.). Boston, MA: Pearson Learning Solutions.

Kyle, T., & Carman, S. D. (2013). *Essentials of pediatric nursing* (2nd ed.). Philadelphia, PA: Wolters Kluwer Health/Lippincott Williams & Wilkins.

London, M. L., Ladewig, P. W., Ball, J. W., Bindler, R. C., & Cowen, K. J. (2011). *Clinical skills manual for maternal & child nursing care* (3rd ed.). Boston, MA: Pearson Learning Solutions.

London, M. L., Ladewig, P. W., Ball, J. W., Bindler, R. C., & Cowen, K. J. (2011). *Maternal & child nursing care* (3rd ed.). Boston, MA: Pearson Learning Solutions.

Potts, N. L., & Mandleco, B. L. (2012). *Pediatric nursing: Caring for children and their families* (3rd ed.). Clifton Park, NY: Delmar Cengage Learning.

Srouji, R. (2010, July 25). Pain in children: Assessment and nonpharmacological management. *International Journal of Pediatrics, 2010.* doi: 10.1155/2010/474838

Wissmann, J. (2007). *Nursing care of children RN edition 7.0* (E-book). Leawood, KS: Assessment Technologies Institute.

Index